Polska Dotty

JONATHAN LIPMAN

Carp in the Bathtub, Throttled Buglers, and
Other Tales of an Englishman in Poland

ISBN: 1478189142
ISBN-13: 978-1478189145

FOR MARZENA,

NATALIA

&

LILIANA

"Poles, what hopes and what designs do you nourish in your hearts?"

Jan Kochanowski (1530-1584)

Orpheus Sarmaticus

CONTENTS

FOREWORD

In the years since the events in this book took place, Poland has advanced apace onto "the West's" radar: first through membership of the EU in 2004, and then, as a result of this, through an invasion of Poles – mostly young, mostly into the UK and Ireland. Poland was again in the limelight when, along with The Ukraine, it jointly hosted the 2012 European Football Championships. Now, Poland is making a joint bid for the 2015 Winter Olympics, this time with Slovakia. In the meantime Polish sports stars fill our airwaves in seemingly ever-increasing numbers (Radwańska, Kubica, Lewandowski…).

The reception of Poles into Western Europe has been mostly very positive. Polish workers are perceived as hard-working, reliable, well-educated and polite. So much so that, at the time of writing, the Canadian Government is making a play to attract them to its shores, to boost their own economy! Poles have brought a sense of style to the UK – in their dress, design and the like – and many a Brit has fallen for and settled down with a Polish girl. Poles have fitted in, and built up a solid reputation for themselves. A reputation even the tendentious BBC TV Panorama programme – "Stadiums of Hate" – broadcast just before the Euros, could not diminish (it exposed genuine racism amongst Polish football fans, but did not give a balanced view of the size and nature of the problem). Yes, Poles are well settled here, and though there is plenty of talk of them returning home due to the Western European economic crisis (Poland's so-called "Brain *Gain*"), this does not appear to be happening in large numbers. Many Poles are staying in UK and elsewhere, and I am sure will enrich the cultures of those countries.

All of this has created a groundswell of interest in Poland and its people: what makes our Polish plumber or doctor or cleaner (or bus-driver, or dentist, or waitress…) tick, and what should we know about Poland before travelling there?

The years 1997-1999, in which this book is set, were a seminal time for Poland. It had to decide in which direction to venture, and this created tensions between old and new lifestyles which were fascinating if at times painful to watch. These seismic shifts revealed much about the Polish condition, which I observed and tried to capture. I suspect these observations are timeless: after all, they reflect a Polish character that has developed over a thousand years, since Poland was founded around the tenth century in Gniezno.

Even so, Poland has undergone change in the years since this book was written. Accordingly I have referenced in the text updating chapter notes, which can be found at the end. This change – modernisation of Poland's infrastructure, slowly changing attitudes of Poles and of attitudes *towards* Poland – as well as our many and varied experiences of the influx of Poles into the UK, I hope will be the subject of a further account.

In the meantime, happy reading, and welcome to the Heart of Europe!

HOW TO PRONOUNCE POLISH LETTERS

In addition to what you may pick up in the chapter *Gobbledegook*, note the following:

"ą" is nasalised, like the French "on"

"ę" is nasalised, like the French "un"

"ó" is like the "u" in "root"

"ć" is like the "ch" in "chop"

"ł" is like "w"
(but note that "w" is pronounced like the "v" in "victory")

"ń" is like the slightly nasal "n" in "handsome"

"ś" is like the "sh" in "sharp"

"ź" is like the "j" in the French "journal"

"ż" is like the "gi" in "gigolo"

Finally, remember to stress the penultimate syllable of the word.

1 MARRIED IN CRACOW

"*Never forget*: in Poland, family is everything!"

These words echoed in my head as my taxi sped away from the flat I had been renting in Cracow, southern Poland, toward the family home of my fiancée-to-be, Marzena. I had been in Poland the whole of that summer of 1995. It was not my first visit to the country, but already the stay had taken on more significance than the previous few trips. A couple of weeks earlier, in a cheap pizza restaurant just off the large main square in Cracow, I had somehow found the courage to ask my girlfriend - my Polish girlfriend - to marry me, clumsily knocking over my beer in the process. *Yes*, she had replied, evidently touched by my nervousness, *of course she would marry me!* But on condition I never forget the above mantra about the family. Its first manifestation would be going through the engagement process. In Poland this meant asking your prospective father-in-law for his daughter's hand in marriage.

Fine, I had said, I was happy to continue such a tradition – but one question: *why* was the family everything? *Well, there were many possible reasons*, Marzena had begun, mopping up with an inadequate paper serviette a pool of beer that had formed. It could be connected with the strong bonds of Catholicism in Poland. Or, it could be Western commercial values had not yet infiltrated a country cobwebbed by Communism for the last fifty years. *But it was so.* I would later discover the truth of her words, at every turn of my Polish voyage, in ever more incredible circumstances. Now, though, they helped guide me on the day's mission. For if the family was all, the introduction of a new member into it was not going to go unnoticed.

I dressed as smartly as I could for the engagement ceremony: cream chinos, a crinkled linen jacket, and a casual white shirt which I buttoned awkwardly to the top to fit the polyester green and white tie I had bought at the last minute in Cracow's market place. I had not packed a suit and tie for my holiday, as I had not expected to become engaged in such formality. It was in this dubious sartorial guise I found myself musing about the family as the taxi headed for a small spa town 20km outside Cracow. But I was soon awoken from my reverie. Hurtling through the outskirts of Cracow at breakneck speed in typical Polish taxi fashion, on a potholed slip road the local authorities had been repairing ever since I had first visited Poland, our car ran over a sizeable stone block. We pulled over to find fluid leaking from the tired old Mercedes. The driver radioed another taxi which took half an hour to arrive, and we continued on our way. I grew increasingly nervous, not because of cracked roadways or maniacal drivers, but because I was crashing along towards that most uncertain of destinations: my family-to-be's expectations. I spoke little Polish at this stage, and had tried to learn by rote the words with which the kindly Polish teacher at the Polish language summer school I was attending had furnished me for "Please may I have the hand of your daughter in marriage?" But it was not easy. Every word sounded like the name of a strange planet out of *The Hitchhiker's Guide to the Galaxy*. My struggles with the Polish language would become the stuff of legend, and get me into some sticky situations in the future. Would I get the right words out now?

I arrived at the house, and found they had laid on a reception party for me. At the front gate stood Marzena, her parents, her sister with husband and new baby in tow and, of course, her marvellous, ninety year old grandfather ("dziadek"). Dziadek still remembered the rule of Austrian Emperor Francis Joseph in Poland, at the turn of the century, about whom he often talked. This was much to the annoyance of Marzena's mother, who took responsibility for dziadek, and had heard his same old stories a thousand times. Everyone had dressed up, the women in elegant summer frocks, the men in smart suits, shaming me. Even dziadek wore a rakish straw boater. Where had I been, they all asked? I tried to explain using my twenty-word Polish vocabulary, but soon gave up, and distributed the presents – traditionally flowers for the fiancée and her mother, and champagne for the father. Choosing the champagne had been simple enough, but the flowers were another story. My Polish teacher, falling perfectly into the stereotype of the family minded Pole, had been most excited about my engagement. I must get the flowers right, she had explained (it was a good lesson, as I would have to do the same at our wedding). Pink, white or yellow roses for the mother (anything but red) wrapped in green foliage; straight red roses (and lots of them) for the "narzeczona" (fiancée). No foliage. More romantic that way. It seemed to work. The women were delighted with their flowers; father, an anticipatory grin on his face, put the champagne in the fridge to cool, for it was a baking hot day, and the champagne had warmed up over the long journey.

We all filed into the house and the ceremony began immediately which was a good thing, because it gave me little time in which to become any more nervous, as if that were possible. The family stood expectantly around the dining table and chairs in the spacious, cool dining-room. I approached Marzena's father, and opened the box containing the ring. Everyone gasped at the diamond and Italian gold number I had acquired - a purchase of such magnitude in Polish terms that the owner of the small jeweller's shop in Cracow, where I had acquired it, had offered me a seat and coffee whilst I completed the deal. I swallowed, gathered breath and… could not remember my line! My backup plan kicked into action. I took out a small slip of paper on which I had written down the magic words and haltingly read out what I saw:

"*Chciałbym prosić o rękę Państwa córki?*"
(*"May I have the hand of your daughter in marriage?"*)

Horror of horrors! Marzena's father replied, calmly, *"No"*. What I did not know at the time is that "No" is Polish vernacular in this region for, "so – well then…". In a flap, I continued on, placing the ring on Marzena's finger, hoping to establish a *de facto* engagement. It worked. Smiles and laughter. And kisses all round. Kisses in this case meant on three cheeks, in the Polish way, which invariably involves pursed lips missing the given proximate cheek – Hollywood style. Everyone then compared my new fiancée's ring to that of her sister's, and it passed the test. Cameras flashed. We all went back outside, and the party started. We drank the champagne on a concrete terrace next to the house, shaded by the upper floor balcony, and chatted, Marzena translating. My future in-laws raised their eyebrows when I explained, in response to their inquiries, that the engagement ceremony had all but vanished in England. The family was horrified at this lack of tradition. The formal Polish way, they declared, was best. Time-honoured, fun, and a source of more photographs, which have iconic status in Poland. When the champagne ran out, Marzena's father fetched a bottle of chilled white wine from the cellar and opened it. I relaxed. Even the discomfort I felt, sweating in a shirt and tie in the intense summer heat, could not detract from the glow of satisfaction I gave off. I knew that the occasion had fulfilled its purpose, and I was at least halfway to claiming the ultimate prize. I would soon become a member of the family.

*

That had been two years ago, when our wedding, which was now imminent, had seemed no more than a distant dream. When it did come, we knew Marzena's local town, which had proven a fitting venue for the engagement party, would double up as the location for the wedding ceremony. But even back then Marzena and I had resolved that some part of our big day should take place in nearby Cracow – in our view the most beautiful city in Poland.

We decided Cracow would be the scene of our reception – an event that Polish history has dictated must be something large, long and gluttonous. In the past, if a wedding in Poland lasted the whole night, it was generally considered a conservative affair. Two continuous days of merriment was a bit more like it. But if you really wanted to impress your guests, you would invite them for a week of celebrations! At the marriage of a magnate, for example, the Polish Nobel Prize winning writer Czesław Miłosz tells us that guests devoured 80 oxen, 300 calves, 50 sheep, 150 hogs, 21,000 fowl, 12,000 fish, plus a proportionate number of barrels of wine and aquavit.

Not surprisingly, Marzena and I decided this was a bit much. Instead, on the last Saturday in August 1997, we arranged to begin our ceremony at four o'clock in the afternoon in the registry office of Marzena's home town. The afternoon timing was unusual: until recently in Poland, there had to be (by law) a registry office ceremony, in addition to a church wedding – the Communists would not recognise a religious ceremony alone. As the church wedding was considered the main event and took pride of place in the afternoon, registry office proceedings were normally relegated to a morning slot. Marzena and I being of different religions, however (Catholic and Jewish respectively) a registry office wedding, transplanted to the afternoon, would have to suffice (the Communists would have been proud). The reception, in Cracow, would be from 6pm until midnight.

By traditional Polish standards, the arrangements were modest and we might have found ourselves boycotted by the more self-respecting revellers. But we had not reckoned on the popularity of this union of a Polish Catholic girl and an English Jewish boy. It seemed to have captured the imagination of both our families. In the end, a contingent of twenty of my family and friends made the journey from England, and most of Marzena's family came. Fair weather arrived on the Friday evening, Cracow sparkled in the late summer sun, and the wedding party prepared for a knees-up.

I had booked most of the guests from England into "Hotel Saski", a rambling, nineteenth century hotel just off the central square, painted a cheerful yellow. It used to be a youth hostel, but had been vastly upgraded, without a corresponding rise in prices. In the lobby stood an old wooden lift, one of those birdcage types with a sliding door and protruding brass buttons to press for each floor. A gentle old man in blue, military-like uniform, with a peaked hat, who never seemed to go home, operated the lift. Often, camera teams came to film the contraption in action, and I suspect the old man did not wish to miss a take.

It was in the lobby of Hotel Saski that the English guests met on the morning of the wedding before setting out in a fleet of taxis for the small spa town where Marzena's parents lived – and where we had become engaged. *Krzeszowice* was only twenty-five minutes away by taxi, assuming the same fate did not befall the wedding guests as had me when travelling to my engagement. On the way, my parents, the best man and I, following Polish tradition, stopped off at the house of the bride's parents to be blessed. When we entered the house, we were astonished to see what seemed like the whole of Marzena's family lined up along the corridor walls, forming with their raised arms a human arch for us to walk through. It was a little like the reception I had received at my engagement party two years earlier, but on a grander scale. Marzena's parents then blessed us, wishing us all the best in our relationship, and my father, never one to miss out on an "occasion", added what he considered a blessing of equal gravity, wishing us luck for the future and many years of profitable electronics hunting. My father, like The Captain in *Nostromo*, by Joseph Conrad - one of Poland's most famous sons - always liked to mark what he regarded as great moments in history, but usually managed to bring in some reference to the transistor or silicon chip. My mother said something more apt, and elbowed my father.

We continued on to the registry office, a fine, two-storey building, painted light brown. It was an impressive small palace, but not as impressive as the immense palace that stood on a hill behind it. This was a stylish, neo-Renaissance building with a pillared front and wings to either side. Unfortunately, the registry office was the only one of the two palaces that had been kept up: the larger palace was so immense that no one from Poland or abroad had the inclination to renovate it. With over one hundred rooms, an orangery and a ballroom, this was a shame. I would later discover, however, that restoration of these old buildings is an expensive and complex business, and not to be taken for granted.

The first thing the English guests noticed was not the palatial setting, but the flowers. It is a tradition in Poland for all guests to bring flowers to a wedding. None of the Polish guests had skimped. They handed to Marzena and me countless bouquets of roses, tulips and lilies, all mixed with green foliage and wrapped in foil paper coloured in various pastel shades, usually with a couple of bright bows attached. This process, accompanied by the noisy whirring and clicking of cameras, took a long time, but no sooner was it over than we were ushered into the registry office, and up sweeping stairs to the room where the marriage ceremony would take place.

Everyone packed inside. It was standing room only at the back. For the benefit of the foreigners the ceremony proceeded in both English and Polish. It was a good thing we had decided to hire a translator. The vows of the Polish civil wedding ceremony are deep and moving, and with the aid of our delightful translator, who stood tall and spoke with a Scottish laird's twang (he often did business in Edinburgh, he later told us) gained something in the translation. I swear I heard murmurs of approval from the bride's side of the family when I vowed to treat her with love and respect and look after her for the rest of our lives. And similar murmurs from the groom's side when the translator announced that any children we might have would take my surname. The ceremony was not without a moment or two of awkward cultural difference - some of the more wedding-seasoned English guests looked perturbed when Marzena and I placed rings, in the traditional Polish way, on the other's right hand - or the *wrong* hand, as they saw it. But, with rings securely fastened and vows complete, the kissing began. Marzena received kisses from everyone. I received the same from all the Poles - male and female - and from the females in the English party. The English men, however, stood back a little, unwilling to participate quite this much, despite being loosened by the champagne that was now flowing freely. They were, after all, English. There's only so much cultural blending at these occasions.

We all jumped back into our taxis and returned to Cracow for the reception, which took place in one of the streets of the old town, just off the main square. We had hired out a mediaeval beer cellar – a feature of the tall old town houses in Cracow. As Marzena and I looked down at the cellar from the top of the stairs, candles twinkled in the darkness, lighting up the brickwork of the barrel shaped ceiling. From down below, the guests stared up at us. The band struck up, and despite weeks of protestations I would never do so, I carried Marzena down the twenty-five or so steps to the cellar to a round of rapturous applause when I reached the bottom. We were both handed glasses of champagne, which we downed before throwing the glasses over our shoulder. The idea is the broken glass brings good luck.

No sooner had we all sat down and begun our first course - a delicate mushroom soup - than I was instructed we were leaving to have our photos taken. This being my third Polish wedding (although the first in which I had acquired a wife) I knew the score: we were off to do the official photos; we would be back in anything up to two hours. I informed my father.

"What!?" he exclaimed. How could I possibly leave the reception at this point? We had only just sat down to eat! There were, well there were things to be done! Aunts to dance with! Speeches to be made! Great Aunts to dance with! Did I know what I was doing!?

Marzena's parents were informed, and didn't bat an eyelid.

Tradition has always interested me, since hearing the haunting song of the same name in "Fiddler on the Roof". It just so happens that, in Poland, the bride and groom often disappear from the reception to have photographs taken inside a studio. While the fun heats up at the reception, Mr. and Mrs. are subjected to the cold flash of a camera bulb. Why is this? It could be because photographs are the memory of a big family event – and we already know about the importance of the family in Poland. Certainly, they are taken seriously.

Wedding parties who can afford it, and many who cannot, hire the most expensive studios, which take a considerable number of photographs. Newly-weds recover the snaps as soon as possible after the wedding, and make copies available to anyone who could conceivably be regarded as a member of the family. Over the years, the pictures are pawed over, and viewed regularly – not hidden in a draw for that once in a decade viewing.

The newly-weds' absence is, some might say, glorification of the memory at a time when they should be enjoying the moment. Like most traditions, though, you get used to it. I enjoyed being out of the commotion of the reception for a couple of hours, and striking Madonna-esque poses directed by the photographer of the most highly-recommended wedding photo studio in Cracow. The only time I felt a little perturbed was when the photographer, who rather fancied himself, asked Marzena if she wanted a few pictures of herself alone. I hoped that, in her white wedding outfit – a patterned lace bodice with small roses sewn on, and a flowing silk dress – she had not outshone me too much during the day's events.

When we returned to the reception, food was continuing to be served. It is no exaggeration to say that, at a Polish wedding, the food just *does not stop*. There is course after course. The meal starts with, well, a meal: soup, followed by charcuterie, hot dishes and dessert. Just when you might expect the end punctuation of a coffee and chocolate mint, you realise that your four courses were really just one big starter. Soon there are more soups ("barszcz" or beetroot soup, "żurek" or sour rye soup, mushroom soup), cold meats, pâtés, fish, more hot dishes (we had veal, duck and chicken), vegetables, cakes, ice cream, fruit - and on and on. When Marzena and I left the reception just before midnight, a fresh helping of barszcz had just arrived at the table. It was paradise for a gourmet like me, and I would in the succeeding weeks drag Marzena endlessly to our favourite Polish restaurant in Cracow – "Hawełka", situated on the main market square – in an attempt to relive the tremendous offering of food that had been put on during our wedding night.

And then there is the drink. Champagne, wine, cognac, beer and... vodka. I can dispel one myth about the Poles and vodka: they do not drink it from big glasses. Instead, they drink from small thimbles of a tumbler design, sometimes perched on long stems. However, I did not say how many of these thimbles they drink, which I leave to your imagination, whilst adding I cannot dispel any more myths. Having said that, at our wedding, with one or two exceptions, no one drank to excess. The two families and sets of friends, separated into Polish and English down the two facing lengths of a U-shaped table, stared respectfully but slightly suspiciously at each other, admiring the alcoholic restraint and studying the class credentials of the other.

As the evening progressed at our wedding the young folk from both parties mixed, thanks mainly to the proficiency of most of the young Poles in English. I noticed a group of them chatting and laughing away. For the older generation, it was more difficult, but with a body language vocabulary that could rival that of Mohammed Ali at his height, my father managed to get across a few basic aspects of English culture. These included the latest computer bargains he had found just prior to flying out for the wedding. Indeed, computer-speak being something of a *lingua franca* (for example, on computer keyboards in Poland, keywords such as "Enter", "Insert" and "Delete" are often marked in English) and computing a massive industry in Poland, my father seemed to make remarkable progress. As he is also prone to exaggeration, I would not be surprised if a few Poles left the wedding with the pleasing impression Marzena had just married into the Bill Gates fortune.

What really got the two sides intermingling, however, was the dancing. The Poles have dancing in their blood. Dancing was a pastime of the Polish nobility ("szlachta"), and Poland has a strong folk dancing tradition. The Poles even gave their name to their own dance – the "polonaise". All generations are able to ballroom dance, and they also know the more modern steps. At my wedding, the older Polish generation, in particular, were delighted to discover the older English generation could ballroom dance too, and no end of invitations between the two parties ensued. At one point, my mother was veritably swept of her feet, swirled around and around like a spinning-top by my father-in-law, who had unobtrusively become Patrick Swayze for the evening. An uncle of Marzena kept up a dancing vigil – usually alone, other than for the accompaniment of the odd innocent child – in front of the band, for the entire duration of the evening. My protestations I knew a few disco steps, and was the next John Travolta, were roundly ignored by everyone who really knew how to dance, including Marzena. I looked back with regret at those ballroom dancing lessons my friends and I had skipped during secondary school because we considered them sissy.

Rapprochement even occurred through one of the more openly Jewish of our guests, an old family friend who sported a long beard and skull-cap, and was wont to say prayers from time to time. At one point, he went upstairs to say some blessings, where a few of Marzena's older family spotted him. They later told how reminiscent this made them feel. Before the war, when so many Jews had lived in Poland, no Polish wedding had been complete without the Jewish band and Jews serving drinks – for at this time, many Jews were innkeepers ("karczmarz"). Marzena's family said it was sad to remember what they were missing. My own discovery of how the Jews disappeared, on trips to places of Jewish heritage in Poland, would be one of the more disturbing aspects of my Polish journey.

At around 11 o'clock in the evening, we introduced the Poles to the phenomenon of wedding speeches - not common at Polish weddings - that they took to with surprising enthusiasm. I spoke a little in English and Polish to attentive and fascinated faces (my Polish had improved a little since the engagement party two years earlier) giving a potted history of Marzena's and my relationship to date.

How we had met studying on a course about the Jews (including the Jews of Poland) at Oxford University in 1994 – when Marzena was over researching her Masters on the Jews of Cracow, and I postponing a career in law by taking a postgraduate diploma in Jewish studies. How we became engaged a year later when I had spent that summer in Cracow. How, two years after this, immediately following our wedding, we would begin a new life in Poland, and would live permanently together for the first time. It would also be my first time living abroad. Having resumed my legal career and qualified as a solicitor, I would continue it a law office in Warsaw. Marzena, after a year seconded to London University, would return to her beloved Jagiellonian University in Cracow where she would extend the subject of her Masters thesis into a full-blown doctorate.

I thought all this background might establish my credentials, and help to explain to Marzena's family how a relative stranger had just become a stranger who was a relative. The tactic seemed to ease the suspicions of my new in-laws, but the coup came at the end of my speech when I turned to my wife, and told her, "Marzena, jesteś moim marzeniem". These words translate as, "Marzena, you are my dream", but make a play on the words "Marzena" and "marzeniem", which both have the same root (Marzena means "dream"). My subsequent, over-elaborate attempts to explain this to the English guests, who had understood the connection pretty quick, caused me a fair amount of grief. However, I later learnt from Marzena that the speeches, and presentation at their finish of bottles of cognac and vodka to the senior member of each wedding party, had gone down well with the Polish contingent, though somehow I doubted they would become a regular feature at Polish weddings as a result.

Tiring with the incredible amount of nervous energy expended during the day, I persuaded Marzena we should go. Soon afterwards, we found ourselves back in the suite my friends had booked us for the night in Hotel Saski. Much to their amusement, the suite's theme was a kitsch Roman baths pastiche. Half naked figures in togas, painted reclining on couches, eyed us from either side of bunches of grapes and tall urns. Entering into the decadent spirit, my new wife and I clinked together two glasses of Moet from a bottle the hotel staff had kindly donated and left on ice. It was not long before we were reminiscing about how privileged we had been to pledge ourselves in this wonderful city, surrounded by so many family and friends. It seemed, after all, the Poles (and The Captain, and my father) had it right: best of all was to remember.

2 CAPITALS OLD AND NEW

After our wedding, we spent a few days' "mini-honeymoon" in Cracow, the former royal town of Poland - and a jewel. Euripides' saying that the first condition of being born happy is to be born in a famous city was never more apt than for Cracow. Unlike Warsaw, which was razed by the Nazis, and rebuilt by the cash-starved Communists in concrete, Cracow was almost entirely preserved despite the war. For this it can thank the speed with which the Nazis were forced to evacuate the city. As the Russian army approached under General Koniev, the Nazis left as rapidly as they could to avoid being encircled by the Red Army. The Polish Communists in Cracow later honoured Koniev by erecting a statue in his honour, in a street named after him. But when Communism finally fell, "General Koniev" street became "The Street of the Polish Underground Army". This pattern continued all over Poland after the defeat of Communism in 1989. We in the West focus on the image of prominent statues of Lenin being hoisted away by cranes in the former Communist states, his form twisted rudely upside down as he is taken to the local quarry or dump. In fact, on being granted their freedom, Poles were busy scurrying all around their country removing unwanted street signs and the like, replacing them with something more appropriate.

From the middle of the eleventh century until 1596, Cracow was the royal capital of Poland. In that year, Sigismund III Wasa (1566-1632), the Polish King, who belonged to the Wasa Swedish royal dynasty ruling Poland at that time, moved the capital nearer to his Scandinavian relatives - to Warsaw. Cracowians still feel a certain jealousy and bitterness the capital was moved to Warsaw – especially as, at the time, Warsaw was no more than a small town of 20,000 inhabitants. They point to the central role Cracow has played in preserving a Polish identity since then as evidence of its continuing primacy until relatively recent times. For example, Cracow was a city-state and "symbolic capital" of a vanished nation after the partitioning of Poland off the map at the end of the eighteenth century by its Russian, Prussian and Austrian neighbours. It became "Free Cracow" in 1815 and received its own constitution, though in reality it was under the watchful eye of its neighbours and was annexed into Austria in 1846. Twenty years later, Austria granted a degree of autonomy to Galicia, the province in which Cracow sat, and Cracow became the centre of Polish political and cultural life. After the Second World War, Cracow survived Communist attempts to crush its intelligentsia through the construction of a gargantuan steelworks on the edge of town at "Nowa Huta" or "New Town"[1]. The Communists thought that proletariat ideology, reflected in the ethos of the steel workers, would balance out the preponderance of middle class in Cracow who had resisted their régime. Cracow buckled under this pressure but did not break: eventually the locals managed to get a church built in Nowa Huta, which had been missing from its original design, and the Communist ploy to parachute in steel workers backfired when most of them joined the Solidarity trade union movement which eventually brought down Communism. But the consequence of this struggle is that Cracow's unequalled architectural legacy is slowly being eroded by smog from these steelworks, sometimes even visible in the air.

One of the spectacular legacies of pre-1596 life is the splendid Renaissance royal castle in Cracow – the "Wawel" castle - built a little way out of the centre of the city, on a rock on the banks of the Vistula. Much of Polish architecture is of the Renaissance style, because in 1518 King Sigismund I (1467-1548) married an Italian princess who brought many of Italy's finest architects to Poland. To this day Poland boasts some of the greatest ultramontane Renaissance architecture, and the royal castle is no exception. It incorporates a cathedral housing the tombs of many members of the Polish royal family, and opulent royal apartments adorned by a remarkably rich collection of tapestries, all commissioned by the Polish King Sigismund Augustus (1520-1572), the son of Sigismund I. There are so many of these – 160 – that at any one time most are in storage or being preserved rather than on display. Outside the castle walls there is a metal statue of the Wawel dragon. This legendary monster terrorised the city and surrounds until an imaginative cobbler's apprentice fed it a lamb stuffed with sulphur.

This caused the dragon such thirst it drank half the Vistula river, and eventually exploded. From inside the statue's mouth, a gas pipe throws flames about once a minute. The kids (and I) love it.

But for me the real glory of Cracow will always remain its central square, or "rynek", situated at the heart of the old town or "stare miasto". It is said to be the largest medieval square in Europe, a mind-blowing two hundred metres along each side, split perpendicularly down the middle by the eclectic cloth-hall building or "sukiennice". The sukiennice was once a centre of international trade, where such commodities as spice, silk, leather and wax were imported from the East in exchange for textiles, lead and salt from the nearby Wieliczka salt mine. Perhaps the square's most famous feature, standing in one corner, is the Mariacki church, a striking Gothic structure consisting of two different towers at the front - both built of dark brown brick - said to have been built by two brothers in competition with each other. The elder killed the younger in order that his tower would remain higher. So remorseful was he after his fratricide, however, that he later jumped to his death from his own tower. From this same tower a bugler plays a short reveille every hour, the "Hejnał" (bugle call) to recall the day when one of his predecessors warned Cracow of the approaching Tartars, who the Poles then beat back in one of their greatest military victories. Before it was over, however, a Tartar's arrow pierced the bugler's throat. In a poignant reminder, today's bugler stops abruptly to imitate his predecessor's demise. No one had much luck on that tower.

Surrounding the four sides of the square are four and five storey houses, mostly coloured cream, brown, sand or light blue, of all different architectural styles, but forming a surprisingly homogenous whole. These are where the wealthy city burghers used to live, whose class grew up thanks to the various trade routes that criss-crossed Poland since the Middle Ages. Many of the burghers were originally German, and hence the architecture and layout of the square, and many other similar squares in Poland, has a Central European feel to it. The ground floors of most of these houses are trendy bars and cafés. One of my favourite pastimes is sitting on a summer's day outside my favourite such café, "Bambus" - where all the chairs are made of bamboo - with a Polish beer and yesterday's *Independent* (if I'm lucky) watching the hordes of passers-by. When I die, I trust they will embalm me and leave me upright in one of those chairs - if it doesn't scare off too many customers.

The square has a life all its own. Either it is quiet and peaceful, despite the crowds, able to retain its tranquillity because of its size, or full of activity, because the Cracowian Council had decided to put on some sort of "event". These can consist of anything from a few grill huts where the smoky smell of BBQ-ing meat is hard to resist, to folk dancing festivals, to full-scale rock concerts, where the noise of twanging guitars and straining voices is deafening. On New Year's Eve, the square fills up with so many people (up to 200,000) all hurling champagne bottles into the air, that the police bring out the water cannon, and you are instantaneously reminded of Poland's inglorious Communist past. But whatever the commotion, the point is there *is* commotion; or at least, on the quieter days, movement. And this is perhaps the best feature of Cracow's square (and the old town in general): it is *alive*.

The surrounding streets run perpendicular off the square. These streets, lined with chi-chi shops which Marzena assures me are amongst the most fashionable in Poland, still constitute the old town, until they end in a circular park (the "planty") surrounding this part of the city. The planty is unexpected, an oasis of calm in the middle of a big city, and a fine place for strolling during Cracow's scorching summer, as its shady trees provide natural air conditioning. Outside the planty there is yet more perfectly preserved architecture, similar in style to the central old town. Here, wide streets and regal house fronts of high windows, balconies and eclectic decoration reflect Austrian style from the nineteenth century, when Austria ruled this part of Poland.

Cracow is a potpourri of architectural gems and styles. The stunning university buildings are the equal of those to be found anywhere. Someone once described Cracow's Jagiellonian University to me as "The Oxford University of Poland", and it is indisputably the finest university in Poland and perhaps all of Eastern Europe, once bestrode by the brilliant Polish astronomer Nicholas Copernicus and (it is rumoured) the original Dr. Faust. The gloriously constructed, endless churches (the Cracowians' favourite remark, uttered with a wry smile, is that every other building in Cracow is a church) and a reminiscent Jewish quarter help round out the magnificent picture.

But it would be in Warsaw where we would live as newly-weds, where investment was pouring into Poland, and where I had found a job. Even Marzena was not familiar with the *present-day* capital, so after our wedding and before we moved up to Warsaw we agreed to meet one of her girlfriends – Zofia – who would tell us all about it. We rendezvoused, at her request, at a fashionable café in one of Cracow old town's narrow streets. Zofia was a trendy girl which presumably accounted for the venue and the futuristic metal mesh chairs on which we now sat outside waiting for her. We hoped Zofia would tell us about Warsaw's hip places.

Zofia arrived, greeted us with a flourish of pecks on the cheek, ordered a gin and tonic, and then tore into Warsaw. She complained (in English) that it was dirty, crazy, noisy, ugly, disparate, featureless and soulless in a flood of adjectives of which a mother tongue English speaker would have been proud. It was as if she had been learning the at once most evocative and provocative English words she could in preparation for our meeting. In contrast, she afforded Cracow not only more salubrious adjectives, but added gestures intended to leave us in no doubt as to the majesty of the former royal capital and its superiority over the present one. In case I had not gathered, Zofia added, she lived in Cracow.

At the time I was taken aback Zofia talked this way of a city in which she knew we were about to settle. But when she left the table for a moment, Marzena enlightened me: *the Cracovians dislike the Warsowians, and vice versa,* she told me. *The Cracovians think the Warsowians uneducated, and the Warsowians that the Cracovians are intellectual snobs and mean.* Zofia returned, and delivered a treatise comparing the toilets of Cracow with those of Warsaw. You can imagine which prevailed. However, the pertinent information absorbed, I did not demur, and spent the rest of the evening grinning amiably at Zofia feeling I had grasped the situation as best I could - for there was never any point attempting to understand age old prejudice.

A few days later Marzena and I packed the car, drove to Warsaw and discovered that our rented flat, organised for us by the law firm I was joining, was a joy. With the fall of Communism, and investment pouring into the country, Poland was now something akin to a building site. That was the bad news. The good news was that Poland was constructing to a generally high standard of architectural form and function. Continental flair, including in the French style (angular roofs, expansive windows, glass atriums), was everywhere.

Our flat, in which we were to be the first occupants, was no exception. It was the ground floor of a three storey building that was clad with white painted walls, topped by an angular roof of attractive red tiles - a popular architectural combination in Poland. The one bedroom flat boasted a garage connected internally to the house (important for those icy Polish winter mornings), an open fire, underfloor heating, an all-glass conservatory and a neat garden with patio. I had never lived anywhere so stylish in England.

In the kitchen, the all white beech wood framed furniture, and oven and fridge, had a modern, IKEA feel about them – but were sturdier than that, having been hand made in Poland. Above the cupboards were swanky display cabinets, lit by halogen lights. Terracotta floor tiles ran through the kitchen and hallway. Tiling also accentuated the bathroom which included an indulgent mirror and glass shelving under lit by more halogen bulbs. Everywhere you looked there was a flourish, brightness or simple elegance: zigzag parquet floors in the bedroom and living room; a wall-sized mirror in the bedroom; a modern fireplace in the living room; French doors leading to a conservatory. And the casement windows featured a convenience we seem yet to have discovered in England: they can either open laterally, or just tilt open at the top. Finally and mercifully, the central heating system was one of the most modern and efficient available on the market, and kept the bills down. This was important considering the price of gas in Poland.

The flat was also conveniently located. We were positioned five minutes drive away from no less than three French hypermarkets – Géant, Auchan and Leclerc. But we soon discovered the food in these shops, though cheap, was not always the best quality – particularly the meat. Also, and unusually for French shops, the range of cheeses and wines was not wide, certainly not compared to the Géants, Auchans and Leclercs in France. Most frustrating of all, we discovered the Western concept of motoring around these shops with your trolley, and minding out of each other's way, had not yet reached the Poles. Sometimes, they would stand in the middle of an aisle, trolley totally blocking the way, apparently in no rush for anything.

The upshot was Marzena and I began to shop at out local food store, one of a chain of small Polish supermarkets named "Rema 1000". There the food was displayed in less orderly fashion, sometimes even in cardboard boxes, and was often more expensive than in the

French supermarkets. But it was of a better quality. The meat counter was situated in a corner of the shop, where you chose the meat and paid for it right away. Here, Marzena got to know the friendly lady running the meat store, who promised her the choicest cuts, which she kept in the back of the shop. On seeing Marzena enter, she would scurry out back and return with the freshest meat of that day, often "cielęcina" (veal) - good in Poland.

The reason for the fine quality and location of where we lived was our landlord, Jan. A genial individual, he was a successful businessman, with an eye for detail, and the sort of determination that alone could create such a perfect dwelling. He took to Marzena and me immediately, and we to him. He was a bit of a father figure to us. Marzena and I liked him on a personal level, and we appreciated his typically Polish pragmatism. He had no qualms about our bolting a monumentally-sized satellite dish onto the freshly painted outside wall of his new flat. And when, a few days after moving into the flat, oil from my car leaked onto the tiled garage floor, this also did not faze him. It would clean up, he said. What was the garage for anyway if not this type of eventuality? In other words, the accommodation he had rented us was to be *used*.

Jan also helped us settle in by providing the antidote to Zofia's critical view of Warsaw. He waxed lyrical to us on the beauty of the capital. Did we know the old Polish Kings had commissioned no less a painter than Canaletto to paint the royal city, and his paintings still hung in the palace at Wilanów? And what beauty those paintings revealed! Why, Warsaw was once described as the Paris of the East! And in the period after Canaletto painted, Viennese Secession architecture was added to Warsaw! We should visit Wilanów, and also the royal baths at Łazienki, and - of course! - the old town, painstakingly reconstructed after the war.

However, rather than visit these attractions, I spent most of the first few weeks settling into my job, and Marzena checking out the local food and clothes shops. She was disappointed by the latter. They did not appeal as much as the unique, quality clothes shops in Cracow, as exemplified by a Warsaw branch of the shop "Gap" – which we nicknamed "Mind the Gap". It seemed to specialise in stocking only the previous year's stuff, and imports of almost every item in size "extra small". We seemed to spend all our time in offices, banks (opening accounts) and supermarkets. The streets in between these institutions we found to be everything Zofia had suggested: cracked and rutted road surfaces, dirty pavements, and by their side, row upon row of dreary, lifeless blocks. It was just as one imagined Communist architecture to be (or "Socialist Realism", as the Soviet architecture of the late 1940s and 1950s is termed). The only advantage we could see at all to the place was that the streets were wide. But when I read the Communists had rebuilt the streets this way after the war (the Nazis had razed Warsaw) so that Soviet tanks could roll down them to quell any Poles foolhardy enough to attempt an insurrection - this rather took away the gloss.

It was certainly strange Warsaw remained so charmless when so much of the investment into Poland had been funnelled through its capital. It appeared all the money had been directed either into steel and glass offices in the centre of town, or villas in the suburbs for the super rich. But there were few facilities for the people: for example, decent swimming pools, gyms, or cinemas[2]. And no *planning*. A modern office skyscraper could be plonked incongruously next to a dilapidated residential block from the Communist era. This was particularly the case in one quarter – Wola, just to the edge of the city centre – because real estate for new build was more accessible there. God knows what the inhabitants of the blocks felt as they watched Western businessman and Polish yuppies rolling up to work in their executive saloons every day, parking outside these locals' windows.

The traffic-jams in Warsaw, particularly over the handful of bridges spanning the Vistula river that divides the city, were getting progressively worse, and not just because of the dearth of bridges: public transport was woeful, there was no integrated system of traffic lights, no ring road for Warsaw, and, simply, not enough roads[3]. No-one envisaged the current popularity of the car back in the 1980s, when it took a ten year wait before one could get hold of even a small Fiat. Completing the dismal scene, in downtown Warsaw two huge central squares – "Plac Defilad" and "Plac Piłsudskiego" - remained undeveloped and ugly[4].

The city planners were not exactly tackling redevelopment enthusiastically. The chief urban planner of Warsaw City Hall, for example, once remarked: "Warsaw is an ugly city, a really ugly city. The challenge is not to make it worse". At best, you might applaud him for a sort of honesty. But then he noted of one new financial centre "looks like someone took a shit in the middle of the city". Suffice to say the chief urban planner of Warsaw City Hall soon became the *former* chief urban planner of Warsaw City Hall.

It was not all bad news in Warsaw. Nowy Świat ("New Street"), was, despite its name, a fine old shopping thoroughfare near the old town, full of splendidly rebuilt neo-Classical palaces, tiled pavements, and old lampposts. It bustled with traditional Polish restaurants and coffee bars, such as "Blikle", famous for its cakes since the nineteenth century. Even though the shops and chic boutiques on Nowy Świat, and nearby Chmielna street sold overpriced ware, they were nevertheless popular with the Poles and tourists alike. One report claimed Nowy Świat contained the most foot traffic in the world, beating Fifth Avenue, Oxford Street and Champs Elysées. And get this: you could park almost anywhere, because there were few parking restrictions in central Warsaw (perhaps another cause of the city's dire circulation problems, as everyone drove downtown). Where you saw a spot, you parked. Rapidly westernising Warsaw had yet to catch on to those Western deterrents: double-yellow lines, congestion charges and extortionate parking fees. Your only caution was to watch out for what Marzena and I coined "Fiat" spaces – apparent parking spaces that disappeared into nothing when, half way into the space, you suddenly realised a small Fiat had got there some time before you.

Almost no Warsowian we met would hear a bad word about the city, and so Marzena and I soon learnt to be ultra-discreet when discussing the capital. We tried to pinpoint what it was about the city we did not like. We hit upon the disastrous centre, so entirely lacking in planning. The central square, said to be the largest in Europe, is occupied by a sprawling wedding cake type building, the old Soviet "Palace of Culture", Stalin's "gift" to the city, which even Warsowians have never taken to, and which constitutes a sickly orange-yellow eyesore right in the heart of the town. Its only semi-redeeming feature is a tall spire that at least constitutes a landmark of sorts. Next to the Palace of Culture, Warsaw's main railway station can best be described as utilitarian in design. An incongruous series of shabby stalls and markets nearby, with barrel shaped canvas roofs painted in thick blue and white stripes, only widen the sprawling urban blemish. On another side of the square, ulica Marszałkoswka ("Marshall Street"), Warsaw's main shopping thoroughfare, is downright gloomy, with end-to-end grey concrete blocks housing downmarket department stores. Outside these street vendors sell tasteless tat – cheap shirts, gloves, bags, wallets, perfumes, tapes and food. There was even one pathetic old lady who offered no more than a tiny basket of walnuts almost all year round, whatever the weather, shivering sometimes in the icy temperatures. She came to represent for us the sorrow of Warsaw. A grating, intimidating commotion fills the air, where other cities might offer an invigorating hustle and bustle. The trams, contraptions from a bygone age that are heavy and bulky, shake the street when they go by. An obstacle course of beggars can knock you off your feet.

Maybe my annoyance was just down to me and my pampered ways, but it was all quite the opposite of the "spokój" or peace and quiet that seems to be at the centre of every Pole's heart, and which would drive us back repeatedly to tranquil Cracow in the ensuing weeks. Was Zofia right about Warsaw, after all?

3 GOBBLEDEGOOK

It was mid-September when I began my job in Warsaw, following our wedding in Cracow the previous month, our short honeymoon there, and our subsequent move up to the capital. Ironically, the problems I had with communication during those first few weeks of work were not related to the Polish language. Polish is legendary for being difficult to learn - the third most difficult language in Europe behind Hungarian and Finnish, they say. There is one prickly tongue twister ("Chrząszcz brzmi w trzcinie") that was even entered in the Guinness Book of Records as being the most difficult for an Englishman to pronounce, until it was trumped by a Czech phrase. No, the problem, as I started work in the small, English law office I had chosen as my first Polish job, was understanding *English*.

I had arrived fresh from completing my legal training at a firm in the City of London. The firm I now joined was very different. Instead of working from a sizeable, modern office block, replete with meeting rooms, canteen and gym, I found myself housed in a horizontal Communist block, four storeys high, appropriately enough named "Grey" building. Conditioned to life in the City, it seemed inappropriate a law firm should present itself this way. Once inside, however, there was no obvious divergence from Western ways. Modern photocopiers and functional office furniture inhabited the place. The only thing revealed you were in another country were the dulcet tones of Polish that could be heard as you wandered from desk to desk (though the business was led by a handful of English lawyers, most of the other lawyers, and all of the support staff, were Polish).

The secretaries, however, *were* different. In the City, secretaries were a rarefied breed, the better ones perfectly capable of taking urgent decisions during their bosses' lengthy luncheons. They certainly knew how to type a letter. In Poland, however – at least in the firm I worked

- typing was apparently not a prerequisite for attaining the post of secretary.

The firm I had joined offered legal advice mostly to foreign companies wishing to invest in Poland. Consequently, any letters of advice or contracts had to be in English. The trouble is many a Polish secretary, though reasonably proficient in spoken English is – understandably – less so in written English. Not ideal for the poor secretaries who had to type up my dictation.

In the first week, I would try to dictate ve-ry ve-ry slow-ly, pronouncing each word with par-ti-cu-lar ca-re - so that my tapes sounded like a recording played back at slow speed, or one of those painful early talkies. I tried and tried, but every time I received the subsequent typed document, it bore no resemblance to what I had dictated. I would frequently receive text that mingled instructions with words, such as:

"Heading No.1 The Taxation of Company Cars Under Polish Law In Bold And Underlined New Paragraph".

I would attack the letter my secretary had typed with a red pen. Suddenly I felt like a teacher correcting homework. I would batter the text into shape, until I had what I wanted. News soon spread in the office of my grammatical and orthographic prowess. Before I knew it, by the start of my second week at work, Polish lawyers were queuing up at the door to have *their* letters knocked into shape.

As for the Polish lawyers, their English was better than that of their secretaries, but with one problem: they were breathing new, unwanted life into the antiquated English legal language of the nineteenth century. In English legal practice there has developed an enthusiasm (in some areas, a necessity) for Plain English – a laudable attempt to get lawyers to draft in easily comprehensible words, jettisoning the user-unfriendly "whereins", wheretofores" and "whereinafters". Legal documents must be intelligible to the man in the street. But young Polish lawyers, deprived of a full vocabulary when they draft in English, would often turn to the language of the old English Courts of Chancery. A "wherein", "wheretofore" or "whereinafter" would often serve as their default crutch.

I did not blame the secretaries for their spelling mistakes, especially as their English was so much better than my pidgin Polish. Indeed, many young Poles, educated or not, speak good English, which they have not only learnt at school, but have grown up hearing in Western pop songs and reading on the labels of their clothes. Their big problem, however, is to distinguish between, or make use of at all, the definite and indefinite articles ("the" and "a") neither of which their language possesses. In Polish, the definite or indefinite is deduced from the context. Poles also express frustration at the number of incomprehensible idioms - Shakespearean or otherwise - that have entered the rich English language. For example, try explaining to a Pole the meaning of "hoist by your own petard".

What did irk me, however, was the *attitude* of some of the secretaries. It was common practice for them to refuse to do work for lawyers, including photocopying, usually with the excuse they were too busy. And yet, however busy they were, this did not prevent them all leaving, like a line of tourists doing the conga, at precisely 4-30pm every day, whatever work remained to be done. When, on one occasion, I asked my secretary to stay late, as I had an important letter to get out, she immediately burst into tears, and I had to let her leave.

Maybe we simply did not deserve it, but there seemed to be an inherent lack of respect towards the lawyers in the firm. The secretaries, in their minds, knew best.

Nevertheless, at least I did not have to produce a letter of advice in Polish. It would have read like an optician's eye chart. Polish is very, very difficult. There are clusters of consonants pronunciation of which it can take a Westerner a lifetime to fathom, unusual letters and acres of verb conjugations and noun endings. Indeed, one famous word suffices to demonstrate how difficult this language really is: Lech Wałęsa's surname.

"Wałęsa" is usually pronounced by the English "Wa-lay-sa". But such pronunciation is not even close. First of all, the first syllable "Wa" is pronounced "Va". As for the second syllable, the "ł" of "łę" has a crooked line through it and such a letter is pronounced like a "w". The "ę" of "łę" has a peculiar little tail on it, which means that, effectively (though not if you want to pronounce it perfectly) the middle syllable reads "wen". The "sa" at the end is pronounced straightforwardly. Result?

"Vawensa".

Now try forming a sentence.

My own Polish is intermediate. However, considering how many courses I have been on, it should be a lot better. I first learnt Polish at Oxford University in 1994, encouraged by Marzena whom I had met there. I then went on an intensive four week summer school course at the Jagiellonian University, during my summer in Cracow in 1995. There I won the summer school prize for the beginner's level, which more or less meant I could pronounce my name in Polish. Next I learnt Polish in London, at evening school, after long, hard days in the office doing my legal training. I was too tired to think, and you have to think when you are learning Polish. I gave this up and took private lessons, which were worthwhile, but prohibitively expensive. I reckon it cost about a pound to learn a new word.

I apparently have good pronunciation. This is important, because Poles pronounce their words with clarity and fire. They are not mumblers. This, perhaps, reflects their character, for such volume and precision makes their speech a perfect vehicle for expressing their manifold opinions on life, including religion and politics. Indeed, it is often said, by Poles themselves: "Two Poles, Three Opinions". But there is a more important reason why they speak so precisely. This is because Polish was (and still is) cherished as the element that kept a whole people together when Poland went off the map entirely between 1795 and 1918, partitioned as it was by its grasping Russian, Prussian and Austrian neighbours. Accordingly, the Poles are proud of their language, rather like the French, retaining many of its archaic and complex features. However, as they also accept its difficulty, and that few foreigners wish to learn it, they are more forgiving than the French. They readily admit Polish versions of Anglicisms into the language. For example, in the business world, "karta kredytowa" means "credit card", "monopolizacja" means "monopolisation" and "gwarancja" means "guarantee". But this can also be necessary, as such words fill gaps in Polish business language which fell behind when Poland stagnated under the rule of the partitioning powers, and then Communism. As for the Communists, they tried to impose Russian on the Poles after 1945. You can imagine how that went down. Post-Communism fewer and fewer young people in Poland were learning Russian, which you might think was just desserts for the Russians. Curiously, though, it became a mini-crisis for the Poles, who did not possess sufficient Russian speakers to facilitate the significant part of their overseas trade which continued with Russia, including copious importation of oil and gas.

There are several dialects in Poland, some of them so remote that even Poles have difficulty understanding them. These include the languages of the mountain people ("Górale"), of the inhabitants of Silesia ("Ślązacy"), whose dialect combines elements of German and Polish, and of the "Kaszubi" from Poland's north-east, whose accent is a strange mix of Polish, German and Lithuanian. My own inadvertent "dialect", picked up through sheer confusion, and involving the use of strange words, perplexes the Poles, apparently bearing no resemblance to anything in anyone's living memory. One Pole once described it to me as the dialect of a one thousand year old man who had lived through all of Poland's innumerable border changes.

Like many nationalities, Poles reveal a lot about their character by the way they speak. The Polish sweetness, affection and willingness to please come through loud and clear in their frequent use of diminutive names. This often involves inserting the letter "k" just before, or at the end of, the word. Thus, "Justyna" (Justine) becomes "Justynka", and

"Tomasz" (Thomas) becomes "Tomaszek". Of the inanimate, "kiełbasa" (Polish sausage) becomes "kiełbaska" and "chleb" (bread) becomes "chlebek".

Diminutive forms are a step too far for me. The closest I have come to colloquialism is to pick up a few of the more common sayings, including "taka jest życie" ("such is life" or "c'est la vie") and "tak sobie" ("so-so", used in just about any context, as I would find out). Instead, I prefer to stick near the basics. I can more or less conjugate verbs, but declining nouns is difficult. In Polish, as in Latin, there is often no use made of prepositions like "to", "of", "with," and so on. Instead, the noun (and adjective, and adverb, and participle, and...) has an ending on it that denotes its relationship to the rest of the sentence. The endings seem infinite. And of course, for every rule there is an exception. Some endings are so elaborate that, to the inexperienced eye like mine, they snuff out any sign of the root noun. I could just about manage this if it were not for the nouns themselves. Not only do they come in three varieties - masculine, feminine and neuter - they also rarely bear a resemblance to their English counterparts. Admittedly, "sytuacja" means "situation", "restauracja" means "restaurant", and "balkon" means "balcony". And we have already seen similarities in business jargon. But no one would ever infer, let alone remember, that "długopis" means "pen", "samochód" means "car" and "pogoda" means "weather". It is not like French where the Gallic pronunciation of an English word with a flourish will often do. In Polish, if you're stuck, you're stuck. You try to mouth words, but emit a series of mumbles. Even if you do manage to say something, your mispronunciation can cause real offence, or mirth. I once inadvertently swore at a shop assistant whilst trying to ask her if the shoes I was contemplating buying were made of real leather – the Polish word for "leather" being not dissimilar to that for the most vile Polish swear word: "whore". I also asked an astonished friend at work whether or not I could see his pot-belly ("wzdęcie"), when I had actually wanted to see his photographs ("zdjęcie"). Another confusion, during my first few weeks at work, was between the similar sounding words "podatki" (taxes) and "dodatki" (extras - including extras added to a sandwich, such as lettuce, tomato and cucumber). I advised several clients on how to reduce their lettuce, cucumber and tomato burden, whilst always being careful to order my lunchtime sandwiches "with taxes". I received plenty of funny looks for my troubles, until a kindly Polish colleague – Paweł, a real Polish gentleman, who later became something of a guru to me on matters Polish - put me right. I was also viewed somewhat suspiciously at work for the tremendous number of times I caught flu, or "grypa". The truth is that grypa was the only word vaguely relating to a cold that I could remember, mainly for its proximity to the French "grippe". I could not for the life of me remember the actual word for a cold, which is "przeziębienie". Through some quirk of fate, I managed in my early days learning the language to pick up the *female* rather than the male word for "goodbye" – incredible though it may seem there is such a thing - and was busy departing from everyone with the equivalent in Polish of, "OK, *ducky*, see you next time". All I needed to complete the picture was to dress up in drag.

I was also hopeless at the complex forms of addressing people. A colleague at a later job I was to take in Poland with a Polish law firm – Antoni - even wrote out for me an explanation on a sheet of A4 shortly after I joined the office. The explanation, which in English might have started with "Mr. Kowalski", and ended a line later with "Mrs. Kowalski", filled the entire sheet of paper. It showed when to use first names and last names, when to use the rough Polish equivalent of "Mr." and "Mrs." ("Pan" and "Pani", literally "Sir" and "Madam"), as well as how to decline said names and titles. Half way down the page, and just as I thought I had got a grip on all this, the explanation went on to cover how to address people with other titles for which we have no meaningful equivalent in English. For example, people with masters degrees are "magister" (master); lawyers are "mecenas".

In general, however, it has to be said most Poles are delighted when you try to speak to them in their own tongue. From the initial smiles or even laughter if you have said something entirely stupid, they soon indulge you, and usually start to pronounce their words slowly and clearly, filling in the gaps in *your* sentence (the words you don't know) as you are speaking to them. Your sentences become like a duet, usually ending with the words, "Pan mówi bardzo dobrze po polsku!" ("the gentleman speaks very well in Polish!"). It is almost as if your Polish interlocutor is unaware of the help he has just given you, without which you would have stood as a good a chance of communicating effectively with him as with a Martian. Why do they help you like this? Because the Poles know they speak an extremely difficult language. Every time you make a mistake, they wave their hands in a "don't worry" gesture, and tell you the language is difficult for them, too. As kids, they say, they had to repeat and repeat the grammar until it was imprinted on them. Even Lech Wałęsa can pronounce little else right other than his surname, they say. And he was President!

Consequently, Poles will rarely criticise a foreigner's attempt to speak the language. What can happen on occasion though is that, on hearing you utter a few basic words in Polish, they will decide you are fluent. They will then proceed to converse with you at breakneck speed, including any and all relevant and incomprehensible Polish sayings. Accredited with such linguistic prowess, you will soon find yourself nodding away at the approaching juggernaut, and at the end of the two minute speech your body language will indicate you have understood every word. The danger is if the Pole's speech ends with a question. You then have to gamble on whether to give a positive or negative reply.

Like in any country, not all people communicate the same. I was struck, for instance by the difference between young and old. By old, I mean those Poles who have lived most of their lives under Communism, and will spend only their dotage in a free society. Perhaps they lost all their life savings in the shock economic therapy of the early 1990s of Leszek Balcerowicz, a radical and liberal finance minister. Perhaps not. But for whatever reason, they are often more unhappy and closed than the young. They do not have time to converse with you in your broken Polish.

In contrast, the young are more likely to be jolly and carefree. Either they see the improvements since 1989, or they are sufficiently young never to have known anything other than bread in the shops and luxuries to purchase or at least aspire to purchase. When you speak to them in Polish, they open up to you, and you feel glad you tried. You just cannot offend them. A young hairdresser once merely smiled and understood my mistake when I rudely asked how many hours she was going to make me wait after she told me she would be slightly delayed. This arose from my incorrect use of the word "godzina", which can mean "time" (as in "what time will you be ready?") as well as "hour" (as in, unintentionally, "how many hours will you be?").

In line with my theory, my young secretary, Anna, was keen to converse with me in Polish, or English (as long as it didn't take her past going home time). As for her shortcomings in written English, these had nothing to do with lack of willingness. On this occasion, the issue at play, I felt, was the division between rich and poor. Secretaries earned around £200 a month before tax. While prices were cheaper in Poland than in England, particularly if you bought food and clothes from street vendors at fairs known as "giełdas", they were not *that* much cheaper as price rises in Poland continually outstripped pay rises. The average annual wage of around £2,500 wouldn't buy much extra kiełbasa - let alone private English lessons.

Despite this, after a few weeks, Anna's English improved. Letters of advice now came back minus my instructions. It was progress. I even got her to use the spellchecker, although with the unfortunate result that letters continued to contain the wrong words - but spelt correctly. This reminded me of the bright spark who wrote "Owed (*sic*) to the Spelling Checker", an amusing piece of verse which demonstrated the tool's shortcomings (it begins: *I have a spelling checker / it came with my pc / it plane lee marks four my revue / miss steaks aye can knot sea*). The "Owed" had landed on my desk one day at work. A Polish lawyer had deposited it there, with the following note:

"Jonathan, if you are not so terrible busy, may you explain this Owed? We are not understanding it's categorisation as "comedic", and wishing on your help to more better understanding the sense of humour presented, therein!".

I noted the last word, and dialled the Plain English Team for urgent assistance.

4 PLANES, TRAINS AND AUTOMOBILES

October 1997. Marzena and I had not left Warsaw since arriving there in September, and were feeling pretty depressed about it, having not really changed our view of the city during that time. We decided to take a long weekend in Cracow, staying with my parents-in-law. We set off at around six o'clock on a Friday evening, in the dark.

One might assume the road connecting two of Poland's best known cities would be the equivalent of what we in UK call a "motorway." Not so! There were only around 200km of motorway in Poland, believed to be a major factor affecting Poland's economic growth.[5] The road from Warsaw to Cracow is instead an indirect route, and one of Poland's dubiously categorized "expressways". Expressways are intricate affairs. Whereas a motorway offers few distractions for the driver, other than the occasional service station, expressways - though dual carriage - can be a minefield.

Every kilometre or two, on an expressway, a pedestrian crossing allows Poles, geese, cows, pigs, horse-drawn carts and God-knows who or what else the chance to cross four lanes of roaring traffic. There are no traffic lights. The brave pedestrian just estimates when he might make it across, and goes for it, whilst bearing in mind no Pole in a car ever stopped for a pedestrian on the road, even at zebra crossings. At gaps in the central reservation – the Poles call them "junctions" - motorists perform ad-hoc U-turns. Torpedoing along in the outside lane of the expressway, they will suddenly slow to a halt, turn into the opening, and wait for a chance to break into the line of missiles coming in the opposite direction. It is, to say the least, precarious. The scattered remains of broken glass at many a junction tells its own story. Add to this limitless roadside signs advertising limitless products and services, and it's fair to say the number of dangers and distractions is high. On one occasion a prostitute even bared her top half to Marzena and me as we sped past.

Every time one of these various types of junction comes up on the road, there will be a sign warning drivers to slow from the 120kmh plus they will be doing to 80kmh, or even 50kmh - which is only 30mph. It had always seemed to me no one ever took any notice of this. Certainly not the Mercedes and BMWs speeding along relentlessly at closer to 200kmh in the outside lane. Why should I take any notice in my little Golf, therefore, putting along at more like 120kph? This is what I thought as we sped towards Cracow that October evening, anxious to arrive there as quickly as possible.

And then - in a flash - someone was holding a lollipop up toward me! A split second later and I registered it was a policeman holding up a wand with a round red reflector on it, as Marzena uttered "Oh, no". She had warned me the police were out to get people on a Friday night. They could make a fortune, she said. I had not understood what she meant.

We came to a stop on a muddy grass verge just after a junction, and the policeman wandered up to our car. He was a huge, imposing figure, done up in full policeman's regalia, topped by an awesome peaked hat. I wound down my window, already nervous. The policeman said nothing, just held out his hand. Marzena elbowed me and told me to produce the car documents. In Poland, a driver must carry his car documents - meaning insurance certificate, MOT, ownership document and driving licence - everywhere he goes, or else face an instant fine. Fortunately, we were wise to this, and I handed them over.

The policeman looked at the documents. He was poker-faced, seeming neither impressed nor unimpressed. He handed back the documents calmly.

"You were doing 125kmh in a 50 kmh zone", he said. "I'm going to have to fine you. Get out of the car, please".

Marzena and I got out. We joined the policeman a few paces behind the car, as he took down our registration number. We were worried. How much would the fine be? We were not exactly rolling in money - the wedding and honeymoon had seen to that. We could not really afford a whacking fine. Our only solace was that at least there was no possibility of points on my UK driving licence.

Suddenly, in what I thought was an immensely unwise move,

Marzena asked the policeman a question. Such impertinence! This was clearly not a man to whom you posed questions, I thought.

"How much will the fine be?" Marzena ventured.

The policeman paused, and stopped writing in his little notebook. He looked up at Marzena, whilst still managing to look down at her from his considerable height. "You were doing 125kmh in a 50kmh zone", he repeated. As if we didn't know. "I'm going to have to fine you the maximum fine. 300 złoty."

Marzena and I shuddered. £50. All we needed. The policeman returned to his notebook. Again Marzena spoke up. Was she mad? She was saying something about it being the weekend. Kindness. Fun. It was difficult to follow everything in Polish. Until now, the conversation had been pretty much monosyllabic. Now, Marzena and the policeman were conversing at faster speed. I drifted into a reverie of being incarcerated in a dirty, cockroach-infested Polish prison, until Marzena elbowed me again.

"Get out 100 złoty!" she said.

"I'm sorry?" I asked.

"Quickly - get 100 złoty". I got 100 złoty. In a trice, she handed it to the policeman, who immediately put away his notebook, the 100 złoty already slipped neatly inside it. He tipped his hat, and offered us some advice.

"There are policemen everywhere on this road tonight" he said. "Go slow at all the junctions". Then he left.

Marzena and I returned to the car and drove off cautiously. "We have just paid off a policeman", I said to Marzena as we pulled away. "How could we do that?"

"Don't worry about it", she said. "They'll make a fortune tonight. Anyway, would you rather have paid the 300?"

"No", I said. "Definitely not. But why was it so easy?"

"No-one here has much respect for the police anymore", Marzena replied, mysteriously. I asked her to elaborate.

"Look", she said, "it's simple. No one has much respect because the police were a main tool of Communist oppression as recently as ten years ago. They know their position is precarious, that they lack authority, and people treat them accordingly. But they can't do much about it. They're happy they stopped us, and got some money, and we're happy we only paid 100 złoty. Maybe, in this way, both sides are achieving a kind of *rapprochement*. But the point is - you should relax about it".

I did. And with a lightness in my heart that reflected the 200 złoty I had just saved – and only slightly dampened by a feeling of guilt that was already diminishing rapidly - I decided I was becoming a true Pole.

People in glass houses shouldn't throw stones. In this respect, it was a disappointment to receive a speeding fine from the police, because I am a critic of Polish driving. "A Pole, when he gets behind the wheel of a car, becomes a little bit crazy", my landlord Jan once said to me, shaking his head and tutting with disgust at the driving habits of his compatriots. My Polish colleagues at work said the same. As with Jan, the emphasis was always on *other* Poles, as opposed to sensible drivers like themselves. It was a Swiftian concept: everyone thought the other was the culprit, which followed to its logical conclusion meant none of them were, when - as I can vouch! – they *all* are.

Warsowians, in particular, drive abysmally: too fast, too close to the car in front, no indicating, never letting other cars in if they can possibly help it, but lane hopping themselves, forever tooting horns and shaking fists. Taxi-drivers have to be certified insane before they receive a licence (other pre-requisites included a lack of rear seat belts, and a meter the customer cannot see). Watch out also in the capital for cars with blue number plates and stickers on their boots saying "CD", for these are not peripatetic music salesmen, but diplomats, whose driving style fully reflects the diplomatic immunity they receive on the road. Almost every day I drove to work, I saw fresh broken glass where there had been another accident. I once saw a cyclist lying in the road covered in blood, not moving, and a perplexed-looking driver standing over him. Every bank holiday weekend, the television news finishes with a map of the country split up into "voivodships" (counties), a figure in each voivodship representing how many people have died in road accidents there that weekend. The figures usually range from 1 to 5 dotted over forty to fifty voivodships. The death toll on the Polish roads is very high. It is said accidents on the roads cost Poland more than its annual GDP growth rate.[6]

In part this can be blamed on terrible road conditions. These include cracked and crumbling road surfaces, and gaping holes in the road which, when filled with water after a storm, are difficult to spot and avoid. Your heart sinks as your precious wheels crash down into the void. Terrible sign posting doesn't help; and then, there are those junctions. Also, many traffic lights have stuck to them a small, green cardboard arrow that allows you to turn right irrespective of the status of the main lights. This is a recipe for disaster, and you will often see cars whipping up to lights and turning right, when the main light is on red, weaving dangerously into a stream of crossing traffic. As for the lights themselves, their poor quality means that green will misleadingly appear to light up in the summer sun, when in, fact, red is still on. Yes, officer, it was the sun wot done it.

In truth, however, driving habits need to change. The problem is that a Pole's car is his pride and joy. They ostentatiously dangle ignition keys and the increasingly ergonomic fobs in front of friends and colleagues. In Communist times, few Poles owned cars, and even to own a small Fiat was a major achievement. Now, sales of cars in Poland have proliferated. All the major manufacturers are fighting to gain control of the market, with increasingly tempting offers. Consequently, many Poles own cars, and big ones. Owning a big car in Poland is more of a status symbol than anywhere I know. The attraction is probably because Poles enjoy finally having the opportunity to own a big car, but also because, as many Poles can still afford only one car, they have to make it one that counts, which means a vehicle that can hold all the family and pets. And if you own such a car, then you *drive* it. It's a little like my landlord's concept of *using* your home. Thus, there is no point piddling along in third gear in town, when you can whisk through the busy streets in overdrive, running amber lights at every opportunity. In Poland, I was constantly overtaken. I don't think I ever overtook anyone.

More culpably, too many Poles drink and drive. I became aware of this thanks to the government campaign to stop drink driving in Poland. Furthermore, it does not take a genius to work out that a nation in which many drink will not change this habit overnight just because it now has more cars. But Marzena and I were never so shocked as when, attending the opening of a new restaurant the following autumn, we refused drinks on the house from our generous host, only to be met with questions from a group of young people sitting next to us. Already half sozzled, they asked why we were not drinking. "Because we're driving" was the inevitable response, that phrase synonymous back home with the gloomy face of someone not enjoying the party as much as the rest. "So what?" replied our interrogators, "So are we!" Maybe not an earth shattering moment, but I can tell you that, in the context, it was worrying, because there did not seem to be anyone in their party who was not indulging. Not earth shattering, then, until they run someone down on their way home. Perhaps we would have been less shocked had we known at this stage of Krzysztof Opaliński's satire *On Drunkards and Unrestrained Drunkenness*. Opaliński was a Pole who lived in the seventeenth century and seemed to take pleasure in chastising his own country and countrymen, writing:

"I affirm that drunkenness has built its nest in Poland. Here it multiplies, and here it raises its nestlings. A kid barely gets his teeth before he is shaking drops out of glasses and looking for something to drink. Sometimes even the cruets used at mass are not safe because after the altar boy pours a bit for the priest (according to the ritual), he drinks the rest behind the altar and thus passes his first test. Poland can be called drunk: bishops and senators drink themselves stiff; prelates, too, as well as soldiers and the gentry; they drink in towns, they drink in manors, they drink in villages".

A little immoderate, maybe, but evidently containing more than a grain of truth to this day. Indeed, in one incident, several drunken doctors turned up in an ambulance to treat a seriously ill patient. The patient later died. The Polish government knew about this kind of thing, and to its credit tried to imitate the "zero tolerance" style of law-making in New York by introducing a bill that would confiscate the cars of drunk drivers, and increase gaol terms and fines for drink driving offences.[7]

Yes, Jan had it right when he told me about crazy Polish drivers. He had imparted that wisdom one day while driving Marzena and me back from the ubiquitous IKEA on the outskirts of Warsaw where we had just bought some furniture for the flat. Suddenly he started beeping his car horn vigorously. As he did so, a full chorus of beeps joined his, and there was pandemonium. I looked around me, and animated Poles were busy bashing the centres of their steering wheels to produce the requisite sound. A few seconds later, the noise died down. "Yes, yes", he said, when there was peace again, "the Poles are a little bit crazy behind the wheel!" I nodded my head, and gave as an example the cacophony that had just passed. "For no reason at all", I added. "Oh, that", my landlord replied, "You don't need to worry about *that*. It is considered good luck to sound your horn when you see the sign for Warsaw".

It was on one of my morning trips to work when, late for a meeting with a client first thing, I inadvertently ran no less than three red lights at a busy junction. Before I knew it, a lollipop beckoned me, this time held up by two unamused policemen from a police Transit van. I slowed down fifteen metres in front of their van and turned the engine off. My knees were knocking. I had suddenly realised, now I came to think of it, that all the lights I had just gone through had been red.

In spite of my nervousness, I still wanted to take the initiative, as Marzena had on the journey to Cracow. I also remembered the words of an old law lecturer of mine from university days. Once stopped by a policeman for speeding, he got out of his car and stood tall in order to show his equality with the policeman. This had not been disrespectful, he said, but a clever subversion of the policeman's authority. Everyone knew the police were superior and talked down to you. Anyway, the net result was my lecturer had escaped a fine.

The problem is that, generally speaking, the police back home are not armed. As I exited rapidly my vehicle, my movements awkward because of my nerves, the two Polish policemen appeared taken aback. Before I knew it, one had his hand glued to the holster containing his pistol, and the other stood menacingly tall and practically up against me. Evidently my lecturer's concept was not portable.

"Hey, calm down, calm down!" I said in my pidgin Polish. Some of the foreigners at work had told me it was better to pretend to Polish police you spoke no Polish. An English lawyer colleague claimed to have been stopped by the police thirty-nine times, but only to have been fined four times - on the occasions when he had attempted to speak Polish, or had been with Polish friends. But, as these guys were young, I decided to rely on my own theory that young Poles are generally glad to hear you try to master their tongue.

The two policemen marched me to their dark blue Transit van, slid open the broad metal door, and sat me down between them on the back seat of the van. I felt like a little boy who had done something very bad at school. They asked to look at my documents, and gave me that look of dissatisfaction that meant they were satisfied with them.

"You crashed three red lights", they said.

"I know", I replied. I was very sorry.

"Why did you do it?"

Because I was late for a meeting, and wasn't paying attention. I really was very sorry.

There was a pause. One of the policemen said:

"We're going to have to fine you".

Weary at having to pay out to the police again, I took out my wallet and opened it up, all the while wondering whether I had sufficient command of Polish, and the nerve, to suggest a reduction in the fine. But before I had a chance to find out, one of the policemen asked me:

"Are you married?"

I did a double take, and wondered for a moment if he was going to ask me whether I wanted to go back to his place, Monty Python style. Then I realised he had probably caught a glimpse of the picture of Marzena I kept in my wallet, and maybe also my wedding ring. I decided to try to capitalise on this moment of friendliness. It was my only possible chance to escape a heavy fine.

"I am married", I said, in halting Polish, "and to a beautiful Polish girl! You know, in my opinion, Polish girls are perhaps the most beautiful in the world. They say Italian girls are the best", I continued, "but Polish girls are so beautiful and so stylish in their dress. They are number one!"

I stopped, and looked at the two young policemen. Would my compliments towards the Polish fairer sex work? They were heartfelt, for everything I had said about Polish girls, who were once described to me by a Polish girl herself, perhaps not so objectively, as "so classy", was true. But the policemen were not to be so easily persuaded. One of them stroked his chin. What about Spanish girls? he asked. I pretended to consider for a moment, and then replied something about their poor figures. And Brazilian? But they were too far away, I quipped. And the English? There was a gleam in the young policeman's eye as he said this. He knew I was English from my car documents. I paused for a moment, and then started giggling, and then laughing more loudly: "are you joking?", I exclaimed. The policemen both started laughing with me, to show that they *had* been joking. Soon the van was shaking with the roaring laughter of the two policemen and myself. It continued for some time, and then died down.

Could they see properly the picture of my Polish wife? I opened fully my wallet and showed them the passport size photo of her. It had been taken by a proper studio. Oh, how attractive she was! they declared. Suddenly, one of the policemen started rustling in his back pocket. He extracted his own wallet, and opened it up. There was a passport-sized photograph inside. He took it out. It was a picture of his wife. Polish, of course. What did I think of her? He handed me the photograph and I set eyes on the most unattractive Polish woman I had ever seen. She was a woman of a plainness I had supposed did not even exist in Poland.

"Beautiful!" I said.

The police let me go with a warning and a fine of 50 złoty - a little under £10, and all I had in my wallet at the time. I offered to go with them to a cash-point and get out a little more money (£10 seemed an unreasonably small fine for running three red lights) but they wouldn't hear of it. I was to hurry up and not miss my meeting. And don't pick up any English girls on the way! I could hear the two of them trying to contain their hysteria as I climbed back into my car and continued on my journey.

There are, of course, other ways of getting around in Poland than by car, but these are not the methods of transport favoured by most Poles. The inter-city trains are comfortable, clean and cheap. On the fast ones, you are even given a free snack, although I have never eaten the sandwiches handed out, which usually contain curled up salami of dubious freshness. The inter-city from Warsaw to Cracow, which Marzena took when she travelled to Cracow for her studies, could do the journey in just two and a half hours, compared to around four by car. Back in Warsaw, there is an underground or "Metro", but it provides a scant service, being the equivalent of just one of the London underground lines.[8] The pride of Poland is Lot Airways, the state aircraft operator which flies a fleet of modern Boeings, and provides a well run and reasonably-priced service. Do not hesitate to fly to Poland on Lot, and relax on your journey. For it is when you arrive at the airport and decide to take a taxi to your hotel that you will require all your strength, and quite possibly some tranquillisers.

5 THE WEATHER

Our October break in Cracow – when we finally got there, having evaded further police cars, radar guns and road blocks all the way – was somewhat spoilt by the weather. It is, furthermore, a measure of the ferocity of the Polish weather (which cites winds from Siberia as amongst its greatest influences) that, by Polish standards, this was to be - mercifully for an Englishman spending his first full year in Poland - a mild winter. The year before, in the famous winter of 96-97, there had apparently been a six-week period commencing around the end of November and lasting until mid-January when the temperature did not rise much above -25C. Even the Poles talk of how the breath was taken from their lungs when they ventured outside during this time. In contrast, the coldest temperature reached in the winter of 97-98 would be around -15C - not much worse than a cold snap in England, but still enough for me. Although Poles compare their weather favourably to that of the British, because the conditions are dry rather than damp, the sheer *coldness* of such temperatures is in my view at least equally unpleasant to our own wind and rain, if not more so. Winter in Poland can also be an ugly scene: sometimes the blanket of snow and ice does not disappear from the roadside and fields for the whole winter, getting dirtier and dirtier until cleansed by the next snow shower. Adding to the misery, it gets dark on winter afternoons at around 3pm, thanks to Poland being at the Eastern edge of a time zone. Indeed, on a gloomy winter's day in Poland, it hardly seems to get light at all, the streetlights flickering bright orange in the murk all day long. Another unpleasant feature of the Polish weather is the rapid, tremendous change in pressure, which Poles tend to blame for every headache they have ever had, a complaint I found myself repeating as I stayed longer and longer in the country. And yet, for the Poles, the one redeeming fact - that the weather these days is getting warmer - is not the cause for celebration but for complaint. They now say, with a puzzling reminiscence, that their winters have changed beyond all recognition. Worried about global warming, you ask? No, no, they reply, explaining masochistically – it's just not *cold* enough.

It was nevertheless too cold for us to sit on the rynek in Cracow, and too cold to spend much time gazing into clothes shop windows - even for Marzena. We therefore spent a couple of days visiting her friends, which opened my eyes to a real, domesticated Poland as fascinating as watching life from a café chair. Despite having visited Poland many times over the previous three years, having married there, and lived there since August, my life in Poland up until now had been all restaurants, cafés, bars, banks, shops and offices. I had not experienced much typical Polish home life. True I had been a well looked after guest at my in-laws' on many occasions - but so well looked after it felt like being at my own parents' home in England. This time, we visited other homes - of some of Marzena's oldest friends in the countryside around Cracow.

We were made particularly welcome when visiting a friend who lived in a small village near Krzeszowice - Marzena's home town where we had married. Setting off by car just after lunch on a gloomy autumnal day, we wound down innumerable country roads, past sprawling, overgrown fields until I felt we were truly in the middle of nowhere. Then, all of a sudden, there was a small village, and a complex of houses into which we drove. It turned out these all belonged to the parents of Marzena's friend, who were building on their extensive property. One house, in particular, seemed to be progressing well, its orange brick walls already formed and some weather boarding erected, and brown roof tiles put in place – but not yet any windows. When we arrived in the main family home, which was being renovated and smelt of fresh paint, the father of Marzena's friend immediately brought cake, opened sparkling wine, and entertained us. He was chatty and joined in the fun. Although this was somewhat to his daughter's chagrin, I decided we were again witnessing the close integration of the Polish family. We later satisfied him by being taken on a tour of the building work. Following the tour, as Marzena and her friend chatted away in Polish, I was left to my own thoughts, and reflected a little on how, famously, first impressions can be misleading. Here was a little village in Polish Galicia, seemingly removed from civilisation, but one family at least had a series of delightful homes, space of their own, a car to get about – and, presumably, a fulfilling life. And not only did they not need the hustle and bustle of Cracow, let alone London, as I had felt sure they must, but in any case, this to them *was* home. I vowed to be more open-minded about such parts of Poland in the future.

Later that afternoon, Marzena and I visited an exceptional Polish home. It belonged to the parents of an artist friend of Marzena's, Olek, who was already well known in Cracow, where he possessed an artist's studio in the garret of one of the old town's grand buildings. Knowing he was at his parents' home that afternoon, we stopped off there on the way back to Krzeszowice. Immediately, on entering his parents' small front garden just off the twisty road that ran through the village, we were struck by what we saw everywhere: statues. Olek's father is a celebrated sculptor, and the range and quality of his work is tremendous. One figure grabbed my attention, an eight foot high, matchstick man, carved leaning forward, an expression on his face like that of Munch's "Scream". I thought he would make a fitting monument to nearby Auschwitz.

We entered the fine old house, a small palace or "dwórek", Olek said (I noted the use of the diminutive – a large palace would have been called a "dwór"). It was painted white, with two solid pillars either side of the front door, which we walked between to find ourselves in a spacious hall, to the left and right of which were the two wings of the building. Immediately we were met by more statutes and plenty of paintings, for most of Olek's brothers and sisters are also artists. Escaping the gnashing "pet" dog that can be found in many a Polish home, we were shown through to a veranda at the back of the house. We looked out into the back garden and saw there, stretched before us - a lake! It was a good size, and included a jetty with small rowing boat attached. Surrounding it was a sweeping landscape garden, very well kept, with thick green grass and an apple orchard. Marzena and I were lost for words. Olek, typically the distrait artist, seemed unconcerned at the lake, but his father did the tour guide bit, explaining that it was a natural lake, being the lowest point in the village. Marzena and I rediscovered our voices, and enthused about the property. Olek's father was clearly flattered, but explained it was not as simple as it all looked. He told us this dwórek was typical of the manor houses and palaces that used to exist in Poland during happier times. Unfortunately, two World Wars and fifty years of Communism had left many such buildings either destroyed or in ruin. A lot of effort had been required by his wife and him to get this dwórek back into shape. I remembered the prodigious but shabby palace behind the registry office where Marzena and I had married in Krzeszowice, and wondered whether we ought not get Olek's parents on the job.

Having already seen the new houses erected by the family of the first friend we visited, and now this little gem, I realised Poland was progressing in modern architecture, but also, little by little, in preservation of the old. Marzena agreed, but explained to me that, as with everything, it's a question of money. Renovating such dwóreks requires a lot of it. Consequently, it is often carried out in Poland by artist folk like Olek's parents, who possess the skills to renovate cheaply themselves and do a job faithful to the original. We had been lucky to see such a fine example of their work.

After our eye-opening local adventures, we decided to head to the famous nearby resort of Zakopane, in the Tatra mountains, less than two hours by car. We would spend a few days there. We would not ski, which was most people's pastime, but for which it was too early in the season, and of which I was anyway incapable, much to Marzena's disappointment, due to an old knee injury. Instead, we would walk the trails, breath fresh mountain air (like the schoolchildren of Cracow, who were sent to Zakopane annually to give their lungs a fighting chance against the fumes of the Nowa Huta steelworks) and eat out by evening. We had not booked a hotel, but would find one on sight. It was an opportunity not to be missed, as I had never been to Zakopane, and as the winter was so (apparently) mild. Little did I know, however, that winter is an entirely different concept at the top of a Tatra mountain.

Arriving in Zakopane, we parked the car and decided to look for a hotel straight away, just in case there was any problem finding a room. We visited the big, spruce hotels in the centre of Zakopane, but found them to be prohibitively expensive - around 600 złoty (£100) a room. Marzena told me this was not the sort of hotel we wanted in any case: better to stay in a "pensjonat", the Polish equivalent of a French *pension*, with good home cooking, comfortable rooms, and equally comfortable prices. We drove out of the centre a small way, and noticed several such *pensjonat*, but they looked uninviting. Uniform, grey concrete squares. Finally, we found one that looked a little more like it - surrounded by trees and with a wooden roof - stopped the car and took a look inside. This *pensjonat* was OK, but it was missing that certain *je ne sais quoi*. It was sizeable, but too much: the refectory, on the ground floor by the entrance, reminded me of where I ate my school dinners. We made our excuses and moved on. We experienced the same disappointment everywhere we went. In the end, we chose to stay out of town at a dilapidated hotel block where Marzena had stayed as a child. I pictured Poles during Communist times feeling privileged to have found a place in such a hotel for their holidays and realised not for the first time that, living in the West, it was we who had been the privileged ones.

It was twilight. We drove into town and walked up the main street, which I had heard so much about. Marzena often talked nostalgically about visiting Zakopane as a little girl, walking in the mountains with her parents, seeing the comical and comically dressed mountain people, skiing as a teenager with friends. Now, though there is still a semblance of the old mountain town about central Zakopane (restaurants housed in old, wooden buildings - all beams and log fires) much of the main street is dominated by shops selling tasteless souvenirs. Marzena was disappointed, revisiting as she was a favourite childhood haunt. However, that night, we had a tasty supper in an old-world restaurant, and slept well after exploring some of the nooks and crannies of the town.

The next day, we decided to take the telecabine up to the top of one of the highest mountains - Kasprowy Wierch - which at 7,500 feet, is much taller than anything we have in England. The cable cars were bulky, made of shining steel. However, they somehow looked past their sell-by date, and as we climbed rapidly up the mountainside accompanied by a loud buzzing sound I became more and more alarmed. I just could not put my faith in these machines, which Marzena said seemed unmodified from when she was a girl, and which I imagined had been put together by work-shy Communists using out-of-date tools and methods. In short, I was scared stiff. However, as I got used to the rolling and jolting of the carriage, I began to look around me, and realised we were passing through some of the most spectacular scenery I had ever seen. Tree covered mountains, some of the trees displaying early winter snow, and valleys, abounded. This was like being in the Alps. Zakopane town may have disappointed, but not its surrounds. As we rose higher and higher, the angle of ascent grew steeper and steeper. After a middle station, we finally arrived at the top, and mind-boggling views of the awesome Tatra peaks.

We left the cabine, and no sooner did I have the pleasure of stepping onto *terra firma* than it hit me: THE COLD. It was *freezing*. Marzena and I rushed into the mountaintop restaurant and, chilled solid, exchanged shocked looks. I had certainly never experienced anything like it. Marzena seemed better off, but also disbelieving. However, plenty of others were leaving the restaurant and climbing up the hundred or so metres to the top of the mountain. There was nothing else for it: we had come this far, we had to continue. As we left the restaurant for the summit, I told Marzena to go on without me if I did not come back, re-marry, and live a happy life. As usual, she took no notice.

We climbed steadily to the peak, and tried to ignore the blizzard that was now hitting us horizontally in the face. Soon, we were at the top, and soon after making ready to turn around and come back. It was just too cold to think. I felt numb all over. The freezing air hollowed out the passage between my nostrils and the back of my throat. I was becoming The Ice Man. And then, as I began my return, I suddenly realised an amazing thing. Signs indicated that the almost sheer drop to one side of the summit masqueraded as a legitimate ski run during the winter season. We are not even talking "off-piste". I could not believe it. The shock, combined with the cold, was enough nearly to knock me out. I hastened back to the restaurant, and downed three hot chocolates to recover my senses.

The telecabine journey back down the mountain seemed a lot less hairy than the ascent. However, for some strange reason, we had to descend with an elaborate Heath Robinson soft drinks machine, which filled almost the entire cable car. It left only just enough room for passengers to squeeze around the outside of it, heads practically forced out of the window. I knew if we fell off the cable, however, that it would be with our thirsts well and truly quenched.

In the afternoon, we walked along picturesque mountain trails, and Marzena told me some of the stories of her scouting days here. I was intrigued by the thought of young Polish girls and boys singing traditional, pre-Soviet patriotic Polish songs around camp fires, which they could only do when away from the party members like this. Before then, during the Second World War, scouts were heavily involved in the Polish underground, comprising half one particular section responsible for "minor acts of sabotage" against the Nazis. Robert Baden Powell – founder of the Scouts - surely never knew he would play such a role in the downfall of Fascism and then Communism.

In the next few days, we took more pleasant walks in the forests, but were never quite able to warm ourselves in the chill mountain air. The snow had not yet arrived, other than at the top of the mountains, which meant there was no blanket of relative warmth to lie under, and no cosy winter feel yet to Zakopane. We were clearly, inconveniently, in between seasons, which perhaps accounted for my perplexity as to why the Poles adore the Tatras. I felt the place had potential, as the eye-catching scenery on our trip up Kasprowy Wierch had demonstrated, and Marzena confirmed this: I should come in the ski season, when the place was abuzz, or in the summer, when the evergreens popped out from under the snow and ice - and things would seem different, she assured me. I would take up her challenge the following summer and change my opinion of Zakopane and the Tatras.

Zakopane in the winter plays to the stereotype of Polish weather. Yes, it can be horribly cold in Poland for six months of the year, but invariably from around April onwards, Poland experiences the other side of a Continental climate. The summers in Poland are extremely hot. The temperature rises way above that in England, sometimes hitting 40C. If you do not have air conditioning in the office, you're lost, and it's a good thing to have it in the car, too. It's *too* hot. In the heat of the day, from around 11am until 4pm, it's impossible to do anything except laze around and listen to the interminable, deafening ringing of what must be giant sized crickets in Poland. It is in such circumstances the Polish habit of beginning work as early as six or seven o'clock in the morning, and returning home around three, comes into its own, allowing the rest of the day for relaxing in the intense heat. Furthermore, such conditions are eminently suitable for holidaymakers, who can wear comfortable, light clothing, slap on the sun lotion, and soak up the heat - or read a book in the shade. The thunder storms that brew for a few days during this hot weather, and then break in all their glory, flooding for a few hours the Polish streets that do not drain properly, leaving small Fiats marooned at almost every street corner, add to the exotic feel. This is the sort of spectacular weather that makes temperate Britain look a little tame. On the other hand, the British, who love to complain about their perpetual lack of a summer, would not wish to swap June, July and August with the Poles if this also entailed accepting the storms. In 1997 and 1998 they caused some of the worst and most devastating floods in Polish history.

The weather can last right up until late September, although by the end of August, the evenings begin to snap cold, even following a day of intense heat. Then, as you grab a sweater and remark it seems to be getting colder a little earlier each evening, you experience a sudden panic and prey unethically for global warming, knowing as you do those biting Siberian winds are once again just around the corner.

6 RELIGION AND FESTIVALS

We found ourselves in Cracow again on 1 November to mark one of the most significant dates in the Polish calendar: All Saints Day. Originally a pagan tradition, in which mourners placed candles on graves to commemorate the dead, and even ate and drank at the side of the graves, it has since become Christianised. Nowadays, candles and flowers are placed on graves and prayers said from the Christian liturgy.

The importance of All Saints Day cannot be overestimated. It is a public holiday in Poland, and many Poles journey back to their home town to attend the graveside. Marzena and I did the same in Cracow. On a bitterly cold November day we drove up the hill on which her parents lived to a bleak graveyard in a high field, and laid flowers (usually chrysanthemums in Poland) and candles for Marzena's grandmother, who had been married to the nonagenarian grandfather – dziadek - who now lived with my parents-in-law. This clearly meant a lot to Marzena, judging from her gentle movements as she placed the flowers and candles on her grandmother's grave, and from the sincere and sad look in her eyes. The day ended with a pleasant family gathering (what else?) where cakes and drinks were served, and the atmosphere was subdued but not overly so. I left Cracow after the commemoration thinking that to honour the dead in this way for just one day a year was the least they deserved. It reminded me of the Jewish custom of visiting the graves of your closest relatives in the month leading up to the Jewish New Year.

Of course, it is at Christmas that the Poles, like many nations, go to extremes. The present-giving, however, takes place before this, in early December, on "Mikołaj" or "St. Nicholas' Day". Children wake up to find presents deposited at the foot of their bed by Santa Claus in the night. Polish employees eager to have some time off then count down the days to Christmas before holding a small party at the office on 23 December ("opłatek") - the last day of work - during which all exchange good wishes. So far, it all appears reasonably similar from a British perspective, but this changes the next day. It is Christmas Eve ("Wigilia" or "Vigil"), not Christmas day, that is the focus of the Poles' celebrations. People travel home the night before Christmas Eve. On the day itself, everyone lends a hand preparing things for the evening meal that is the equivalent of our Christmas day lunch.

But preparing for Christmas Eve starts a long time before this - other than for the Christmas tree which is put up shortly before the holiday. House cleaning breaks out on a truly grand scale, including the beating of rugs, the washing and waxing of parquet floors, and the cleaning of windows (inside and out, whatever the weather). Plates of food start filling fridges, including herring, barszcz (the beetroot soup), "uszka" (literally "small ears", named after their shape - small dumplings filled with mushrooms to be eaten with the barszcz), "pierogi" (larger dumplings) and "makowiec" (poppy seed cake). But worst of all for a man like me - the turkey's nemesis, and a fish-hater to boot - it is *carp* that is eaten for the Christmas Eve meal, because the Poles are fasting at this time; that is, not eating meat during Advent, the season of penance, that ends at midnight. The carp is often bought live and stored in bath tubs at home, and then prepared on the day before Christmas Eve. Even though I do not like it, I have to admit its preparation is something special: it can be breaded in strips, fried, and served with horseradish, or eaten cold in its own jelly, or poached, or eaten "Jewish style" (without bones). And so valued by the Poles is carp at Christmas that it has been known for employers to offer prize live carp as part of the Christmas bonus to employees – who are always grateful because it means they don't have to queue up for the freshest specimens.

Marzena and I decided to spend Christmas 1997 in Poland with her family, as this was such an important time for her as a Pole, and as I wanted to experience the occasion for myself. We arrived early on Christmas Eve, and after a day of interminable preparations in which I began to despair of any celebration ever taking place, formal proceedings finally began in the evening with more breaking of the opłatek (from the Latin "oblatum", meaning sacrificial gift) - a Christmas wafer made from unleavened bread. This was the real thing, rather than the token opłatek I had experienced on 23 December at work. The ceremony dates from mediaeval times, and entails members of the family exchanging blessings and good wishes for the coming year. It is a happy time, when individuals struggle to keep a straight face at the sincerity of the wishes offered them. This was not a problem for me, however, as, due to my lack of linguistic skills, I was not quite sure what I was being wished. The good will is sealed with kisses on the usual three cheeks, again including between men folk. The meal then begins once the first star is seen in the sky, symbolic of the star the Three Kings followed, and up to *twelve* dishes (to represent the twelve apostles) are served on a table incorporating a little hay scattered under the tablecloth to recall the manger.

After the breaking of the opłatek I felt a little left out during the remainder of the evening. I ate a fried egg instead of the breaded fish which was piled high on a big plate. I then stayed at home as the rest of the family trouped off courageously in the icy cold to midnight mass or "pasterka" (literally, "the shepherds' mass") at the local church, just up the hill. The local church is a moderate affair, but the locals are fiercely proud of it because, though built after Communism, their priest tried to establish it before then and was arrested for his troubles. It boasts a high angular roof, and is painted a bright white. The exterior is tasteful, in contrast to many churches in Poland, which are concrete monstrosities built in the name of modern art (one, on the road into Cracow, resembles a ship). Inside it is elaborately adorned, mostly in gold, which is typical. The embellishments include innumerable crosses, carved angels and cherubim, candlesticks, and stylised paintings and statuettes of the Virgin Mary. Indeed, it is the Virgin Mary who occupies the commanding position behind the altar, with Christ relegated to a position to one side of her.

Church royalty, however, can be found at Częstochowa, a monastery in central Poland. This church is more like a castle fortification - of which any of the various violent religious orders of the Middle Ages would have been proud – consisting of a series of defensive walls and towers, as well as an arsenal and treasury. Its *pièce de resistance* is a small painting of the Black Madonna, by an unknown artist, that is said to have magical powers. As you enter the area of the monastery where the Black Madonna resides, you see before you a sea of crutches discarded by those who have thrown off their disabilities. It's a good job I'm not disabled, however. On the occasion we visited the monastery, the next unveiling of the Black Madonna (which was for the rest of the time kept behind a screen) was not due for another two hours. We did not have the patience to wait, as we were on a return journey from Cracow to Warsaw. I would have had to keep my crutches. But the defence of Poland has not been so compromised in the past. During the siege of Częstochowa of 1655, 250 Poles held out for six weeks against 4,000 superior armed Swedes. This sparked a national revolt by the Poles who by 1660 had regained almost all the territory they had lost in the Swedish invasion of Poland known as the

"Swedish Deluge". The miracle of Częstochowa was put down to the incredible powers of the Black Madonna, whose painting had been paraded everyday on the battlements in front of the Swedes.

That first Christmas Eve, with the others off worshipping, I decided to watch television. Maybe I would get a glimpse of the Black Madonna, it being Christmas Eve, and all? It turned out I had an inspiring choice between the Pope's midnight mass from St. Peter's in Rome, and a programme featuring Polish Christmas carols ("kolędy"). I opted for the carols, consoling myself with the thought people had been singing carols in Poland since the fifteenth century – so I would certainly not be the first to suffer. In fact, they were melodic and peaceful: children dressed in long white surplices sang a number of hymns in soprano voices in perfect unison, as studio lights shone off baubles hanging from small Christmas trees. I even thought I recognised a Polish version of "Silent Night". I lay back and relaxed, sipping a little too much of the delicious "miód królewski" or honey vodka. As the alcohol descended, I felt a little guilty I was relaxing in this way as my relatives stood in a parky church making their final apologies for sins no doubt smaller in number than those that I had committed throughout the last year. *But not too guilty.*

POLSKA DOTTY

A unique feature of Christmas in Cracow are the "szopka" models constructed by children and adults alike. Szopka means "little barn", and the models are supposed to represent the place of Jesus' birth. They actually resemble more churches, particularly the famous Mariacki church in central Cracow. These models, many made from wood and the shiny foil used to wrap up sweets, are sparkling, rainbow hued constructions – spectacular in appearance. They are mostly coloured red, white, blue and green, and consist of many small church towers and spires, and sometimes miniature exotic palm trees, figures of animals and people. These can include Jesus, Mary, Joseph, the Three Kings, shepherds, the Wawel dragon - and even political figures, modelled with a strong sense of irony. Some students who build szopka even include models of themselves. Many of the szopka also feature lights, sounds and movement. This is how models were supposed to be. The best examples are displayed in the main rynek in Cracow, and entered in the Christmas competition arranged by the historical museum there since 1937. Once the public, including parents with excited children (and sometimes children with excited parents) have been allowed to pass by, a winner for the adults' and children's categories is chosen. Some of the szopka can be bought, for small fortunes. Not a surprise when you think of the work that goes into them, for the construction of many szopka begins in January, just after the previous year's display.

Marzena and I also spent the following Easter, another significant Polish festival, with the family in Cracow. As with Christmas, the first day - Good Friday - is spent going to church and, once again to my disappointment, eating fish. On the Saturday, a wider selection of food, including painted eggs, bread, salt, pepper, fruit and meat, all prettily packed in a basket, is taken to be blessed in the church. Afterwards, the contents of the basket, including the meat, are eaten for breakfast. This is more like it. Easter Sunday consists of church and another family breakfast, including "mazurek" cake filled with nuts, raisins and two layers of cream, and topped with icing, and "sernik" (cheesecake) for which the Poles are renowned.

But the best part of Easter is Easter Monday, or the bizarre sounding "Śmigus Dingus" ("Wet Monday") as the Poles call it. This being the day of the patron saint of water, it is a tradition to bless water in the church. But it is also an excuse for anyone and everyone to throw buckets of water at each other with impunity. Young men will try to douse the girl of their dreams, hoping in this strange way to affect a process of attraction between them. Walking in Cracow on Śmigus Dingus, you take a real risk of ending up soaked to the skin, and would be wise to wear a cagoule and waterproof trousers - if you can handle the resultant verbal flak. Marzena has another problem: she has to dodge the various types of aftershave thrown at her by her doddering but cheeky grandfather.

It was important to celebrate these festivals with Marzena and her family because such occasions are taken so seriously in Poland. At first, I was tempted to put such respect down purely to the strong Catholic tradition in Poland. Most Poles are born Catholic, and many practise the faith. The late Pope, John Paul II, was Polish and revered throughout the country, including for the brave and effective role he played in the downfall of Communism[9].

I found out, however, that it is not the case that all Poles are staunchly Catholic. When the AWS coalition (one of the two main political groupings in Poland) tried to incorporate references to God in the new Polish constitution, there was an outcry from the rival SLD, and a compromise had to be found.[10] Indeed, many centuries ago, Poland was even considered heretical, due to the tolerance it showed to many different religions. In the sixteenth century it was termed *Paradisus Hereticorum* – a paradise for heretics. The rabid Teutonic knights once wrote of the Poles:

"If someone advances a schism, the Poles ally themselves with him.
If anyone scorns the Christians, look and see if he's not a Pole;
And when priests are slain, see if Poles are not in it again.
If someone insults the Pope, he is sure to be a Pole.
If someone insults the Holy Virgin and Saints
Or tramples upon the body of Christ
Or refuses the Sacrament and destroys the holy vessels,
See if his companion is not a Pole".

I was confused. What was the role of religion in Poland? As usual I asked Marzena for an explanation – and received the usual explanation: *the family*. The religious festivals, she said, are really treated as an opportunity in which to have time off, be with the family, and relax. Having been with Marzena's family during Christmas, I realised what she meant. I witnessed this as a time for playing with the kids: taking them for walks in the woods and to playgrounds, and presenting them with presents on Christmas Day (sampling a little from the West here) in addition to those they received on "Mikołaj". For maybe giving dziadek yet another bottle of Cognac for his collection; for thrilling mum once again with flowers and dad with whisky; as well as indulging in the statutory eating and drinking. There is also perhaps time to enjoy a good movie with your partner, and explain to the grandchildren what type of animal "Big Bird" is on the omnipresent *Sesame Street* show – a more unintelligible creature than ever when dubbed into Polish. None of which could exactly be described as worship. All in all, it is a question of quality time in which religion, though certainly not the after thought it has become for many back home, still has to compete. Even in Poland, therefore, it seems Catholicism - so much a part of the fabric of society – takes second place to that most popular of all faiths: The Polish Family.

7 ENTERTAINMENT (AKA WARSAW REVISITED)

New Year, 1998. Marzena and I resolved: more time in Warsaw, less in Cracow. After all, we lived in the capital, so no use in escaping it every free moment. The obvious place to start our Warsaw renewal was the old town. We had already visited it fleetingly, but never given it its due mainly because, having been totally reconstructed after the war, we could not escape the notion it was not genuine. This time we went on a crisp, January Saturday, cold but bright, and appreciated it a lot more.

Not as extensive as the old town in Cracow, the old town in Warsaw is nevertheless, we realised, enchanting. It dates from the thirteenth and fourteenth centuries, when the Mazovian Dukes – nobility descended from Polish royalty - left their castle to transfer their seat to the later site of the royal castle. In the seventeenth century, after the devastation of the Swedish invasion, many old town houses acquired Baroque fronts during their reconstruction. Then, after the even worse damage inflicted by the Nazis, the Poles reconstructed the place so intricately that fragments of portals or window frames found amongst the rubble were utilised. But most of the original Gothic architecture was lost, due to the small number of relics that existed at the time, and now the features of the old town are mostly Baroque and Classical. There is also a so-called "new town", which dates from the turn of the fifteenth century, in which the winding streets create an ambience of long ago which is the equal of that in the old town. The new town even has its own main (though irregularly shaped) square, in which stands the brilliant white St. Casimir's church, a late Baroque structure with a bold green dome.

The more important main square in the old town is much smaller than that of Cracow, but size isn't everything, and this square has plenty going for it. The various burgher houses that align its four sides are all connected, making for an intense and intimate feel. They are painted more brightly than in Cracow in a variety of bright colours - blue, pink, lime green, dark and sandy brown, and have attractive patterned stuccoes on their facades. The combined effect of this mélange is greater than the sum of the parts. As we walked around, I remembered when it was late summer in Warsaw, and chairs and tables had been spread across the square, and people sat at them drinking frothy beers. It had been a pretty scene. Today, it looked equally pleasant. So what if it wasn't genuinely old? Was it any more unreal than us, renewing our cells day by day? What surely counts is the *essence* of a thing. And as most of the dates carved on the keystones of the old town houses are from the previous three centuries, there is no obvious sign the old town has been reconstructed at all. We carried on walking, past the remains of the city defences - the Barbakan, with its castle turrets and half-destroyed but lengthy red brick walls - and saw numerous churches (their domes covered in verdigris) and quaint restaurants. We passed the bronze gilded statue of Sigismund III Wasa, the Polish King who made Warsaw the capital of Poland, and who now stands on a column above the old town – supposedly the oldest monument in Poland. His statue is virtually unique because the King holds a cross in one hand and a sword in the other, and thus is glorified in a manner usually reserved for saints. Next to Sigismund's column, we passed the magnificent "Terracotta" royal castle, and marvelled that this building, burned in 1939, and blown up by the Nazis in 1944, was once again whole. We went on and were able to walk for ten or fifteen minutes before we reached the edge of the old town. It was not so small after all, and was architecturally a pearl. All you could really criticise was that, at its furthest points, and unlike the old town in Cracow, it seemed deserted and lifeless.

We also visited, a fifteen-minute walk from the old town, an evocative place - Próżna street. The two or three buildings on this street, though now slightly derelict, survived the war reasonably intact. Here, we saw atmospheric old Warsaw: faded red brick buildings, iron balconies, and old lampposts. The wooden scaffolding of current reconstruction even seemed of another era. If we still had any doubts about the genuineness of Warsaw, of what it used to be, then here it was, plain for us to see – even before we witnessed the Canalettos of which our landlord had spoken so lovingly.

We wanted more, and decided there and then to make it a weekend habit to explore Warsaw. The next Saturday we visited the Royal Palace of Wilanów, to see those self-same Canalettos. In the past, Warsaw had been famous for its palaces. As Johann Bernoulli, a Swiss scholar wrote, in a letter of 1778:

"What is striking in Warsaw is the host of beautiful and shapely palaces, which quite astounded me. I must confess that, while Berlin possesses many more lovely burgher houses, Warsaw boasts at least as many buildings that may be called palaces".

Of course, since then, Warsaw and Poland has lost many of its palaces, especially during more turbulent recent history, as Olek's father had explained. But the Royal Palace at Wilanów had survived the Second World War better than most, and we looked forward to going there.

Wilanów, from the Latin "Villa Nova" meaning "New House" - an upmarket suburb of Warsaw traditionally favoured by expats - was only ten minutes from where we lived in Warsaw. It is on the edge of the city, a magnificent palace built by the Polish King Jan III Sobieski

(1629-1696). He achieved a famous military victory over the Turks, finally repulsing them from Western Europe for good, at the Battle of Vienna in 1683. The victory was a typically romantic Polish one, gained despite an inferior number of troops, mainly thanks to the famous Polish "Hussars", a formidable cavalry that wore the characteristic two rows of eagles' feathers on the backs of their armour. The Baroque style palace is a celebration of this and other victories. It is basically a quadrangle, surrounded by appealing gardens with sculptures, fountains and small pavilions. These include English parks to the north and south that are at their most resplendent in the spring, and that drop away at the rear of the palace to a wide, sweeping lake. What caught my eye were the frescoes on the walls of the southern galleries, painted in the sepia of old photographs, and depicting scenes from Homer's *Odyssey* and Virgil's *Aeneid*.

Given the cold that day, we decided we would enjoy the beauty of the outside architecture and gardens later in the year. In the meantime, we would take a guided tour of the palace. We shuffled inside fast as we could, and stamped the snow from our shoes. We were lucky. A guided tour in English was leaving in ten minutes. Just time to change into our slippers, the lady who took our ticket explained. I was not sure what she meant, until I saw a crate of scummy looking footwear, that looked like a cross between flip flops and Jesus creepers. First, Marzena and I tried removing our own shoes and putting on these replacements, but they were much too big. No one was there to help. The lady whose job it was to collect tickets had, well, collected her tickets. Now she was gone. So, with devastating initiative, I slipped my shoes back on and put the flip-flop-Jesus-creepers over the top of them, with some improvement, though they were still too big. Marzena did the same, but was still swamped, and had to shuffle her way around the tour. We decided it was a security measure. Certainly no thief would make off at speed, a Canaletto under his arm, wearing these things.

Our guide for the one-hour tour was a diminutive Pole, whose hair looked like it had last been washed when royalty inhabited the palace, at the end of the eighteenth century. It was jet-black, and slicked back, and with a narrow face, he had something of a look of Hitler about him. But how wrong can you be! The man hated everything to do with the Germans, and indeed the Russians. I had long been aware of the traditional suspicion of the Poles for these two nations which flank them. But never before had I seen it in such action. It seemed that every priceless artefact of the palace had at one time been looted (and then returned, not that they deserved any credit for *that*) by the despicable Germans or Russians. I almost expected our guide to spit every time he had to mention the words "Germans" or "Russians", and prayed there were none in our group.

For all that, our guide was a lively individual, who brought the palace to life. Full of clever little quips and tales, that he told in a sweet, slightly aristocratic English accent, the only problem was he was so dead-pan no one dared laugh, which seemed to annoy him slightly. His finest feature, which gave him the air of a mad professor, was the pointer he used, which he would telescopically extend and retract when he was nervous. It looked like an ordinary car aerial, and I spent most of the tour wanting to nip back to the car just to check he hadn't taken mine.

The rooms of the palace, which all connect by the one corridor that looks out onto the main quadrangle – are exquisite. On the ground floor, the ceilings are high, decorated with paintings and sculptures. Gold painted crystal chandeliers hang down. The floors are either marble or wooden, and on them stand antique furniture, including tables, chairs and cabinets. Every room is full of works of silver, glass and ceramic, vases and ancient stone sarcophagi, and ornate golden clocks. Most walls are adorned with colourful friezes, stuccoes and paintings. The King's bedroom boasts a magnificent red bed, canopied with seventeenth century Turkish fabric – by the side of which hang armour, suits, shields, swords and hatchets, all set with precious stones – showing him to have been a true warrior-king. Upstairs, the rooms are smaller and the ceilings remarkably low, with the exception of a long room housing the only permanent Polish portrait gallery.

It was upstairs our guide showed us what we had been waiting for: the Canalettos of Warsaw. Canaletto had indeed been invited by Polish royalty to paint Warsaw, as our landlord had said - but this was the "other" Canaletto, namely Bernado Belotto, his nephew, who painted in his uncle's realistic style and often used his name. But no matter, for what a city he revealed. Painting a view of the capital from the far, right bank of the Vistula, eighteenth century Warsaw looked unrecognisable from the Warsaw of today. It was all green domes and brown Baroque steeples and Gothic bell towers and the magnificent white facades of palaces and the rococo royal castle and sailing-boats on the Vistula - their white sails and Polish red and white standards billowing in the breeze in front of the simple wooden houses of the poorer right bank. The Vistula had clearly earned its title as the "Queen of Poland's rivers" in such bygone days. All in all, the town looked more like Cracow does today. Maybe Belotto painted with a romantic eye, but there did not seem to be an ugly building in sight. Warsaw was once a jewel too, I realised. And Belotto was not flattering the Polish Kings, our guide added: these were accurate drawings, later used to rebuild the old town after the devastation inflicted by the Nazis. I sensed our guide holding back a globule of spittle.

The tour lasted exactly an hour. Our guide had been splendid to the last, kindly reminding us several times not to miss the concerts given in one of the larger downstairs rooms of the palace - August II's Great Dining-room, which even had a small balcony attached. I wanted to thank him at the end by way of a small tip, and had the feeling he wanted this, too, but no sooner had he pronounced the tour at an end than he disappeared, like a bat into the night. I imagined him sitting back in the staff quarters bemoaning to his fellow guides that no one laughed at his jokes or gave him any tips, and felt sorry for him, but helpless. He seemed to be too proud to accept a tip. All very laudable, but not very pragmatic. But as I would later learn, for many reasons the Poles *are* a proud people, and I would not change this. So in the meantime, I just hoped he would learn Western capitalist ways, which would certainly overcome any feelings of honour he may have.

Now on a roll, and keeping to our master plan, we decided the following weekend to visit Łazienki park. This is the royal park, the name of which means "Baths", which was brought to its glory by the last Polish King Stanisław Augustus Poniatowski who – as well as controversially ruling over Poland at the time it was partitioned - built a number of stunning neo-Classical buildings housing, in particular, baths and spas. The water is said to be medicinal.

Thousands of people visit Łazienki every weekend, so we expected crowds, even on a winter's day. However, when we got to the park, which is more like a forest, we realised it would take a lot of visitors to crowd such a vast area. No wonder these had been the hunting grounds of the Mazovian Dukes. We wandered around the park, every now and then encountering ornamented buildings that were said to have housed baths in the days of the Kings. There was no rhyme or reason to the location of the buildings, or their type, which gave the park immense charm. We came across an amphitheatre for summer plays and concerts that romantically featured – something I've never seen before or since - a stage built on an island, separated from the semi-circular amphitheatre auditorium by water. We saw the small "Temple of Sybille" (an ancient female prophet) and also a bronze statue of Chopin now speckled green with corrosion. Art Nouveau, it depicts the composer under a willow and has an austerity about it of which the Socialist Realists, whom I was in the process of learning about, would have been proud. However, its history tells a different story: it was torn down by the Communists, and only pieced back together and re-erected after '89. For once, maybe the Communists had the right idea. Even the Poles of 1926, when the statue was unveiled, did not like it. But the monument honours one of Poland's most exalted sons, and there is an inherent popularity in that.

What we were really looking for, however, was the famous "Palace on the Water". We had seen this building looking spectacular on a postcard in the town: Corinthian columns standing straight and true, reflected in the water that lapped up to the palace, the middle ones supporting a triangular pediment, above which stood carved figures. We arrived at a central area, where more than the usual number of walkers seemed to be milling around, and noticed one or two interesting looking structures. But where was the palace? It had to be somewhere near here, because this seemed to be the main focus of the park, and we had seen a sign for the palace pointing this way. Marzena asked a gentleman who was passing by if he could direct us to the Palace on the Water. There were a few small buildings around here (Marzena pointed at one nearby) but we could not seem to find the palace. Could he help? The man explained the "*small building* around here" (he spat out the first two words) to which Marzena was referring, *was* the Palace on the Water, and walked off in a huff - a Warsovian insulted. We felt chastened, and stood back to look again at the palace. Now we realised our mistake: we were not seeing the "postcard" side. We rushed around the palace, and there the columns confronted us, looking stately, but not glorious. The building was dirty, and in need of renovation. The stone was a mucky brown, instead of cool grey. The lake in front of it was half frozen over, and rubbish gathered on its surface. It was a real pity. Marzena put it down to lack of funding – that conundrum of what happens to the millions of dollars of foreign investment pouring into Warsaw. Could there be any better cause than to spend some of the money on renovating the Palace on the Water? We hoped in the summer the full potential of the palace would be realised.

But Łazienki had not disappointed. Along with thousands of others, we left feeling refreshed and invigorated, if a mite chilly. Come the summer, in the intense heat, we would learn that the park, thanks to its canopy of trees, is an outsize and welcome cooler box, and the Palace on the Water would return to its picture-postcard glory.

In the summer we would also come to understand that the Chopin monument was more apropos than we might have thought when, on the last Sunday in June, we would go to hear one of the free, outdoor concerts of the composer's music given under the statue. This would turn out to be an important element in our reassessment of Warsaw, but also in my voyage of discovery of all of Poland, for as we have already noted, Chopin is one of Poland's most admired and best loved sons. Indeed, until the present Pope came along, he was probably unchallenged in this position. Furthermore, he got there by pure genius, as anyone who knows his tremendous variety of music will vouch. To this day he is honoured by his countrymen, and can be found on the side of frosted "Chopin Vodka" bottles, on countless street signs, and in the form of numerous statues, including the one in Łazienki.

The concerts were at midday and four o'clock. As it had rained both of the previous two days, we thought we had better take the earlier showing when it coincided with a break in the weather. By the time we reached the rose garden surrounding Chopin's monument, the sun was beating down. Many of the audience sat in the shade, but we took a bench in the sun to warm ourselves after the two days of summer chill. There were seats everywhere, so many that there was room for everyone who wanted to attend. And crisp red roses as far as the eye could see, some in orderly flower beds, others on gently sloping banks or cuddling up to the benches.

In front of the statue stood a pool of water, calm in the still day, and to the side of it, a grand piano under a canopy, its lid hinged, and a microphone. Dead on 12 o'clock, our host, a slightly robotic old chap in a brown suit, conveyed himself up to the microphone and introduced our pianist for the lunchtime concert, a middle-aged lady wearing a long flowing dress of greens and blues. She looked majestic. She stepped up to the piano, sat down, and composed herself. She proceeded to play a rousing and melodic polonaise No. 6 in A flat major (always a good number to start with, it already had some of the audience humming along) met by an enthusiastic round of applause at its end. Then through mazurkas, impromptus, nocturnes, études, fantaises, and more polonaises. It was a dreamy. By the time she moved on to my favourite Chopin piece - his light waltz No. 1 in E flat major - I had met heaven on earth. I closed my eyes. The sun beat onto my face, the scent of the thousands of red roses wafted across me, and waltz No. 1 played out from speakers perched on the grass in the form of tinkling piano keys. Occasionally, a gentle breeze cooled me, and the pianist's hands, when I opened my eyes, were a rhythmic, soothing blur. What was better? This, or drinking a beer in Bambus café on the main square in Cracow? I opted for this. This is where I should be mummified and laid to rest! For in enjoying a Sunday concert like this in Łazienki, I knew I was getting closer than ever to discovering the "real" Poland, almost at one with the hundreds of Poles around me also taking in the moment. Waltz No. 1 ended, and we all - that is, my fellow Poles and I - gave a loud round of applause to our performer.

The occasional interruptions annoyed me, but this was Poland, after all. Forster's India, it turned out, did not have a monopoly on the famous "muddle". A couple of old ladies walked down one of the main paths near the monument, loudly gossiping about something, seemingly unaware of the concert taking place in front of them. A group of yobbos swayed to one of the polonaises as if it were a football chant. A car alarm went off on the edge of the park near to the monument, an alarm that was able to run through a series of warnings from straightforward beeping to "nuclear attack imminent" to "the Martians are coming" – dying away after two minutes. But nothing could break the spell. Eventually, after fifty minutes of paradise, the recital was over, the lady in the flowing dress took a final round of applause, and the man in the brown suit invited us to come for the afternoon's recital. By the afternoon, however, one of those spectacular Warsaw storms had arrived, everything was flooded, and there was no chance of another concert. We had been lucky. And through it all, Chopin gazed serenely down at us. The face of Chopin, and the dandyish nineteenth century coiffure that sits above it, is the most lifelike part of the statue, for the rest of him is cloaked. It stares towards where the pianists play and we were seated. I stared back at it for a minute during the recital and tried to imagine that the statue was Chopin alive, watching the pianist, listening to this interpretation of his music, and taking in the audience's appreciation of his tunes. It was not difficult, looking at those realistic facial features. I soon felt his presence. And I swear that - just for a second - I saw him smile.

That would be in the summer. It was in February, however, that we began our Chopin leitmotiv by visiting Żelazowa Wola - the small estate where Chopin was born and lived until his exile from Poland. We took the opportunity to beat the crowds that would undoubtedly flock to this place in 1999, on the 150th anniversary of his death, which had been officially declared the "Year of Chopin" in Poland.[11]

Żelazowa Wola lies about 50km west of Warsaw, and so we still regarded this trip as part of our rediscovery of Warsaw – or, at least, "Greater" Warsaw. We arrived there late on a Sunday morning, walked through sizeable manor-house gates, and found ourselves in a park. We followed a path strewn with pine needles and heard music. It seemed to be coming from around the side of a small outhouse. We edged around the two storey building, which was painted white with a gently sloping roof of dark brown tiles, and realised the Chopin melodies were not live, but coming from loud-speakers attached to the house. The music was playing onto a terrace, and we later learnt it was on this terrace, surrounded by trees from the extensive gardens, that live Chopin piano recitals were given in the summer. They must have been blissful, though we never got to one, because the prospect of attending a concert in nearby Łazienki always proved more inviting. In an embarrassing carbon copy of the Łazienki "Palace on the Water" incident, we asked an attendant where the Chopin manor house was, and met with a frosty reception: *this was the manor house.* However, on this occasion, we felt justified in our ignorance, because it transpired this *was* only an outhouse, the original manor house having been burnt down in 1812 by the passing Napoleonic army.

The Chopin family home is not so impressive inside - though there are some interesting artefacts - and Chopin actually left there aged 7 months. But he was enchanted by his old family home, and often spent his summer holidays there where he came into contact with the Polish country and folk music he later transposed into his own pieces. It is my bet Chopin was most taken with the park surrounding the house. Although laid out differently in his time, it cannot fail also to have pleased then. Today, there is abundant greenery, in the form of trees, bushes and flowers, a river running through (with a small bridge over), pergolas, and criss-crossing lanes and paths. Near the outhouse the garden is laid out in more orderly fashion, consisting of a circular garden parlour. Seemingly as with all monuments to Chopin, perhaps because he is such a famous Polish son, controversy surrounded the new laying out of the park in the 1930s. The park is unconventional, not classically manorial. Many Poles wanted the latter. But however it started out, the influx of donated plants and vegetation from around the globe, reflecting Chopin's international popularity, now make it an unusual and enjoyable spectacle. Its variety perfectly complements Chopin's musical variety, which can be heard over loudspeakers not only from the terrace, but in most parts of the park. The effect, as you wander through undergrowth, is romantic, and lifts the spirit in a way a sedentary concert cannot.

Back in the metropolis, even some of the more drab buildings took on a new lustre in our reappraisal of Warsaw. Some of the Socialist Realist construction held a certain fascination. Socialist Realism, a form of art used for propaganda, was developed in the Soviet Union under Stalin, and imposed on Poland until the mid-1950s. Monolithic buildings, and sculptures and murals on a colossal scale, are its architectural traits. The Palace of Culture is a good example, and also the Warsaw Stock Exchange (the former Communist Party headquarters), an uninspiring grey block pitted with row upon row of small rectangular windows. The sheer size and austerity of these buildings and monuments somehow impresses, as do their blatant glorification of Communist party workers, hearty wenches and muscular labourers. The memorial to the Warsaw uprising is another good example, unveiled in 1989 by the Communist authorities. It combines heavy rectangular concrete blocks stood at acute angles with large effigies of soldiers. All of these structures were too big to be removed by ordinary Poles after '89, when, as we have seen, street signs, and anything else moveable which could be identified with Communism, were whisked away. Where did all these smaller Communist icons go? Perhaps to Lublin, where there is a museum housing the most complete collection of Socialist Realism art in Poland. When we discovered this, we did not exactly hop on the next bus down there. But the discovery gave a certain justification to this strange form of art/ideology - which no less a sage than Miłosz said indicated a soul lost to the black hole of the *New Faith* (Communism) on the part of those who practised it.

No, Marzena and I had better things to do than jump on a bus to Lublin. Better things, right here in the city that was rapidly growing on us - Warsaw. We discovered the Polish opera. It was Marzena's suggestion, and it caught my attention when she mentioned the tickets were known to be exceedingly cheap. Music (as it were) to my ears. How cheap? Go and find out, she challenged me. It was no challenge.

I arrived in "Plac Teatralny" (Theatre Square) one Sunday

morning, and was met by the Grand Theatre, an aptly named Neo-Classical building with wide porticos to left and right. I pushed a high, heavy door, which swung open slowly, and was met by a tall curtain in which I got caught up for a moment. I thought I was entering Kafka's *Trial*. Inside, however, at the end of a long foyer was, somewhat incongruously, a small ticket office. I asked the lady behind the desk if there were any tickets left for tonight's performance of Rigoletto, and what was the price range of the tickets. Hardly an opera buff, or frequenter of Covent Garden, I nevertheless knew these events booked up very early in London, and were exorbitantly priced. The woman, somewhat surly because I had interrupted one of her most exciting chapters yet, put down her book and tapped away at her computer. A number of seats were available, she replied. Prices ranged from 7 złoty (around £1) third balcony to 39 złoty (£6) at the front. I don't know how long I was out for, but when I came round, I purchased two tickets on the fourth row of the stalls and rushed home to tell Marzena what I had just achieved. Though not surprised, she was excited, too.

The night of the opera, we drew up to the square in front of the theatre shortly before the performance, parked, and walked toward the entrance. We soon realised we were taking part in an "occasion" (my father would have been proud). Everywhere we looked there were smartly dressed couples and families arriving in taxis, the women in long fur coats, and some of the men even wearing top hats. Once inside, we observed every man was wearing a suit, and every woman a ball-dress or something akin. Marzena was dressed appropriately in a full-length black Laura Ashley number patterned with red roses. As for me, well, I thanked the Lord (and Marzena) I had been advised to "at least put on a jacket", but still wondered if I would be ejected and told the construction work started again Monday.

Once inside, the building really came into its own. Its straight lines, marble floors and walls, abundant crystal chandeliers and bright lighting leant it a grandiose air. I imagined all the "nomenklatura" (as the Communist elite were termed) meeting and greeting here in darker times. The excitement built up tremendously: the huge audience in the capacious auditorium, made up of stalls, an amphitheatre, three levels of balcony and numerous boxes, produced a loud hubbub; exotic perfumes wafted around; and there was a spontaneous round of applause when the conductor arrived, dressed in full black tie. Our seats were magnificent. We could almost reach out and touch the divas and tenors, who sang with a verve and personality I liked. The colourful, textured backdrops were breathtaking, and the party scenes full of vigour with jugglers, dancers, small bands, fire-eaters and stilt-walkers. The only peculiarity was the translating board, a digital screen converting the singers' words into Polish positioned so high above the stage that most of the audience must have had cricks in their necks by the time the performance was over. However, blissfully unaffected, my Polish still not sufficient to benefit from this facility, I could not take my eyes off the stage and, ever emotional, was practically in tears when Rigoletto's daughter died in his arms at the final curtain. We both left the theatre buzzing, and in the ensuing months managed to take in, amongst other performances, La Traviata, Don Giovanni, Carmen (including a humongous wooden bull that filled the stage), the ballets Swan Lake, Zorba the Greek and Romeo and Juliet, and a rousing version of Fiddler on the Roof.

The final chapter in our discovery of Warsaw was the cinema. Never a great one for going to the movies in England, here it became essential. Although I had satellite television, there were few English-speaking channels I could receive, and almost none on which I could watch movies. The cinema became a must, especially as I was fortunate enough that most of the movies were not dubbed, but screened with English sound and unobtrusive Polish subtitles. The subtitles were at the bottom of the screen - maybe in an attempt to ease the crick necks of those who had previously been to the opera.

The odd thing about most of the cinemas we went to in Warsaw was that... they were odd. From the first one we went to, Polonia, where the screen sat high above you, but the rows of seats were angled stubbornly down towards the ground, and where the lights came on within one second of the film ending, destroying immediately any atmosphere the film had taken around two hours to engender; to the most modern complex, Femina, where if you sat in any of the front four rows (and there were only eight in the whole room) you were more inside the screen than the Woody Allen characters in Purple Rose of Cairo; to Muranów cinema, where the absence of seat reservations created an almighty scrum to get the best place once the door opened, leaving you recovering your breath for the first half hour of the picture;

to the aptly named "Wars", where apparently long-standing heating problems (so the thickly sweatered usher said, with a shrug of his shoulders and a shiver) meant that, in the winter, there was no danger of falling asleep during the movie, but every danger of frostbite.

Still, the range of movies showing in Warsaw was wide, and the Poles showed they had a film industry to rival that in the West. For example, the Polish comedy "Killer", at the time the most successful film in the country's history, was sold to an American studio for a small fortune, to be re-made there for Western consumption.[12] Its successor as the most successful Polish movie and also the most expensive – an adaptation of the famous historical novel "With Fire and the Sword" by Nobel Prize winning Polish author Henryk Sienkiewicz – was keenly expected to export successfully, and maybe even pick up an Oscar or two.[13] Its director Jerzy Hoffmann is already internationally renowned. This builds on a Polish film industry that has been strong over a long period of time. Most Westerners are familiar with Roman Polański's work (Rosemary's Baby, Macbeth, Chinatown, Frantic) but there have been plenty of other famous Polish film-makers. For example, Andrzej Wajda made films that were constantly getting him into trouble with the Soviet authorities, but did not flee to America like Polański. Perhaps for this reason it is he who is now a cult figure in Poland, not Polański. Travelling back in time, I have noticed inter-war Polish cinema was evidently very sophisticated, because most Sunday afternoons I can catch Marzena in front of a black and white weepy that resembles the old Fred Astaire/Ginger Rogers features in everything except language. Nowadays, the Film School in the Polish city of Łódź, which gave both Polański and Wajda their breaks, is still one of the most successful elements in Polish cinema. But pride of place in my tribute to Polish cinema goes to Krzystof Kieślowski, another of the Łódź film school alumni. This is not only for his amazing surrealist films such as the three colours trilogy, but because he possesses an uncommon surname which is so close in pronunciation to Marzena's that almost everyone in Poland (and many film buffs elsewhere) who hears Marzena utter *her* surname draws instantly the wrong conclusion and treats the two of us as if we were royalty itself.

*

Marzena and I were certainly more settled in Warsaw. So much so that when, at the start of February, my father asked if he could visit us for a week (my mother was visiting my sister in the US, and he would therefore otherwise be home alone) we felt ready to accept. *Note*: you do not accept such proposals lightly. Grandparents talk of being exhausted when the grandchildren have left after staying for a period. Grown men and women talk of being exhausted after my father, himself a granddad, has visited for a *day*.

We were, however, delighted to have my father come stay. He would no doubt add much jollity (and anxiety) to our lives, and in truth we respected him for visiting a country still regarded by many as off the beaten track - and what is more, during its legendary winter. What I did not foresee is how he would cement our Warsaw revival.

My father had heard me moaning by phone about the greyness of Warsaw in our early days here. Now, as things had started to improve, I felt slightly the sulky child, and wondered if I ought explain to him we were currently having a good time. In the end, we decided just to show him the city and let him make up his own mind. He had the same plan.

"Now, I want to see the old town, where I was nearly arrested by the *ZOMO* motorised riot police fifteen years ago on my PUGWASH trip - awful buggers you know, those Communists, son; have I told you that story?" PUGWASH is an international group of invited scientists who tried to thaw East-West relations during the Cold War, and who strive for world peace. "And I want to see Łazienki park, Wilanów palace, the royal castle, the city walls, the marching square, the university, and where you work. Oh, and those three big French supermarkets near you".

I had long suspected my father would visit us some time just to get a good look at the electronics sections of Leclerc, Géant and Auchan.

Unfortunately, I was busy in work the week my father came, and left Marzena to look after him. As it turned out, I may as well have kept them company, for my father would regularly interrupt me at work, phoning in from some new area to which Marzena had taken him. But I was glad, because he was almost certainly having a good time. And if I had any doubts about how he would consider my early, gloomy reports from the capital in the light of his visit, I was not to have for long.

"I just *do* not know what you've been complaining about, son!" went the first phone call. "What a place! Changed so much since I was last here! So many beautiful parts! So much to see and do! *Much less grey!* I am enjoying myself tremendously, son! This is an occasion!"

And then:

"We're in Łazienki Park, son, and…" he paused for effect, "the sun is spreading through the trees adding sparkle into our lives. As is your lovely wife!" My father could be quite a poet when he wanted.

And finally, the call that left me pleased to be in the office, after all:

"Here I am, son, I'm standing here opposite the President's residence just where the *ZOMO* tried to catch me and the other professors on the trip". I pictured my father, mobile phone in one hand, ubiquitous rucksack in the other, a group of confused onlookers, and poor Marzena. "But they didn't catch me! Remember they'd already stopped me once, but I had said, "NO! ME MEMBER OF PUGWASH – INTERNATIONAL GROUP OF SCIENTISTS! ME BRITISH!" and refused to let them have the film from my camera! And now, as the other professors got caught up in the dangerous, anti-government demonstration, I slipped under the *ZOMO* cordon - nasty buggers, those *ZOMO*! - and hotfooted it back to the Victoria Intercontinental where I was safe and sound, had a Coca-Cola and gave a call to your mum." Here it comes, I thought: "just like Yeltsin on a tank, or Wałęsa on a fence".

"Just like Yeltsin on his tank, or Wałęsa on that fence!" my father yelled down the phone.

He was definitely having a good time.

My father loved all the sights of Warsaw, and was genuinely impressed by the colour that could now be found there, in contrast to his last visit, during Martial Law, in the early 1980s. He noted - in addition to the absence of the *ZOMO,* the most notorious of Poland's Communist police forces - the centre was now lit up at night something like Piccadilly Circus. When he had visited it before, it had been pitch black as soon as the sun went down. But, in addition to such welcome sights, my father wanted to take part in some "occasions", too. We took him to a typically lively production of La Bohème at the national opera, but *pièce de resistance* was to be the concert at the Warsaw National Philharmonic on the final night of his stay.

My father and Marzena picked me up from work and we drove to the National Philharmonic building. It was another Socialist Realist piece, although, apparently, at the turn of the century, the original building had been something much more, an eclectic structure embellished with allegorical figures and statues of the great composers. I saw a picture of the original building in the foyer: the broad, ornate edifice, featuring columns and dainty towers on its four corners must have fitted perfectly into Warsaw's pre-war architecture.

We arrived in the foyer, but no one seemed to be there to take our tickets, even though it was only twenty minutes or so to the performance. We were to see a concert of Bach, Mozart and some Polish composers - although, unfortunately, not including Chopin, whose lively polonaises, waltzes and mazurkas even I felt expert in. The concert was to be given by that well-known group - the *Kalinigrad* Symphony Orchestra – which perhaps should have been early warning the evening might turn out to be unusual. Marzena and I finally found an attendant, who told us we were not in the foyer at all: we had come in the back entrance. We both turned around to find my father and make for the front entrance, but he had gone. We heard something from down a distant corridor. It was a man speaking in slow, questioning English: "How-much? How-much-are-the-CDs-you-are-sell-ing-here? How-ma-ny-zlo-tys?" It was my father: he had found the National Philharmonic's CD shop. CDs were not as pricey in Poland as in England. Tapes were even cheaper. Fortunately, we got to my father before he found the tapes, and proceeded together into the main foyer.

We handed our tickets to the usher, who ripped them in half and pointed down to the basement. Marzena queried her. Was the main concert hall in the basement? We had tickets for seats in the main hall. No, she said, the concert had been moved to the basement. Not enough people for the main hall. Were the seats reserved in the basement, Marzena asked? No, no reservations in the basement, she said. And - typically - no apology; no smile. I was annoyed. But my father took it well. It was peanuts, he said, what we had paid for the best seats in the main hall. Anyway, he would make sure we got the best seats in the basement. I had every confidence in him. I knew his scrumaging skills.

We waited with a few brave souls outside the basement hall, and could hear the orchestra warming up. The funny thing was, the muffled sounds that came through the closed doors did not sound like a conventional orchestra. There was more of a guitar-based sound to what we could discern. My father's curiosity was aroused. He sidled up to one of the doors into the hall and pushed it ajar. In the split second before an irate attendant grabbed him, scolded him and slammed the door shut again, my father was able to discover that this was no symphony orchestra. He reported his findings to Marzena, who approached the usher and asked whether the Kaliningrad Symphony Orchestra was playing tonight. No, she replied, they had not been able to catch their plane due to the inclement weather in Kaliningrad. Instead, the touring Kaliningrad Folk Orchestra, which happened to be in the vicinity, would fill in. Again my father was calm, but I was beside myself. I probably felt responsible for the disaster the evening was becoming. But my father had clearly seen something he liked in his brief incursion into the basement hall.

We were summoned into the hall by the noise of some high-pitched bells that sounded like something from the bridge of the Star Ship Enterprise. Before I knew it, we had the best seats, a little way back from the front and right in the middle. My father had done his stuff, without breaking sweat. We waited for ten minutes, and heard some more bells. I wondered if the Klingons were preparing to attack. On this evening, it would not have surprised me. Then, the conductor walked out onto the stage, and held his arm to one side to welcome the musicians. They filed in one by one, wearing a variety of brightly coloured blue, red, green and yellow costumes that made them look like the *crew* of the Enterprise. Maybe the Klingons *were* going to attack? However, instead of carrying phasers, they held delicately carved old wooden instruments - mostly balalaikas - and cellos and violins. We were clearly in for something... different.

The conductor, a small, sprightly fellow with a cheeky grin, sporting an ample black velvet bow tie, addressed the audience. Would they mind if, in between pieces, he explained a little to them in Russian about what they were about to hear? Would they understand? Following fifty years of Russian domination in Poland, everyone nodded except for my father and me, and the conductor proceeded, accompanied by much gesticulating and posturing, to say a few words in his mother tongue. Marzena translated. The conductor told that these were Russian folk songs, interest in which was rekindled in the nineteenth century by the Russian music academy. Marzena added herself that this type of initiative was followed up by the Communists who liked to stress the folk culture of peoples (i.e. the traditions of the peasant class they wished to enfranchise) rather than ethnicity. The conductor spoke for a couple minutes more, and when he had finished, tapped the lectern with his baton, and there was silence. Slowly, he moved his wand to one side, and a strange sound started to fill the room. It was a sweeping, humming noise - enchanting and dreamy - a little like the sound the sea makes as it rolls onto the beach. It seemed to come from nowhere, until I looked closely at the orchestra and realised the ladies with the balalaikas were beavering away at their instruments, strumming at this stage, not plucking. Soon, the rest of the orchestra joined in, including a solid drum, beating faster and faster, until the sound crescendoed and the percussionist banged down the cymbals. It was exhilarating. Later, the balalaika players began to pluck their instruments, more and more speedily, until their fingers were a-blur. The sound was amazing, cleanly picked strings making clean, harmonic noises. One young girl, clearly the leader of the substantial balalaika section, and something of the conductor's pet, was able to produce an incredibly loud noise on her balalaika, despite the speed with which she was frantically picking, without error, at the taut strings. The first piece ended to a stirring round of applause. Bravo! Bravo! my father shouted, clearly in seventh heaven. In all his sixty-five years he had never heard a sound like it before. I was glad, but wished my mother were with us to shush him when his "Bravos!" became too noisy.

The evening continued spectacularly. The music was not only alluring, but there seemed to be a surprise around every corner. At one point, the conductor, his back to the audience, suddenly swivelled round to face us and began singing during one of the numbers. I think it was intentional, and not a sudden fit of karaoke fever brought on by how well the orchestra was going down. In another piece, the percussionist would stand up high above the orchestra and "clack" together two pieces of wood every half minute or so, a broad grin on his face. The first time I heard it, I thought somebody had been shot, and realised the percussionist probably stood up ostentatiously in this way so the audience would be reassured.

The concert, with a break, lasted for upwards of two hours. By the end, my father was ecstatic, shouting "Encore, encore!" at the top of his voice - until I suggested to him maybe the Russians and Poles did not know what encore meant. He quietened down for a moment, and then returned to "Bravo, bravo!" explaining to me this was *lingua franca*. We left the hall, and my father was full of the concert, and of Warsaw.

"I want you to know", he said, "this has been the most wonderful holiday for me. This place has changed a thousand-fold since I fought my battles with the *ZOMO* here. So much greyness has gone, and been replaced by so much colour and light. You two are very lucky. You must enjoy yourselves here!"

By now, however, my father's gentle warning was not needed, for we were already enjoying ourselves in Warsaw. His presence, furthermore, had cemented our new way of life, providing that vital second opinion we were doing the right things, forming the right opinions. We were sorry to see him go, but looked forward with anticipation to spring in the capital – and wondered if there were any aspect of life in Poland that could frustrate our exciting new lifestyle.

8 CUSTOMER SERVICE

As it turned out, there was something that would cause disquiet, especially for an impatient individual like myself: namely, customer service – or *lack* of it. Customer service can, of course, go too far. The Americans are expert at this. Shop assistants there so frequently tell you to "have a nice day" that it begins to seem disingenuous. But at least they try. In Poland, you met the other extreme. The notion of "customer service", or "the customer is always right" had, like many ideas from the West, not yet penetrated Poland's frontiers. There was also no concept of service with a smile, or attempting to develop and preserve goodwill. When I came to Poland, therefore, and was met everywhere by such indifference, and indolence, on the part of those who served me, it began to get me down. And the poor service I received buying tickets for the opera, or in the weird and wonderful cinemas I frequented in Warsaw, was only the half of it. It was in banks, restaurants and shops that I would have some of my most unseemly battles – starting on day one.

The affair at my local bank was one of the best examples. It began immediately on my arrival in Warsaw, when I was frequenting many offices in order to set up my life in Poland. This is a process not to be sneezed at, as Poland retains much of the bureaucracy of its Communist (and earlier) past. I had to open a bank account in Poland, in order to be paid by the firm I was working for, and so, one day in September 1997, I chose the nearest branch of Marzena's bank, and set off with her to arrange everything. It was good I even knew which bank to choose from. There was a plethora in Poland, and it helped to be directed to one. This one was the most well established retail bank on the Polish market, and Marzena and I, though aware that banks in Poland were not as well developed as in England, expected things to go reasonably smoothly.

When we arrived on the first floor of the utilitarian building housing the bank – an unimpressive structure looking like one enlarged portakabin plonked on top of another - we were met by that favourite of Polish pastimes: *the queue*. There seemed to be two queues, both equally long. We wondered which one to join, although, already twitchy and with an eye to beat the crowd, I was hoping we could go to a separate desk altogether to set up our account, as seemed sensible. Surely they did not expect us to wait with all the people taking money out and paying money in, ordering account statements, and so on? What would happen, if we did this, when it was our turn? Would the remaining customers have to wait for half an hour whilst we filled in forms, showed passports and carried out various other formalities in order to open an account? It seemed ludicrous, especially as each queue had only one assistant serving it. I asked Marzena, who was already anticipating maximum embarrassment, to find out if there was some separate place for us to go. She did, and there wasn't. We joined the relevant queue.

For some strange reason, our queue backed down the stairs that reached to the ground floor. I had rapidly bypassed this queue when I arrived in the bank, hoping it would not pertain to me. Now I found myself edging down the stairs to the end of it. I wanted to rearrange things somewhat, and request in my broken Polish for everyone to move themselves onto the first floor, where there was plenty of room to wait. After all, that was where the other queue was. It would not have required much initiative for the members of *this* queue also to have ensconced themselves there. But they showed no such initiative. There was simply no way to move these people, who were clearly well used to queuing from Communist times. These were connoisseur queuers.

We waited and waited. And waited. Finally, after forty-five minutes, we were approaching the service desk. Suddenly, a young buck in a denim jacket walked straight to the front of the queue and stood waiting there, ready to go next. I was incredulous. Not only do I dislike queuing - I can't stand queue-bargers. But what was remarkable was no one else in the queue batted an eyelid. What did they think? That this guy had special dispensation to go to the front? Anyway, I was having none of it. I stepped up to him and told him in Polish to get to the back. He demurred momentarily, until the evident anger in my eyes persuaded him to retreat fairly fast. Only at this point were there a few murmurs of approval from those surrounding me. Amongst them was a smart Polish gentleman who spoke perfect English (I later learnt he taught English) and we began talking in English about queues, queue-barging and the slow service in Polish banks. The gentleman explained that this ability of the Poles to queue without objection was a result of Communist times, when you could queue all day for a loaf of bread. Furthermore, shop or bank assistants in those days were kings, and you did not challenge them in any way, as this put at risk your chances of procuring what you wanted after the day's queuing. This included not challenging a queue-barger, who may have had some connection with the assistant. Though you wouldn't know it from today's performance, the gentleman said, the service industry was gradually improving, and with it, paradoxically, there was less willingness on the part of the average Pole to wait and wait in a queue. I would see this in time, he said.

We finally got to the desk and requested to set up a joint account. We had our battery of documents with us, we added. I could not resist adding we had just queued up for nearly an hour. However, the girl serving us was totally unfazed, and offered no apology. Instead, she told us it was not possible to open a joint account, as I was a foreign national. Not a good move on her part. I ranted and raved, first in English, then in the assistant's mother tongue – this time receiving no compliment that "the gentleman speaks very well in Polish". Everyone stared, including an agitated-looking security guard. I called for the manager. I told these people how long I had been queuing. I asked them, what sort of service were they running here? To no avail. We finally compromised by opening an account in my name, and Marzena had to sign a declaration she permitted her salary to go into my account. We showed passports, identity cards, work permits, temporary residence certificates, birth certificates - the whole process took forty-five minutes. Behind us, the members of the long and winding queue, by now probably extended out into the street, stood and waited. Towards the end of the transaction, I asked the girl serving us what the other long queue was for. *It was for getting money out,* she explained. This is the point at which I knew I would be a model saver in Poland.

I complained to the manager at the main reception - on the ground floor, beside which stood another security guard - about our ordeal, with only one apparent result. Next time she went to the bank, a week or two later on her own, Marzena told me the security guard on the ground floor chuckled. He approached her, and asked if she was the one married to that difficult Englishman.

The lack of initiative of the Pole who finds himself in a queue may be resignation to the poor service he has received over the years. I experienced such poor service myself not only in the bank, but also on one occasion when I went to buy a pair of gloves. It was a couple of months after the incident at the bank, and I needed a new pair of gloves as it began to get very cold in Poland, around November time. I drove into the centre of Warsaw on a Saturday, careful to get to the shops before 2pm when most of them closed for the rest of the weekend. I headed straight for "Salon Futer" (House of Fur) a shop specialising in leather goods and furs, not the cheapest, but not charging the exorbitant prices of the shopping complexes – and stocking good quality, hand made items.

When I entered the shop, the tall, thin lady behind the glass counter, all cheekbones and swept back hair, seemed aloof. She was middle aged, edging on elderly. Could I see a good pair of gloves, I asked her? She said nothing, but reached sulkily into the glass and extracted a beige pair. They were nice, made of leather as smooth as new born skin, and fur lined. They fitted, too. But I realised the price - at 140 Polish złoty, a significant proportion of the average monthly Polish wage – was too much. Did the assistant have anything cheaper?

"No".

The answer was definitive - but strange. I had spotted a ticket on one pair of gloves under the counter with an "8" on its left side. I couldn't see the right side. Surely this pair was priced in the eighties? They were black, too - my preferred colour. I asked to see them. The woman whipped them out, her jerky movement presumably intended to demonstrate her annoyance at having to extract *two* pairs of gloves for the same customer. What was the world coming to?

The gloves were 85 złoty. They again were made of smooth leather - but were too big. Did she have a smaller size?

"No", came the inevitable reply.

What were those, then? I pointed at identical looking gloves, but smaller. The "assistant" (I now had her name in inverted commas even in my head) took them out impatiently, and it turned out they were identical. I tried them on, and they were a perfect fit. I was going to buy them, but spotted some cheaper. Exactly the same process then repeated itself, the woman becoming more and more uptight, until finally I managed to purchase a perfectly good pair of gloves for 70 złoty instead of the initial 140 złoty. When I left, the sales assistant looked mortified she had managed to make the sale. Some months later, my Polish colleague at work Paweł explained to me that a Pole prefers not to make a sale at all than not receive his initial asking price. Only then, thinking back to this incident with the gloves, did I gain some understanding of, if not sympathy for, the assistant's behaviour.

Not having been used to such poor customer service, I tended to lose my patience quickly. For example, I complained in numerous restaurants throughout Poland, sometimes with good cause and sometimes without. From the waiter in the Chinese restaurant in Cracow who tried to improve the warm beer I had complained about by placing several lumps of ice in it, to the Mexican restaurant in the same city that served Marzena and me such a large appetiser of nachos and guacamole, when I had specifically asked for us to share one portion, that I complained vociferously to the poor waitress. She was at a loss, for she had served us one portion, divided up into two. They were simply big portions. The problem became one of being too ready to complain, from force of habit. When the service turned out to be good, I found myself complaining about nothing, and making a fool of myself. Or complaining when there was reason, but no real need. For example, I once argued over the translation of a menu into English, which admittedly included the puzzling dish "Pork-Mat-Disc-Chop". Furthermore, every Indian restaurant in Poland (even Marzena's and my outstanding favourite in Warsaw, where we would later attend a fascinating ceremony) has got it into its head (and its menu) that lamb dishes are best described as "mutton". A case of "lamb dressed up as mutton", maybe? I also used to complain when Polish waiters removed my dish the second I finished my last mouthful, irrespective of the fact Marzena was invariably still eating. This happened almost everywhere. Now I say "tant pis" and join in the boorish behaviour, resting my weary elbows on the table where my plate had rested. I must be mellowing.

At other times, my complaints were more justifiable. Like when Marzena, my then fiancée, bought a pair of shoes in the summer of 1995, during one of my stays in Cracow. They were ankle high lace-up boots, made of canvas coloured brown and white, very pretty and intricate, and ideal for the summer. Marzena wore them for only a week before the lacy, web effect on the surface started developing a hole in it, soon wearing right through to the inside of the shoe. Within a day or two, it was a gaping chasm. We took the shoes back to the shop where we had bought them, on the first floor of a tall building on the rynek. The shop assistant, of course, was not interested. Stony-faced, she told us to go upstairs to the top of the building and speak with "the office". We climbed up the stone steps of the dark hall until we reached it. Inside, an old man with a white beard ignored us. Undeterred, we complained. The man informed us the shoes would have to be sent away to the manufacturers for repair. They would be back in a minimum of one month, maybe six weeks. Just in time for the onset of the colder weather! It was ridiculous. All he needed to do was offer us a refund of a relatively small amount. But the old fella' was not to be persuaded. My assurances the goodwill of his shop would be damaged if he did not give us better service fell on deaf ears. Eventually, I complained so bitterly that the old man started to look nervous. This was a deliberate ploy on my part. I had noted that often you could overcome a Pole's obduracy if you did not let his initial hard stance put you off. I went on and on until, sure enough, the old man offered us our money back there and then.

Clothes shops provided an equal challenge to shoe shops. Buying a shirt for work has always been an ordeal for me. As well as having to be the right design, colour and fit, *I must be able to try it on first.* A typical conversation in even the best Polish men's outfitters went something like this:

    Me: I'd like to try this shirt on, please.

    Assistant: I'm sorry sir, but shirts can't be tried on.

    Me: Why not?

    Assistant: I'm sorry, sir, they just can't. I don't make the rules.

    Me: But there are changing rooms here!

    Assistant: Not for shirts.

    Me: So what if I need to take it back?

    Assistant: Why should you want to do that?

    Me: If I decide I don't like it!

    Assistant: But you can decide now.

    Me: OK - so what if my wife doesn't like it?

    Assistant: She'll have to come in to see it.

    Me: This is crazy! Can I speak to the manager?

    Assistant: (after glancing around the shop for an instant) There's none on duty.

    Me: I can't believe it! I bet you only have this policy because you don't want to have to fold the shirt back up using all those pins and all that tissue paper!

    Assistant: (shrugs)

    Me: (storms off).

But it was not only an Englishman who was prone to lose his patience at the sorry state of the service industry in Poland. As my bank queuing accomplice had correctly suggested, the Poles themselves are finding they have had enough. For example, Poles are fussy about the contents of what they eat. As far as I can ascertain, this arises from three causes: that in Communist times, you never knew if what you were eating contained what it was said to contain on the packet; the parlous environmental state of Poland (and Polish soil, more than half of which is acidic); and an ongoing campaign in Poland to improve the population's excessively fatty diet. Thus, in any supermarket, you can usually find individuals making a beeline for the nearest packer, accosting them and asking them to clarify the exact contents of the packet they are holding. As the packers prefer to pack, and only know how to pack, they usually offer no such clarification, and the inquisitive shopper is left to utter a few curses and decide whether to purchase the item or not. Furthermore, the queues in the large French supermarkets that have invaded Warsaw are horrendous, as people swarm in to take advantage of low food prices. They can stretch so far down the aisles that those waiting to pay invariably interrupt the process of others shopping for food. Strangely, unlike in the bank, people *will* confront any queue jumper and force him to the back. Looks like my Polish queuing companion from the bank was right.

Of course, to describe customer service as universally poor in Poland is a generalisation. There are plenty of assistants whose eyes light up when you ask them for help, particularly when you try to address them in Polish. At hairdressers, aside from the time they kept me waiting, the young staff are generally polite and efficient. They always wash your hair before cutting, however basic the joint, and then go meticulously to work with scissors. This precision came as a shock to my curly top and me for I was used in England to being attacked with a shaver in a process that lasted about ten minutes. Back home, I often considered it might be simpler to enter sheep-sheering competitions playing the part of the sheep. There is, however, one peculiarity. Polish hairdressers *tape* the cloak to your neck. The tape resembles a dog collar. Walk into a Polish hairdresser, and you might think you are attending a vicars' convention.

It is also possible to eat well in Poland, and receive tip-top service whilst doing so, despite my experiences with warm beer, mutton, and "pork-mat-disc-chop" dishes. "Hawełka" stands on a corner of the rynek in Cracow, adjacent to where the horses and carriages ("dorożki") line up in the summer ready to take you on a romantic tour of the city. Works of art in their own right, dorożki can cost the price of a small car. As you walk past them, and are knocked out by the pungent smell of dung, you momentarily lose your appetite. But all that changes when, passing through an arcade, you enter the paradise that is Hawełka. Staff take your coat and show you to your generous table covered in a lace tablecloth on which will sit wide, round metal under trays ready to accept your plates of food. There will be oodles of space between you and the next table. Within minutes, your first course arrives: perhaps the fanciful mushroom soup, contained in a small bread urn which can itself be eaten, but allows none of the soup to leak out; or my own favourite, żurek soup, containing pieces of kiełbasa and a whole egg; and then maybe on to Russian ravioli ("pierogi ruskie"), delicate dumplings of sweet, hot, white cheese topped with fried onion; or, *pièce de resistance*, and the house special, "Kotlet Hawełka", a piece of lightly fried pork so jumbo-sized you have to try to envisage which one of the world's continents it resembles this time. Two waiters will simultaneously remove the lids of your respective dishes with a flourish and a smile. At the end, the whole things with drinks and side dishes, will cost a mere £10 for two.[14]

In the basement just below Hawełka is one of the best *toilets* in Cracow. For your one złoty, you get clean facilities, and can listen to Ella Fitzgerald crooning, and take in pictures of models in various states of undress, as you relieve yourself. Afterwards, you can dry your hands with as much soft tissue as you require. But, be warned! Such luxury is the exception not the rule in Poland. I noticed this on my first trip in 1994, when I contemplated using a toilet in a Cracow restaurant that appeared to contain a week's worth of waste – but thought better of it. I was later given an oral treatise on the issue of public toilets by Antoni, the same colleague who had given me a written explanation of forms of address in the Polish language, and with whom I shared an office at my second job in Poland. Clearly, these two topics inspired this young man.

I remarked to Antoni one day about the toilet in Cracow, and was told I had not seen anything. This young man was currently training to be a lawyer, which meant he often attended the courts in Warsaw. *You should see the state of the toilet at the Registry Court,* he told me. *One toilet for the whole court! And as for the Land and Mortgages Court – what a disgrace!* I knew what Antoni meant. I had once visited one of the major court complexes in Warsaw, and noted the terrible working conditions. Three judges shared a decrepit room, and received next to nothing in wages. However, there was one court – the Supreme Administrative Court – where conditions were slightly better. It even had quite a good canteen, cheaply priced offering staple Polish food. What did Antoni think of this place, I asked? *Ah, the Supreme Administrative Court!* Antoni became animated. *The Supreme Administrative Court! What a place! This is more like it! For at the Supreme Administrative Court – there are two toilets!*[115]

There were further signs that customer service was improving, as competition improved. Two of my local hypermarkets – Géant and Auchan – had dry cleaning facilities. I became unhappy with the Géant service when it returned a suit to me without having pressed the lapels of the jacket in the remotest way. When I tried the jacket on, they just hung down limply on either side of me, like two kitchen tea towels. As a consequence, I decided to start using the Auchan service. But here I was afforded even worse treatment. I took in one of Marzena's padded jackets and after queuing up for nearly an hour just to hand it in, pay in advance and get a receipt, was told it would be available the next week. I duly turned up the following week, when the clerk informed me the padding effect in the jacket made it impossible to dry clean. In vain did I show the assistant the words on the label that read "Dry Clean Only". She returned the jacket - but not the money! The assistant insisted she could not return it. The scene that followed has been officially cut by the censors, but suffice to say many Poles now go around saying, "that Englishman – he *swears* very well in Polish". I got my money back, eventually, and returned to Géant. The woman remembered me, and I told her I was back in her fold. She was delighted. We both now had a common enemy. I asked her to promise me she would make sure the lapels on my jacket would in future always be properly pressed, which she saw to.

As we have seen, the phenomenon of customer service can be an ageist one, with the young folk generally more willing to assist than the old girl looking forward invidiously to a penniless retirement. Certainly there should be some degree of improvement in customer service as the older generation fade, and there will have to be if Poland is to progress. Poles themselves agree on this, particularly young ones, nodding their understanding when I talked to them about the poor service I received in such and such a shop or restaurant. One colleague at work empathised, telling me the obtuseness he sometimes met from those serving him was so pronounced he often asked himself if *he* was being stupid. Another colleague told how she phoned no less an august institution than the legal department of the Polish Parliament to get hold of a Parliamentary Bill where the unhelpful lady at the other end put the phone down on her. Her umbrage confirmed to me Poles can offend Poles, as well as Englishmen. Her dig (it seems digs are the way you retain your sanity) was to tell me the woman probably had to go because her coffee was getting cold. And yet, in spite of such daily frustrations, one has to ask whether the cloying "have a nice day" culture would fit into Poland, or whether Poles want this. A survey of Polish students by the international student organisation "AIESEC" showed that over the top customer service was one of the aspects of American life they most disliked. It might even be a shame were Poland ever totally to lose its characteristic, East European version of "mañana". But then something tells me I won't need to worry about this for a while...

9 HOTELS, HOLIDAYS AND HOSPITALS

Easter 1998. Marzena and I were settled in to life in Warsaw. With this newfound rootedness, we decided after the festivities to set off on holiday to Poland's only coast – the Baltic, in the north. Who knows, we might even take an early spring swim? However, after our debacle in Zakopane, we decided to book up in good time, to make sure we had somewhere salubrious to stay, and were not left with a last minute choice between the most expensive hotel in town and someone's spare room. We took a room in a small hotel, the equivalent of a B&B, with a view of the beach, and at a good price. We would stay in "Sopot" one of the "three (connected) towns" (the others being Gdynia and Gdańsk of Wałęsa fame) and the one that was supposed to be more developed as a resort than the other two. It boasted a long pier and the "Grand Hotel", apparently a magnificent sight, at its height when Sopot was a famous holiday destination peopled by movie stars and politicians, including General de Gaulle, back in the 1930s and 1940s. It would be enjoyable to visit such a classical resort, with a chance to breathe some fresh air and get away from the dirt and grime that populates any capital. We would go for ten days. We would come back invigorated.

We went by train, knowing the inter-city service in Poland is efficient. The journey was quick, three and a half hours or so. First we entered the main city of Gdańsk, a historical town that we would later visit, home to now mostly defunct shipyards and the Solidarity trade union, from where the train continued on to Sopot, the second of the three towns. Eventually it would make its way to Gdynia, a modern town of large harbours and more active shipyards. When we arrived in Sopot, and bundled our luggage onto the small platform, the heavens opened. An inauspicious start. As we travelled to our hotel by cab, Sopot appeared a small town, consisting more or less of one long, broad street lined with restaurants, cafés and tacky souvenir shops, leading from the station down to the beach.

We reached our hotel in minutes - an old, decrepit building, six or seven storeys high, with a small, decaying turret in one corner. And surprise surprise - it did not look as it had in the travel agency brochure. There, in what we had been able to see of it in the small black and white frame (which was in itself a bonus: most Polish travel agents won't show you any picture at all) it had looked English Victorian seaside. Now, in its black and white striped paint, it looked more Adams Family Home.

The rain continued to pelt down. We wanted to stay in the taxi, but the meter jumped at an alarming rate, so we paid the driver and rushed into the hotel. Inside, like the small hotels we had seen in Zakopane, the porch gave immediately on to a school-dinner dining-hall. The landlady's kids ran in and out of our legs. Rough-looking types came and went. Our hearts sank. We were shown to our room, up a wooden staircase that looked down onto the foyer below. We passed the public toilets on the way - I peeped in the gents and saw toilet paper all over the floor. There was a foul smell. Our room was at the top of the staircase. It was a corner room, and reasonably big. Those were the good points. Otherwise, it consisted of three scraggy-looking single beds lined up on three of the walls, on which lay grubby blankets; a small coffee table in the centre of the room, every leg of which I guessed had originally come from a different item of furniture; and, surprisingly considering it was the corner room, only one window, out of which one might have been able to see a grain of sand on the beach in the distance - but not today in the rain. The landlady left, *and so I hatched my cunning plan.* I was acutely aware the only money this lady had got out of us so far was a 200 złoty deposit - about £35. She could keep it. Tomorrow, a relative of mine would take seriously ill and we would be forced to return to Warsaw via any decent hotel in Sopot that had a room available for the next nine nights at a reasonable price.

After a bladder-bursting night in which I was too fearful to use the toilet for worry as to what I might find there, I unwound the plot. Leaving the hotel smiling at the landlady, Marzena still in our room, I returned (having found a public toilet) ashen-faced, and rushed up to Marzena to tell her the bad news. I then rushed down to tell the landlady the bad news. She took it well, which was good news - but was obviously deeply suspicious. We packed our things, and descended the stairs in the manner of a couple focusing hard on a father/father-in-law whose very life hung by a thread. The landlady still seemed annoyed, but astonishingly, offered us the deposit back, less one night's board, which we accepted ungraciously. Ever a Pole, and family minded, she said she was concerned about my father, having evidently decided we were telling the truth. As we left the hotel, and trying not to picture my father athletically swatting 100 *ZOMO* militiamen with his rucksack, I explained he had always been a weak one - it was his heart, you know. I just hoped he would make it through.

The feeling of relief as the taxi swept us away was immense. All intact. No financial loss. The sun had come out. And now, a taxi-driver enthusiastic to find us a hotel. He would take us to the edge of town where three or four pretty hotels were situated opposite each other, he said, a lovely green area, convenient for the beaches and popular during the summer months. He would find us something!

We cruised with our driver-guide, by now suspicious as to what "pretty" and "lovely" meant in this town. But we need not have been. The taxi turned down a wide road edged with clean-cut lawns and forest, and soon we were - sure enough - in hotel land. They were mostly modern blocks, three or four storeys high with neat balconies. They had vacancies, and were not too expensive as it was not yet the season. But they lacked something, looking utilitarian. We wanted something more swanky for our ten day stay. We asked our driver-guide if there was anything a little more... exciting. Oh yes, he said, *of course* - but we would have to stay with the Mafia! I knew all about the Polish Mafia from Marzena's horror stories. Apparently they operated half the taxis in Warsaw, often taking the best positions outside the main railway station and airport. But I did not really take seriously what the driver had said, and as much expected to see anyone recognisable as Mafioso as I did General De Gaulle strolling languidly in front of the Grand admiring the sea view.

We drove slightly further out of town, whereupon we came across what we had been looking for: a charming two storey hotel, broad and white, with a red roof. Flowers, chairs on the covered veranda with men in shorts sipping beer, and even a couple of palm trees. This was no block! We took a whole apartment at a good price, thanked and paid the driver who whisked off apparently in a tremendous hurry, and then carted our luggage in past the men in shorts, all of whom seemed to be in earnest conversation on their mobile phones. Once up the sweeping, Hollywood style white stairs, we entered a wonderful room. It contained the closest we had ever come in Poland to the heretical double-bed - two single beds pushed together, but part of a set with a common head board. There was also a living area complete with stylish (if plastic) white table and fresh flowers, cable TV and en suite. We both heaved sighs of relief, and, at last, relaxed.

That day, our second in Sopot, we took in the town itself. Fortunately, as we were a ten or fifteen minute walk from the centre, the weather was now fine, and surprisingly balmy. Sopot relaxed with us in the warm air. It had a casual feel about it. The main street was indeed a little tawdry, but the beach - a bona fide beach of yellow sand, stretched out endlessly. People sat on towels, still well wrapped up. Children played. Grilling burgers and kiełbasa gave off inviting smells. There was chitter-chatter in the air. I liked Sopot. I also had the feeling it was better to be at one of Poland's main resorts on its only coastline now, rather than in the summer crowds. On the other hand, we could not swim: no one was to be seen in the Baltic in the spring. I understand even in the height of summer it's a mite chilly.

We discovered Sopot also had a second side to it - a number of scenic backstreets, cycle tracks, paths and greens. As well as the part of town where we were staying, the western side was clearly a wealthy area of lavish villas that we later found out were mostly owned by entrepreneurs, artists and architects. This area, with an Art Nouveau influence in the architecture, including an abundance of castle turrets tacked on to the sides of houses (though in better condition than the one on the Adams Family Home) has been described as the "Polish Hampstead".

Two things to see in Sopot are the Grand and the pier. The Grand is a well proportioned, wide building, secessionist, built in the 1920s. It has an aristocratic, palatial air about it, and a sleek red roof. I could easily imagine De Gaulle ambulating around there. Or maybe one of Thomas Mann's patients making it his very own Magic Mountain. What is romantic is how this huge construction is built right onto the beach. You fall out of the back of it onto the sand, and it has, of course, its own, exclusive sunbathing area.

The pier is wide, with small jetties on either side where flash wooden yachts come and go. Its most intriguing feature is its end. I was always used in England to high piers, the ends of which stood a good twenty feet above the waves lapping beneath them, which you could stare down at endlessly from the safety of a railing. The end of the pier in Sopot, in contrast, is almost at the same height as the water. There is no rail. It would be easy simply to keep walking and splash gently into the blue-grey froth. This, of course, brought on from me a lecture about safety standards in Poland, to which Marzena paid no regard. I spoke meaninglessly for a moment on hidden currents and eddies before we returned to the safety of dry land.

When we arrived back at the hotel that evening, the men with the mobile phones were still jabbering away, and there seemed to be a plethora of top of the range Mercedes with dark windows screeching in and out of the hotel drive. That night, I slept soundly, but Marzena swore all sorts of shenanigans went on in the small hours, and at one time even claimed to have heard what sounded like a gun shot. On subsequent nights I heard some faint screams, but not much else. However, it is quite possible our hotel was some sort of retreat for the underworld, or a money-laundering joint. I would certainly inform Al Pacino about the place if ever he had the urge for a bit more method acting before his next instalment of *The Godfather*. But I was just happy to be somewhere comfortable, whomever the neighbours.

On the subsequent two days, we tackled Gdańsk and Gdynia, respectively.

Other than being well-known for its famous son Wałęsa, Gdańsk has had an identity crisis over the years. It was once the free port of "Danzig", for a long time a German city, and also a part of the Hanseatic League (the commercial association of northern European cities formed in the mid-fourteenth century to protect and control trade). It was another group, the Teutonic Knights who – despite their taste for death and destruction – developed Danzig into one of Poland's richest mercantile cities. One thing Gdańsk has always been is a famous shipping town, doing business with the rest of the world. Even the Scots traded here, allowing us centuries later to have lunch on our visit to Gdańsk in "The Scottish Pub". Many of the rich burghers of Gdańsk brought in Dutch and Flemish architects to design the buildings and show off their opulence. The consequent Hanseatic appearance of Gdańsk, combined with its numerous canals and waterways, lead many to compare the city with Amsterdam.

The most dazzling aspect of Gdańsk is its long main thoroughfare, the aptly named ulica Długa ("Long Street"). Entering through a high stone gate, once part of old Gdańsk's fortifications, an extremely broad cobbled street lined with magnificent burghers' houses, many featuring gabled facades, stretches before you. The ground floors of the houses are mostly jewellery shops and restaurants. Here, unsurprisingly, amber abounds (Poland's Baltic coast is known as "the Amber Coast") which, belying its name, can be brown, yellow, white, red or earth coloured, translucent or opaque. It is prettily carved into all sorts of shapes (hearts, crosses, small elephants) and cheap. This variety is no surprise: although the largest amber mine is in Russia, Poland is the centre for amber products. As such, it can only have been pleased when Jurassic Park popularised DNA perfectly preserved in amber. One of the best ever such examples was a lizard encased in amber which was washed up on Gdańsk beach a few years back. Street artists also ply their trade here. Polish families stroll down ulica Długa, past the stunning, late fourteenth century, reconstructed Town Hall, like the Italians parade down their main concourses showing off the latest *bella bambina*. And why not? For this, believe me, is a street made for promenading. Nothing even in Cracow rivals the proportions and aspect of Gdańsk's Długa street.

At the end of the street, you meet a maze of small lanes surrounded by water, from where you can take a boat ride, should you wish. This is where the Amsterdam feel comes in. Here there is a Maritime museum, and the SS Soldek is moored, the first steamship built in Poland after the Second World War. Walking these streets you begin to understand why boating is so much in the Poles' blood, and how Joseph Conrad was able to write with so much feeling and verve about life on the ocean wave. Skirting past this area, Marzena and I found the rest of Gdańsk a little disappointing - traffic, blocks and some modern structures, much like the grey parts of Warsaw, which was not what we had come for, and we headed back to the beach. We did not even attempt to take in the shipyards, once so thriving and the groundswell of support for Solidarity and Wałęsa. Now, apparently, they are so run down it is sad to see and almost pointless to invest in them – although since Communism some money has been injected.

Gdynia, on the next day, was a pleasant surprise: a wholly modern city in Poland - or, at least, a wholly modern centre. I later learnt from a colleague at work who used to live in Gdynia that it is mostly the centre that is well developed. There is a long shopping street with one of the best arrays of shop window displays I have seen in Poland. We walked back and forth along it picking out what holiday bargains we could. At one end of this street there stand, in Kościuszko square (named after the eighteenth century Polish military hero) some grand post-war buildings, and adjacent a green area of immaculately kept grass, exotic palms, a fountain, and flags on tall, white flag poles. Standing in this groomed main square, the sea and cranes in the distance make for quite a backdrop. It is also comforting to know these metal giants are still active, decades after they and the harbour were deliberately constructed as an eye for Poland onto the Baltic. This was at a time, just after the First World War, when Gdynia and the few kilometres either side of it was the only coastline Poland possessed.

By the time we had seen the three towns, half the holiday had gone. All we seemed to have done was walk and walk and walk in the course of sightseeing, and so it was I began to get a twinge in my dodgy left knee - a badge from my college days, when I ruptured half the ligaments in it playing football. It has never been the same since, but the key is for it to be passable, not cause me too much gyp. It is no significant loss my football playing days are over, but I do take exception to not being able to walk about. This is what began to happen in Sopot. Even though we resolved conservatively to spend the rest of the holiday pottering around Sopot itself and on the beach, with the weather now so conducive, as we walked around on the sixth day of our trip, I soon found I could hardly move. Furthermore, and what alarmed Marzena - every time I took a step, my knee made a tremendous clicking sound. People even looked at me as I passed by. I was rapidly becoming the best street musician in town. The South American pipe bands that abound on the main street in Sopot didn't stand a chance.

"If you're ever ill in Poland, get the next flight back to England", had been the advice of a fellow ex-pat in my English law firm. Another friend – this time Polish, but living in England – who was involved in a serious road accident on a return trip she made to Poland, claimed she would have ended up disabled if she had gone through her rehabilitation process in Poland rather than England. But even had we wished to heed these warnings, returning to England was not practical in the middle of a holiday. Instead, we returned to the hotel, and Marzena began frantically to phone up the doctors and hospitals listed in the Sopot telephone directory. With little effect. It was a bank holiday, and everything was shut. Except, it transpired, for one specialist. He worked, conveniently enough, just near to the main promenade in Sopot, and so we jumped and hobbled respectively into a taxi and made for his surgery. We would see him privately, but that would not be a great expense in Poland where, if you wanted decent medical treatment, so they said, you always went private.

When we arrived in the waiting room, around twenty pairs of eyes fixed on us. The place was heaving. Clearly, this specialist knew how to make his money - on a bank holiday, when no one else was working. He probably took the next two weeks off to count his takings. A medical entrepreneur in a land just brimming with entrepreneurs. We registered with the nurse, who sat at a small wooden table in the waiting room, and waited - but not for long. Within ten minutes, we were asked to go through, and found ourselves in a second room, with more patients, a kind of antechamber. Five minutes later we were before the doctor. He was a handsome, middle-aged man, who spoke excellent English. We told him what had been going on, and the history of my knee, and he nodded all the while as we spoke, and then examined me. He gently moved my knee around in exactly the same manner as the specialists did in England, which instantly relaxed me. He seemed to know what he was looking for. He then sent me off for x-rays, which did not take too long, and we returned, x-rays in hand, into his surgery. He pinned the x-rays up on one of those light boards that reveals bones in their full glory, and I stared at the structure of my dodgy knee - ignorant as to what I saw. After a few minutes of looking, the doctor turned to me.

"Your knee will never be the same as it was before your accident", he said. My pulse quickened. This guy really knew how to break it to you, I thought. What next?

"However, I can see no new damage with your knee to worry about. You have slight laxity of the co-lateral ligament, and your posterior cruciate is as damaged as it ever was, but otherwise everything is fine. Maybe don't walk too far for a few days. You are OK. Go home".

Marzena and I breathed sighs of relief, thanked the doctor profusely, and left his room. My resolve strengthened, I got into a battle with the administrator who tried to charge me double the normal fee because I was a foreigner, and not registered with the Polish health care system. The administrator claimed my only way of avoiding this - to have the good fortune to come from a country that had signed a health treaty with Poland - was not applicable here, as she could not find "Anglia" (England) at the start of her alphabetical list of treaty countries. It took us several minutes of gesticulating to convince this lady that the words "Wielka Brytania" (Great Britain) at the end of her list included England. She eventually backed down. I paid just £20 for the doctor and the x-rays (though bear in mind £20 ate some way into the average Polish monthly wage). The whole thing had taken less than an hour, which shows - amongst other things - that customer service can be excellent in Poland. More importantly, I now had peace of mind. I would certainly use the Polish medical service again, I said to myself, although I would stick to going privately. What I did not know was that I would be using it quite so soon.

We spent what remained of the day on the beach. It was not a pleasurable afternoon. Marzena was having a go at me, complaining either I did not answer her when she addressed me, or, alternatively, kept asking her to repeat herself. It was only in the early evening when we got away from the hubbub of the sea-front, and back to our hotel room, that I realised something: I was going deaf in one ear.

I told Marzena, who asked me what I expected if I never used cotton buds to clean my ears. I hated the things, because I was always terrified they would break off and leave the cotton-wool part incarcerated. The fact is I simply have ears that wax up at intervals, and when I lived in England, was forever having them syringed. But Marzena was not to be outdone. She took one of her cotton buds, and poked it around in my bad ear. Nothing happened. She poked some more, and suddenly - hey presto! - I could hear again. Everything, *everything,* became crystal clear. Oh, how I thanked her! Could she poke around a bit more? Of course, she said, happy to be proven so utterly right, and began again. Then, as quickly as my hearing had returned, it disappeared. Something slurped back into its unlawful place, and I was deaf again, but this time - totally. I could not hear a thing in this ear. It was most distressing. Quick! Quick! We would have to find a doctor, I said. It was just before seven in the evening. After the day's events, Marzena wanted to wait until the next day, but I persuaded her to have a go. She picked up the phone and began calling around - *again.*

There was a hospital, operating on an emergency basis, somewhere between Sopot and Gdańsk, which would take a look at my ear. It was open, but only for another hour. They were waiting for me. Unable to believe my good fortune, we ordered a cab immediately, and told the driver to step on it. That was our mistake.

The driver seemed typically gung-ho for a Polish taxi-driver, but I had not realised when I stepped into his car that this man was the insanest of the insane. He seemed to be going at a noticeable pelt in his Mercedes as we left Sopot, but then we entered some bypass between Sopot and Gdańsk. Next thing I knew, we were flashing along at the speed of light. Street lamps and buildings rushed by in a blur. We practically took off when there was a bump in the road. All the while, the driver would flick buttons on his radio, uncannily finding up-tempo "driving songs" on every station that seemed to encourage his speed. Bill Withers' "Lovely Day" and Dexies' Midnight Runners' "C'mon Eileen" struggled to be heard above the roar of the engine. At one point, a policeman, sat in his car perpendicular to the road, watched us pass, and didn't even blink, obviously deciding he would not be able to keep up. All in all, I did not know whether to be elated or terrified. We would definitely get to the hospital in time - if we got there at all.

I saw the needle on the speedometer rapidly decrease from 180 kmh to zero. We were there. We both got out, legs like jelly, and paid the driver, who sped off, ready for his next victim. We entered the hospital, and saw no one except a cleaner polishing the floors with a cumbersome, electric polishing machine. She directed us to the second floor. We waited – inevitably - outside room no.13. What with room no.13, the taxi ride, the carry on with my leg, and the fact I could not hear at all in one ear, I was what you might call *a little nervous*. Furthermore, having some national health doctor poke around inside my ear was not my idea of fun, and much worse than the afternoon when there had merely been a few manipulations of my leg by a private medic.

We were called in. Here goes, I thought. An elderly doctor greeted us, sitting next to a glass cabinet containing what looked like instruments of torture from the French Revolution. She spoke little English. Marzena told her the problem. She smiled, and took out one of those ear torches that allow doctors to see what you're hearing. She peered for a minute. Thankfully, it didn't hurt. She smiled again. "Wosk - dużo wosk", she said. I understood. "Wax - much wax". I knew the word for wax from the car washes in Poland. She would have to syringe. I didn't mind. I'd had my ear syringed many times before. I knew what great lumbering things the ear syringes were. She took out a great lumbering syringe. I panicked.

The doctor blasted warm water into my ear, and I re-lived the syringe experience - an ocean swimming in your ear. "Tut, tut, tut", she said at the end. No progress. She repeated the process. "Tut, tut, tut". This was getting difficult, she said. If she tried too many times, it could damage my eardrum. What then, I thought? Deaf forever? I imagined my leg problem recurring, and it being amputated, and returning to Warsaw with one leg and one good ear. Some holiday. She tried again, but this time with much hotter water. "Ah -

something", she said. I had hope. Finally, one more firm push of the syringe, and out it came: a lump of wax that could have blocked the Channel Tunnel. I could hear again. "Voila!" she said, a polyglot pleased with herself. I was also pleased with her. She soon knew it, as I reeled out every word I knew in Polish for "thank you" and "it's very kind". But the fun did not stop there. She was now on a roll. She reached into the glass cabinet, and soon was poking in my ear with an instrument last used to murder Marat in his bath. It was a strange thing, a long, thin metal implement, the length of a scalpel, that looked like it ended in a sharp point. She poked it into my ear through another long utensil that had a loop at its end, and seemed to prevent the sharp instrument from slipping out of place and rupturing my eardrum. The process was apparently intended to scoop up any remaining wax, and gave me a mildly tingling sensation. It was expertly done. These two weapons of mass destruction had left not a sore millimetre in my ear. She finished.

The rest of the holiday was tame by comparison. My leg improved, and I skipped happily around Sopot with a youthful vigour, hearing with crystal clarity – in both ears - the South American pipe troupes. They were no doubt pleased that this strange, sickly Englishman, rather than stealing their thunder with his amazing clicking leg, had once again become just another member of their audience.

Later I would come to understand that the health care system in Poland, that had so far seemed so accomplished and been of such assistance, did have a down side. It all came to a head in the late spring and early summer. I had been suffering from an upset stomach for about four or five months, a common occurrence for foreigners in Poland who are often affected by the water. My bowel movements during this time had been - shall we say - *fluid*. However, intermittently so, and so I had never got round to doing anything about it. In Sopot, precedence in keeping my ramshackle body in one piece had been given to my dodgy knee and blocked ear. Only after a few weeks back in Warsaw did I realise the noises coming from my tummy every time I ate food sounded like the film score from a thriller - which meant it was time to do something about it.

Fortunately, my firm – the Polish firm of lawyers I had joined in the New Year - gave private health care to all its employees and so I was able to see a doctor at *"WarsawMed"* knowing the cost of any consultation and diagnostic tests would be covered. Furthermore, WarsawMed boasted staff who spoke English, which was important. Trying to speak the lingo is all very well, but when you're concerned about your health, it's another matter. You just want to know what is wrong (and how it can be fixed) as soon as possible, and in a language you can understand.

The first doctor I saw at WarsawMed looked all of 15 years of age. I told her in detail about all the problems I had, which I shall spare the reader, but which centred around this intermittent upset stomach, on and off for a period of months. When I had finished talking, the teenage doctor replied in such broken English that it was apparent she could not have understood a word I had said. Nevertheless, this did not prevent her wanting to do tests: urine, stool and blood. Then we would see. But at this point, it looked like a pancreatic problem. The pancreas produces enzymes that digest food. In my usual, neurotic way, I decided I had cancer of the pancreas, and it was all over bar the shouting. After all, how could one manage without the pancreas, something of which one had only one? In the meantime, the doctor said, I was to take *three* pills: one type for one week, one for two, and one for a month. They should settle the stomach whilst we awaited the results of the tests.

We completed the tests and I swallowed the pills, without any beneficial effect. The most noteworthy event in the whole process was, when taking blood - or, should I say, when *trying* to take blood - they could not get any to come out. Apparently, I had low blood pressure, to boot. Only when a strapping, more experienced nurse came to help a young one did my blood pressure rise with alarm and the red stuff start to flow.

They also lost the stool tests which meant more embarrassing trips to the WarsawMed Centre, carrying my stool samples suspiciously in a plastic bag like I was about to enact a scatological stick-up. The tests also took an interminably long time to come back. There were apparently no facilities for WarsawMed to carry out tests on site. This, combined with the inattentive receptionists, who considered it some kind of failure if they did not hold you up at the reception desk for at least half an hour, in one way or another (answering phones, making photocopies - anything but serving you) did not inspire confidence. Eventually, three weeks after seeing the first doctor, I saw another one (the fifteen-year-old was not available - probably taking her GCSEs).

The second doctor, whom I guessed was at "A" level stage, sat me down. "The blood tests say you have very high cholesterol", she told me. "Not good". She was so serious I wanted to ask her how long I had left. I must go on a strict diet, exercise, and take some pills - *Kreon* - the enzyme produced by the pancreas, in which I was probably deficient. I most likely had a damaged pancreas, for which there was no cure, she said, echoing the opinion of the first doctor. I would have to take Kreon all my life, two after every meal. The damage to my pancreas was irreversible. However, I should count myself lucky I did not have acute pancreatic disease, in which case I would certainly be in hospital by now. In the meantime, she would do more urine, stool and blood tests to check my alarmingly high level of cholesterol.

What could I say? I took the prescription for the Kreon, to be added to the other three types of pill that had so far done nothing for my stomach condition, and left. I was not convinced, however, and managed to persuade the doctor to let me have an ultra-sound test the following week, to look at the pancreas.

I took anti-gas pills for the ultra-sound, to enable the ultra-sound doctor to see my pancreas more clearly. Half an hour before the appointment, I was instructed to drink a litre of water. The ultra-sound began, predictably an hour late, by which time I was bursting for the toilet. But the doctor would not let me go. She said she needed the water to facilitate her scan, and the test would not take long anyway. She spread gel onto me and with a white plastic wand dug and dug around the area of my stomach and bladder, until I felt like telling her if she carried on like this I would wet myself for the first time in a long time. But I need not have worried. She stopped the test abruptly. "Too much gas", she declared, as if judging the sum of my life until now. "I cannot see your pancreas. But you have damaged kidneys".

We arranged another ultra-sound test for a week later ("when there might hopefully be a little less gas", the ultra-sound doctor had said). I spent the intervening time worrying about my latest catastrophe. What was wrong? Were the problems with the kidneys *in addition* to the pancreas? And what was the connection with my low blood pressure and high cholesterol? What was the prognosis? The only saving grace was that, unlike with the pancreas, at least I had *two* kidneys. Unless they were *both* damaged?

The second ultra-sound revealed as little as the first about the pancreas. My kidney problem was adjusted to a diagnosis of too much fat around the liver, and clear on the kidneys. I breathed a deep sigh of relief at being cured of the condition I never had. I was now to see a gastroenterologist, which I did at a private clinic outside WarsawMed – but courtesy of them. The gastroenterologist was, at around 35 years of age, probably one of the most experienced doctors in Poland, I decided. She listened carefully to my description of all of my ailments, and wrote me prescriptions for three types of drugs. One of them was "Kreon". Kreon is very, very strong, she told me, before I had a chance to interrupt, and tell her I was already on it at the rate of 6 pills a day. I therefore should empty all the grains out of one capsule and take only one third of the grains after every meal. One complete pill should last me one day. I told her I had been taking six pills a day. She was astonished. I changed tack. Was there a problem with my pancreas? No, she replied, certainly not. I wondered why I was taking the Kreon, then. What was the problem, I asked her? "Stress", she said. I reflected – despite the need to adjust, my Polish life was actually relaxed and pleasant compared to hectic life back in the City. I wondered where the stress part came in. If the problem continues, you might consider having a "CT" scan, the gastroenterologist added - a computer scan - on the stomach.

We left, bewildered, after an hour. I had tried to pin the doctor down using my fabled powers of cross-examination, but was met by the stock diagnosis of "stress" every time I seemed to be about to clarify anything. As Marzena and I sat in the car just outside the hospital, after the appointment, suddenly we saw the gastroenterologist, hitherto composure personified, waving vigorously out of the window and calling for us to wait. She ran out to explain. We had taken the piece of paper with us that permitted her to be paid for our visit. Another entrepreneur.

The only really useful thing we seemed to get out of the visit was to discover that the laboratory which did the blood, urine and stool tests had made a mistake: it had put the decimal point in the wrong place on the cholesterol test results. Twice. No one could possibly have cholesterol that high, the gastroenterologist said. We were glad to have that cleared up, Marzena and I, until, driving home, Marzena asked the inevitable question: how did we know the *gastroenterologist* was right?

I stormed into the room of the next doctor with whom WarsawMed gave me an appointment, and told him I was not happy with anything. From the receptionists right through to the specialists. But this doctor, though as young as all the others, was a collected individual. He listened to all my complaints, looked at my myriad test results, and asked me to describe my condition in full. He was not in the least alarmed by my agitated state (I now became stressed every time I entered WarsawMed: perhaps the gastroenterologist's diagnosis of stress had been more of a prognosis?). You probably have a damaged pancreas, declared the doctor, who I now realised resembled in manner a young Clint Eastwood. We'll do blood, urine and stool tests. I'm also sending you for a CT scan. Finally, Clint said, you should take this enzyme - produced naturally by the pancreas but probably deficient in you - *Kreon*. It's very weak, he said. Therefore, take two after every meal, three if it's a heavy one. Six to nine a day, then.

I didn't even bother to tell Clint about the Kreon. I didn't want to make his day.

The CT scan again took place in a private hospital outside WarsawMed's surgery. I was rapidly coming to realise that WarsawMed's surgery could handle not much more than patients with the common cold. It was also adept at inconclusive ultrasounds. I had the scan, of course, at my second attempt. For my first, WarsawMed had told me to drink one litre of water before I arrived at the test, as for the ultra-sound test. It turned out, however, when I got there, that I had been supposed to bring one litre of water with me, which the CT scan people were then supposed to mix with various chemicals to facilitate the scan itself. Another appointment had to be made to prevent me exploding like the Wawel dragon.

At the second appointment, I found myself seated in a decrepit corridor with a number of fellow patients. We were all given cups of water, which tasted of chemicals, to drink every 20 minutes for the best part of two hours. Some of the patients were ahead of me in this process, and went in before me. One lady came out in tears, another with some contraption plugged into a vein. Eventually, after four or five cups (I lost count) I went in, quaking. I was confronted by a contraption consisting of a long piece of flattened metal, looking like a horizontal children's slide, around which, two thirds of the way along it, was a fat metal ring. *Great,* I thought, *time travel at last.* Dr. Who came out, and informed me immediately that he disagreed with my diagnosis from WarsawMed. Chronic pancreatic problems never occurred in one so young! His test would prove it! I lay on the slide, after having had a needle painfully poked into my arm, attached to a tube, "to insert dye, to improve clarity", the doctor said. He added he had never had to use the dye in twenty years of practice, which made me wonder what the point of such an injection was in the first place. Dr. Who left the room. I was automatically run a couple of times through the ring, as the slide on which I was lying moved me back and forth. All the while, I was addressed through a loudspeaker in the ring by the time traveller, who kept telling me to hold my breath for inordinate periods of time. In front of my eyes, for no apparent reason other than effect, a red strobe danced around the ring with a frantic life all its own. I was becoming increasingly disorientated and nauseated by such *son et lumière* when Dr. Who suddenly burst into the room shouting, "You see, told you so, told you so! No problems at all!" Dr. Who spoke perfect English as he had lived for five years in Canada, and five in the UK.

By now, though relieved, I had really had enough. What was this all about? Who, or what, was WarsawMed? What was wrong with my stomach? Dr. Who sat me down, and explained all. WarsawMed was a legitimate but scammy sort of medical organisation, one of a large and growing number (both domestic and foreign) that operated in Poland at this time. It offered cheap private health care, but using young, inexperienced doctors who would otherwise have to work in the national health system, where they would earn next to nothing. WarsawMed's desire to produce good quality service was genuine, but their glorification was not of this but the bottom line – particularly in light of the fierce competition on the market - with inevitable results. The national health programme was equally crummy, massively underfunded (anaesthetists, for example, earned £100 per month) and in desperate need of reform. Best of all was to go to a doctor who had a reputation and his own, private clinic. He gave me the name of just such a doctor - a professor - who was a gastroenterologist. He suggested I go there if my symptoms persisted. Actually, the story is what Marzena had been telling me all along, but I had not wanted to hear, so mesmerised had I been by the thought of free private health care. It seemed that in Poland, as in England and probably everywhere, there was nothing to beat a good personal recommendation.

I left thanking Dr. Who profusely. My only worry was the "Groundhog Day" effect - that I was simply experiencing the same thing again and again. What if I went to the gastroenterology professor and he told me that Dr. Who was a little "spaced out", and, as it turned out, I had a chronic pancreatic condition, and should take *Kreon*? Who would I believe then? But Dr. Who seemed genuine. So much so that when, as I was leaving, he leaned through the door and told me he had forgotten to say: the only other possibility was gallstones, but the scan had proved inconclusive - it did not even register.

I went back to WarsawMed for a follow-up consultation now that I had the CT scan results. I was given an appointment with a new doctor, of course - but this time I was in luck: I would see the most experienced doctor in WarsawMed. Unusually, the doctor I saw was genuinely older-looking and more experienced. He even had a little grey hair. He explained he had worked for 10 years in the US, such foreign service evidently being *de rigeur* for any doctor in Poland hoping to achieve high rank. I was immediately filled with confidence. For a moment. But then, amazingly, the doctor started pouring his heart out to me. He was back in Poland now, he said - but should he be? Yes, he had his family here, but – like many Poles - he had relatives in Chicago, too! The standard of living was higher in the US. What should he do? Did I have any suggestions? I wondered whether this was some kind of disarming tactic: relax the bothersome Englishman before he begins to complain again. Perhaps his staff had told him about me. Or maybe another tactic - make the patient feel there is always someone in a more unfortunate position than him. Either way, I lost confidence as quickly as I had gained it. We chatted a little about my results, getting nowhere fast. We did not even have a chance to discuss that old favourite - Kreon - which was now irrelevant following the CT scan, which had not revealed any pancreatic problems. Then, the doctor, eager to keep up his record of wrong footing me at every turn, did so again. He said I was looking tired, probably a result of all those medical tests and appointments. Would I like to take the rest of the week off, therefore? He would happily write me a sick note. *After all,* he said, on this Monday afternoon, to a disbelieving patient - *it's practically the middle of the week now.*

Through the next few weeks, too disillusioned to see any more doctors, as I either lay pole axed in bed or marooned on the toilet for days on end, I kept thinking of the English colleague at work who had given me the warning about Polish health care. I always pictured him flying off to England to have some common illness treated by a Harley Street physician, laughing at my medical mishaps and shaking his head at my stubbornness as his plane jetted towards Heathrow. I felt like a fool, but at the same time satisfied I had tried it out with Polish doctors, and not simply hot footed it back home at the first sign of ill-health.

10 WORK AND ENTREPRENEURS

Returning to work as a trainee at my law office in England after a holiday had always been a demoralising experience. The thought of re-entering that old routine of rising early in the morning, slaving all day and then returning home late in the evening exhausted and often unfulfilled by the menial work I'd been given. By contrast at the *Polish* law firm ("kancelaria") I had joined in the New Year, I soon discovered how much I fitted in, and how much I enjoyed Polish working life. This being the case, it was easy to slip back in even after ten days' Easter break on the beach in Sopot.

My firm was much larger than the English firm I had started out with in Poland a few months earlier, and one of the most prestigious in Poland. This was one reason I had decided to join, as well as a desire to work wholly amongst Poles. Yet, though the practice was consummately professional, it also had a very human air about it. As you walked down the corridor, people smiled at you, were interested in you, made jokes with you, helped you, and generally had a good time. But this did not affect their diligence, as most of the lawyers could be seen beavering away in their offices in between times. I say they smiled and did all these things at "you" and not specifically at "me" because it soon became apparent that, though the firm was keen to welcome its first foreigner into the fold, these were courtesies they extended each other, and on an ongoing basis. They made a special point, for instance, of celebrating an employee's "Name Day" – "Imieniny" – a tradition of honouring people whose names are attached to a date in the country's calendar, that has more significance than birthdays in Poland. Our firm would fête the luckily named person with flowers and chocolates, and offer bubbly and cake all round. For my first few Name Days, I did not really cotton on and remained constantly baffled as to why the people I was congratulating with a handshake or peck on the cheek all shared the same name.

Our weekly team meetings also exemplified the convivial working conditions. Often the boss would bring in fresh cream cakes, cherries and, on "Fat Thursday" - a Christian celebration associated with Carnival - "pączki" (like donuts but more delicate, filled with rose petal jam). We'd have lively, productive discussions among much chewing, wiping and the noisy expulsion of pips. Lawyers interjected jokes into the discourse, and lightened the mood where the opportunity arose, even to the degree of one-upmanship as to who could tell the most amusing stories. I liked this; it was a welcome, stark contrast to the sober office conditions back in England. It took me a little time to get used to such behaviour. The boss was pleased to see me eventually loosen, explaining he preferred the "relaxation" of the East to the rat race of the West.

In this respect, the parties held from time to time with the major American firm with whom kancelaria was associated were an unwelcome return to Western formality, consisting of the usual canapés, alcohol, false smiles and amateurish band. Nevertheless, the biggest such event – the American firm's annual ball - was an outstanding event, and turned out to be a little different. It was held in the Warsaw Polytechnic, an exquisite building of eclectic style boasting a pentagon shaped "aula" (or auditorium), cloisters, a glass roof, and sweeping open staircase. As we entered the Polytechnic on a sultry June night, dressed to the nines, we were snapped by the official photographer for the evening (we were later given the photo). We then managed to eat till we burst and drink our way through almost every aperitif, spirit (including, of course, vodka), wine, cocktail and liqueur known to man. As it also seemed to be *de rigeur* to smoke a cigar at least twice as fat as your neighbour's, I was coerced into puffing my way through half of Cuba's annual cigar export. Cigarettes and alcohol. I spent the rest of the weekend and the first three days of the following week hung-over in bed. I then returned to work to find that, to my relief and surprise, the enforced absence had done wonders for my cachet – particularly with the boss! In England, I'd probably have got the sack.

During the ball I had an interesting conversation with a go-getting female lawyer – Joanna - a senior manager in our firm, who summed up the East-West difference well. She was an advocate, the broad equivalent of our barrister. I told her how relaxed I found working life in Poland, and she agreed. Earlier in her career she had been seconded for several months to a "Top Ten" law firm in the City of London, and had not enjoyed the experience. As a young Polish lawyer, no-one had taken any interest in her, she said. Faces had glazed over as she passed them in the corridor. Only when a senior partner took her under his wing and involved her heavily in a major project did the previously unfriendly lawyers start to take her seriously, and be communicative. She never forgot this valuation of purely her work potential rather than her self. And nor did I. For the warmth shown to me in the office did not at any time seem to be conditional on my work prowess. Indeed, how could it be when I was qualified in English not Polish law, and so there was a limit to the business input I could have? The Poles seemed to value me in broader terms. Yes, I was an asset because I could introduce Western legal technique into the office. But also because I was someone with whom they could have interesting and challenging discussions about the West, and whom they could educate on the ways of the East - even if such co-operation was hardly quantifiable in terms of profit. They – and I – were interested in the contrast in cultures. All in all, I was thankful I was an Englishman in Warsaw and not a Pole in London.

The ball would not have been complete, of course, without the amateurish band. And so it remained incomplete, for this wasn't any old band but "Elektryczne Gitary" (Electric Guitars), big in Poland. I had heard them several times on the radio, and liked their lively, upbeat rock. The lead singer had a definite air of Mark Knopfler about him, right down to his dulcet voice and fingers a-blur on his guitar's fret board. The band went down a storm, including the manic, sweating, long-haired saxophonist who looked like something out of the Muppets, and made the sax scream. They worked brilliantly together. After the gig, I was surprised when an on-stage karaoke competition took place using Elektryczne Gitary's set. It was won by a colourful lawyer from our office, Henryk, a boisterous young man with a bush of curly hair, fetching dimples and evidently a very loud voice. Slightly embarrassingly, the consensus was that his performance – of one of Elektryczne Gitary's own songs - had been better than the real thing. But it had not detracted from the wildest work evening I could remember.

When not attending office parties until around six in the morning, Poles keep working hours that are wholly reasonable in that they reflect their work load. In the West, we suffer from "presenteism" - staying in the office just to look diligent even if you have no work left to do. In Poland, it's different: if you have no work, you go home, or if it is the middle of the day, listen to music at your desk on headphones and read the newspaper. Or perhaps take a two hour lunch break. If you have enough work to last the whole night, you stay and do it. Simple and effective. People are also more honest about how they feel at work. They will skulk around, telling you openly they are trying to wind down and avoid work on their last day in the office before a two week holiday. They won't necessarily run about the office like a lunatic to show everyone how busy they are - how many projects they have to tie up - before they can get away. On Fridays, work permitting, they leave as early as possible, and at 5-30pm on the dot at the latest. After all, it's the weekend. I remember one lawyer being shocked when, deep into a matter, we discovered it was 5-45pm on a Friday afternoon. Immediately this lawyer told me she was leaving. Not that she had anything planned, she said. But she was not paid to be there at a quarter to six on a Friday when the weekend had already begun! And such attitudes are universal. After being shocked by the attitude of the doctor who wanted me to take the "second half" of the week off on a Monday, I later learnt from colleagues at work that most Polish doctors will do the same. Sign a certificate giving you more or less as much time off to recover from an illness as you wish - however minor.

But such working practices should not mislead you as to the nature of Polish working life. When I put it to another manager in my office – Oliwia - that the Polish office seemed so informal, and the Poles so relaxed, she corrected me, apparently contradicting Joanna's theory about easy Polish working conditions. In fact, she explained, the Poles are a terribly stressed people. True, they do not find it difficult to pop out of the office when they wish to arrange their personal affairs – but this was a necessity not a privilege, a result of the poor service industry in Poland where arranging things by telephone was a virtual impossibility. Instead, if you wanted something done, you had to turn up in person at the relevant office during its restricted opening hours, and probably queue up for hours as part of the process. In other words, you had no choice but to leave the office.

No, Oliwia said, the Poles are stressed, and this comes from the dramatic changes that are taking place in the way of life of the typical Polish family. When she was a girl, her parents had worked from 8am until 4pm, and so by 5pm the family was together for the rest of the afternoon and all of the evening. Now, it was common practice for Poles to work until 6, 7, 8, 9pm or later, and they had no choice but to do so if they wished to keep their precious jobs in a country where unemployment was high. The Poles were still adjusting to this change, which even threatened the traditional importance of the Polish family, she said. They wore the stress on their faces as they pushed and shoved each other on the streets of Warsaw. Another work colleague concurred, contrasting the politeness of people on the streets in Brussels and Amsterdam, after a visit he made there, with those in Warsaw. Oliwia said she envied the position in the West where the population had got used to the intensity of working life, and thus such stress was kept to a minimum. She wished it could be like this in Poland, she added, because when she talked in this way about stress she was talking about her *own* stress, too. She had left an American law practice in Warsaw to come to our Polish firm precisely because she could not get used to working until 11pm every night, and because there would come a time soon when she would wish to settle down and start a family. Although she would not expect to be home for her children at 5pm every day, as her parents had been for her, she still wanted to maintain an acceptable level of interaction with them as they grew up. I sensed a convergence with Joanna's views, working for a *Polish* law office being the common preference.

This newfound conflict in Polish working life was precisely mirrored in the relationship between my own firm and its American parent. The Americans wanted a regime of work work work in line with their famous work ethic. Whereas many in the Polish law firm accepted such an approach, many did not. I once discussed the issue with my landlord, himself a success in business, working for a German company. He criticised the young Pole who, like his Western employers, thought only in terms of profit. He even went so far, perhaps tenuously, to suggest it accounted for the critically low birth rate in Poland. To work late every night and all weekend – what for, my landlord asked? To make a fortune and then drop dead of a heart condition at 55? But my landlord need not have worried that all young Poles were selling out. A newly qualified colleague in my law firm, when I asked him about the attitude of the Poles to work, made a comment of which my landlord would no doubt have approved. He said it was sufficient for him to have money in his pocket to buy a "Żywiec" (a staple Polish beer) and have time to drink it, than afford a Stella Artois but not.

It wasn't just the Americans who were imposing a hard work ethos. Daewoo, the South Korean conglomerate, invested heavily in Poland, building automobile factories. Daewoo management was at a loss when it found that Polish workers preferred playing around on the internet all day, including looking at pornographic material, over work. And they were totally puzzled as to why Poles prioritised the family breakfast over the business breakfast. The South Korean bosses criticised such behaviour and blamed it for low output - Polish factories produced only 23 cars per person annually compared to 70 in

South Korean factories. There may have been some truth in this, but the South Koreans shared in the blame by introducing some ill-considered techniques into the Polish work place. They placed pictures of successful workers on the walls, and introduced slogans such as "work makes profit". Both devices backfired. They simply reminded the Poles of similar tactics employed during Communist times, and stifled productivity rather than increased it.[16]

The most shocking aspect of working in Poland is the corruption. For example, making use of connections and bribes is not uncommon in bidding for business. I once won a prestigious European Union tender for my law firm, and was even sent a letter confirming the win, only for the project to be transferred to a rival firm. I later learnt the boss of the "new" winner was a close friend of the responsible Polish government minister. I was told this by a partner in my law firm who seemed to take the matter for granted. In light of such nepotism, or "crony capitalism", many a firm has a "cwaniak", best translated as a "fixer" who basically has the job of giving and receiving bribes. The success or failure of a firm in winning important contracts depends to a great extent on the talent and connections of this fixer. There is even a Polish saying for the type of qualities a cwaniak should have: namely someone who, if you throw him out of the door, he'll come back in through the window.

Of course this sort of thing happens in the West, but it is hard to believe to the same shocking extent as in Poland. Transparency International's Corruption Index at the time placed UK as the eleventh least corrupt country in the world, showing Poland back in 39th place, keeping company with Mafia-ridden Italy, and according to its indicator rating, 50% as corrupt as such moral luminaries as Venezuela and Columbia.[17] In addition, a Polish Interior Ministry Report of April 1999 concluded there was bribery in every sector of the Polish economy, including government agencies, hospitals, customs offices and the courts. By way of further example, I learnt that, in addition to bribes in business, bribes can help you pass your driving test, get on the training course that leads to qualification as a solicitor, and even win court cases. Indeed, on some occasions, two bribes may be the requisite for success. There are, of course, historical reasons for such corruption. In the past, Poland, without a powerful monarch, was effectively governed by a small number of magnates, all well connected. The lack of an industrial revolution in Poland, and the corresponding lack of the emergence of a strong middle class or bourgeoisie meant such magnates retained their influence to a very late period. After the Second World War, at a time when meritocracy might have taken over, the Communists took power, and they were the embodiment of nepotism. So the Polish mentality has been shaped in this way, and Polish business practice, too.

And yet, all in all I enjoyed my laid back working life in Poland. I found it healthy. People were permitted to have other lives. I liked the way the leniency of the bosses, though capable of being abused, was not - and the way it did not damage entrepreneurial spirit. For Poland is a land just brimming with entrepreneurs whose activity contributes much to Poland's growth. It is on display everywhere, along with the indomitable spirit of the Poles. This includes the rotund old woman whom we chanced upon in the powerful heat of a late summer's day in the Zakopane mountains, when we revisited there, attempting to sell us the thickest woolly winter sweaters we had ever seen (and stubbornly wilting in one herself to show how suitable they were), to the young girls who tried desperately to sell us drinking water at the exit to a supermarket at the same time as the heavens opened dropping more rain on Warsaw soil than any Pole could remember in living memory. I admired their determination. Somewhat more successfully, my closest colleague at my first job in Poland, Paweł, who had explained to me the difference between "dodatki" and "podatki" (taxes and extras) would often go off late at the end of his working day and give private tax and legal advice to clients - despite the fact he was a young and inexperienced lawyer. But because he was exceptionally clever, and well presented (almost more the English city gent than the Polish gentleman he was, in his dark blue three piece suits and spotted blue and white ties) clients already respected him, and instructed him. As a youngster, he could undercut the more experienced lawyers, and make a quick buck, which he did. I would never have had the confidence at his age to have tried the same thing when I worked as a lawyer in the City. Last thing I heard, he had set up his own law firm in his mid-twenties and was bringing in significant fees.

And, of course, the entrepreneurial, architectural exploits of our landlord should never be forgotten. For in addition to having built the marvellous home in which Marzena and I lived, Jan managed to organise the construction of a whole square of delightful maisonettes during the dark years, in one of which he still resided. Their construction took seven years, but at a time when there was virtually no building material available in then Communist Poland (Jan's grimaces when explaining all this left us in no doubt as to the absolute dearth of materials there must have existed in Poland at the time). Furthermore, he said, the square was constructed by government workers, who did not exactly have an incentive to produce under the old Communist régime. No performance related pay for them. As the old Polish rhyme of Communist times ran:

"Czy się stoi, czy się leży
wszystkim równo się należy",
"It doesn't matter what you do,
You get the same reward".

However, I do not think the young lad who fixed my computer when it went wrong can ever have heard of such a saying. The computer, which had not worked with its modem since being in Poland, had baffled everyone. The internet company I belonged to - the largest in Poland, which meant a shack run by a couple of young, pony-tailed nerds - had not been able to get things working, complaining that my modem was not "homologated" (i.e. conformed to the Polish market). The problem would later be diagnosed as partly caused by the Polish telephone system – an antiquated network which specialises in cutting you off mid-sentence, crossed lines, not allowing you to get through in the first place, and exorbitant bills. But as I did not know all this at the time, I phoned the ubiquitous "Office Depot" and spoke with a young lad there who had given me small pieces of computer advice on previous visits to the shop. He told me to bring the computer one evening, and he'd take a look.

Taking up his offer, I carted the computer box into Office Depot one midweek night, slapped it down on the customer service counter, and the lad, blond-haired and looking about 16, began to take a look. I soon realised he was an electronics whiz. Whatever problem any customer in the store had with any electronic item, this lad could solve it. In between helping them, he bashed keys and added commands and software into my computer. Which was fine, except the elderly supervisor was clearly not too enamoured of it. The young lad was running around fixing items on the shop floor, serving Office Depot customers at the customer service point, and simultaneously serving one of his own, private customers on Office Depot territory. I felt dreadfully guilty. Every time the supervisor approached, I had a word with him, praising him for having employed such a complete young man. Gave Office Depot a good name, don't you know? I even bought a filofax while I was waiting, which I only half wanted, to mollify him. It seemed to do the trick. The supervisor relaxed. He said there was no stopping the entrepreneurial instincts of the young, these days – as if it were a crime. I realised then it would take a long time to change the attitude of everyone in Poland, and thought again of my own theory about the division in attitudes between the old and young.

Within half an hour, after plenty more key bashing, the computer was done. It worked with the modem like a dream. I'll just add a brief command to make Windows run faster for you, the lad added, and did so (since when it ran like a flash) and we were finished. I gave the young prodigy the equivalent of £10, with which he seemed happy. I felt like telling him to use the money to run along to the cinema with some friends - and not spend any change on sweets. As I left, I saw him, hands outstretched and elbows slightly raised making a "what'd I do?" gesture to the supervisor. I guessed the young entrepreneur had fixed a hundred such computers in his time at Office Depot, and earned a whole lot more than his frustrated boss.

But the computer whiz kid proved to be a mere warm-up act to some entrepreneurs I encountered when seeking new software for my laptop. Marzena was frustrated that our English versions of Word and Windows did not allow her to produce Polish letters. I needed to find these programmes in Polish, but in an old version for a laptop that was out of date and not too powerful. One Saturday morning, I went along to a giełda or "fair" in order to try to track down the relevant software. A "giełda" usually consists of shacks selling any kind of goods - computers, cars, clothes – much cheaper than in shops proper. This was supposed to be the main computer giełda in Warsaw. A colleague at work had told me about it. It was held Saturday and Sunday mornings right outside our office.

I entered the giełda, which was taking place in a yard bordered by a high wire grated fence. The place looked like a building site. It was raining hard. I darted from shack to shack, but no-one had the programmes I was looking for. Finally, one shifty young lad said he could have Windows for me tomorrow morning - Sunday - price, 100 złoty. His eyes were a-gleam. I told him it was a deal, but I was peeved. My colleague at work had told me I should be able to get the programme cheaper than this. And I still needed Word. I went back to one of the first stalls I had come to, near the entrance to the giełda, and asked the guy who ran it to elaborate on something he had said earlier - that in the adjacent school I might find all the programmes I wanted. This was confirmed, and so I ran through the rain past walls covered in graffiti and into the school. I found myself in a narrow, dark corridor. I was requested to pay 3 złoty to go in. I asked, if I paid, could I buy software inside? Upstairs, they said, and so I paid my 3 złoty and climbed the stairs.

I got to the top, and stared across a large, almost empty room. All I saw was a man in each corner with a desk and a computer, a few CD-ROM holders scattered by the sides of the computers - and nothing more. At the far end of the room was a man selling snacks from a table. I was frustrated. Where was the selection of software? Feeling the exercise was likely to be pointless, I nevertheless approached one of the four men and his computer. Did he have Polish Word and Windows, I asked? Old version? Yes, came the reply. I was encouraged. Could I see the disks, I asked? There are no disks, came the mysterious reply. I was nonplussed. How could there be no disks, I asked? The young man, who had looked uneasy from the moment I asked to see the disks, now became even more uncomfortable. He began to ignore me and started serving another customer. Excuse me, why are you ignoring me, I asked him? He continued to ignore me. Hey! Hey! Give me some service, here! The young man turned to me: go to my colleague opposite, he said.

His colleague was a little older and more relaxed. I explained what I wanted. He also had the programmes, it turned out. Could I see the disks, I asked? No disks, he said. But he went on to explain. He was a little more forthcoming than his associate - though he still eyed me up and down suspiciously. It turned out I had to bring my own floppy disks. He would then copy the programme from his computer onto my disks. Now I was clearer! These guys were home copying - breaking all the licensing rules - and charging for it. Not unknown for friends to do for one another, maybe - but in a public place? As a business? No wonder I had aroused the suspicion of the first copier, who was still looking at me intently. He probably thought I was the Polish undercover police - or even Interpol. Nevertheless, the thought of incurring Marzena's wrath for not having found the correct programmes for our laptop was not a pleasant one. I told the second copier I had no disks. Don't worry, he said, with a wink. Go and buy some peanuts - *two packets*. Before I knew it, I was speaking code, asking the old gent behind the sweet stall for two packets of peanuts. He immediately reached behind him and handed me two boxes of floppy disks.

The copier charged me 5 złoty (about £1) for each disk I used - two and a half for the programme on the disk, and two and a half for copying it, he said. It turned out his plastic box of CD-ROMs contained just about every piece of software known to man. He would insert into his computer the CD-ROM of whichever programme the customer required, and copy the programme onto floppies. I used twenty disks, and so paid 100 złoty for both the programmes I required - about £17. A fraction of their new cost, and doubly useful in my own case as such old versions of the programmes were not available to buy new anymore. The process of copying went reasonably smoothly and quickly, but I could see the copier was all the while nervous there would be a police raid on us. There was a particularly sticky moment when Marzena rang me on my mobile. As "The Toreador's Song" from Carmen blasted out at full volume, the first copier, evidently thinking this was the rest of the police squad phoning up to ask if I needed assistance, looked on the point of lynching me. But the story had a happy ending. When I got home, both programmes loaded into my laptop and worked like a dream. And I came to realise that, in the entrepreneurial stakes, the young lad in Office Depot was a mere beginner.

Care of cars, so central to human endeavour, and in constant need of attention like the human body, can say a lot about a country. They are a microcosm of a country's attitude to business and its level of entrepreneurship. In Poland, the car industry is significant, on both the manufacturing and retailing side. This is because the potential car market, for a population of 38 million Poles, is huge. When Daewoo began its massive investment into Poland in 1995, building production plants and new car showrooms seemingly on every street corner, it very nearly blocked Poland's road to EU accession. The West Europeans were furious Poland had given Daewoo this jump-start over their own car manufacturers who also wished to invest on the Polish market. However, by the time we arrived in Poland, other car manufacturers had caught up, and their new car showrooms were also everywhere.

As for car repair centres, interspersing official franchised workshops were an even greater number of independent establishments skulking in back streets and down dirt tracks. Furthermore, on some streets in Warsaw, the sheer number of tyre shops, lined up one after the other, was baffling. One wondered how they all made a living, until one remembered the hazardous state of the Polish roads.

As a foreigner in Poland instantly recognisable as such when he opens his mouth, the key is always to try not to get ripped off when I need a car repair. Such is the entrepreneurial spirit of the Polish car mechanic when he sees and hears a rich Englishman before him (all Englishmen – indeed, all foreigners - are rich in the eyes of the Polish car mechanic: an old Polish saying goes that it's good to have a Western salary but to live in the East). Fortunately, over my garden wall lived an affable mechanic who was genuine to the core and did not rip me off in the slightest. His prices were a fraction of the money charged by mechanics in England. On one job, I once tried to offer him a bit more money, as the job had been so cheap, but he would not accept. "50 złoty is 50 złoty", he said, as if I had offered him the King's ransom in this alone.

In more desperate situations, others have tried to make as much lucre as they can out of me. A local car spares shop tried to sell me four litres of oil for more like the price of an engine. I educated him in a few of the more popular English expletives. Another garage charged me nearly £100 to replace a wheel bearing and wheel they assured me was causing the worrying vibrating noise that had brought me to them in the first place. When the noise did not go away, I returned to the garage in the same week in which the work had been done, only to find the whole enterprise – from owner through to mechanics – had changed hands. None of the old employees were to be seen. The new mechanics identified the problem as a loose screw holding the car's front wing down, which they tightened in thirty seconds without charge, and the problem was gone. I have no idea if the original work needed doing.

This is not to say all repairers are enthusiastic to take your money. Not long after we got back from our holiday in Sopot, I had practically to beg an electrician to do a job on my car. I had purchased a Polish car, partly in the hope of avoiding being continually stopped by the police to have the documents of my foreign car checked, and needed to have it insured. In Poland, comprehensive insurance is only offered if you have enough security devices on your car to make it impregnable as Fort Knox. Fortunately, the car I had bought came with a Mul-T-Lock (a device which locks your gear stick in reverse) and car alarm. The problem was the alarm did not work. Never mind, our neighbour-mechanic said, drop round to his friend the car electrician.

The car electrician was to be found not far from where we lived, at the end of a dirt track. I rushed round to him on the first Saturday morning after I had bought the new car, as had been arranged, as I had limited time within which I could continue to drive the car on its old insurance. I had to arrange the new. I was confronted at the end of the dirt track by a colossal wire gate. It was shut. There was no sign of life, other than the inevitable Alsatian barking at me incessantly and gnashing its teeth, from between which saliva dribbled out. What to do? Was he not there? We had an arrangement! I beeped my horn. Nothing. I beeped again. Eventually, a depressed looking chap came out from a small workshop on the other side of the fence. He was wiping his oily hands on a cloth, head poised questioningly to one side. I got out of the car and walked up to the gate. He stared at me a little from the other side of the wire, still near his workshop. What did I want, he asked? I could barely hear him above the barking of the Kraken in his garden. I had come for the repair to my alarm, I said. Did he remember? We had an appointment. The car electrician looked at his watch. I was half an hour late, he said. *Too* late. Again, I was encountering that initial obstinacy of the Polish worker. But could he not do something now, I asked? Please? It's urgent! The car electrician swayed gently from side to side. He was considering the issue. He walked, very lazily, a couple of paces up to the gate, and opened it. I jumped back into the car, as much eager to drive into his workshop as I was to be inside four sheets of metal with a monster in the vicinity. I drove in. He chained the Kraken to a formidable metal post. I got out. We looked together under the bonnet.

It was a problem, he said. The alarm box needed replacing. It was a specific type, made by Silicon. He didn't have it here. I should go to a Silicon dealer. Open Monday. He looked at me poker-faced, as if challenging me to show him any way in which he could possibly be of assistance to me. It seemed the entrepreneurial spirit was not yet endemic in Poland. Or maybe he wanted his weekend. I sensed two of the prime motivators of Poles – relaxation and profitability – pulling at each other. Was there nothing he could do, I asked, appealing to his professional pride? After all, alarms were important, I said. It was my big mistake. There followed a lecture on the uselessness of all forms of car security except for the famous engine immobiliser. He could fit me an engine immobiliser if I wanted. 600 złoty (£100). He would do it today. It seemed the entrepreneurial spirit was returning, as the potential reward became higher. But I needed a car alarm in order to take out comprehensive insurance, I explained. That was the reason I needed a car alarm - specifically. I agreed, of course, that an engine immobiliser was the thing (a little bit of sycophancy never harmed anyone). But could he not, just for now, sort out the alarm somehow? Do a quick repair job so the insurance people saw it working? I would return later for an immobiliser (I had no intention of doing so, but was learning how to "haggle"). Stroking of the chin. I had woken him up a bit. The car electrician walked slowly to one corner of his workshop, dragging his feet like an unwilling schoolboy. He returned with a small box that had holes in one side. Some kind of loudspeaker. This would do for now, he said. It was a separate alarm box that he would wire into the old system. It was not the correct box. For that, I would have to go to Silicon. But it would do the job for now, he reiterated. He brought some tools - a wire stripper, a soldering iron, solder, and set about the job. And a funny thing happened. Now he became enthused. His hands worked steadily as he did the sort of job he had done a thousand times before. Yes, this would work for now, he assured me. *Very well*, in fact (no use of the famous Polish "tak sobie" – "so so" – here). There was really no need after this job to go to Silicon. This alarm box ("alarmek" – again, in came the use of the diminutive to make the job even more appealing to me) would make the same sort of noise. He continued to strip, twist and burn. He stood up from the bonnet. It's done! he said. And sure enough, as I pushed one of the buttons on the car alarm fob, the alarm set with a loud, bird like cheep. When we tried to "steal" the car, it then sounded off noisily. Great job! Now, a smile broke out on the face of the car electrician. He looked pleased with himself. I paid him £10 for the job. Come back again, next time, he shouted, closing the gate after me as I reversed out the drive. I turned the car round, and as I left saw the car electrician in my rear view mirror releasing the Kraken once again. I felt relieved to get out with a working alarm and all four limbs intact.

So, the Polish entrepreneurial spirit, though often manifest, does sometimes require a little "activation". At other times, however, it can be hard to find at all.

Pan Leszek is the local taxi driver on the hill where my parents-in-law live, near the small spa town 20km outside Cracow where Marzena and I were married. He personifies Poland's entrepreneurial paradox. He is both the best and worst entrepreneur I know. His positive credentials include setting up a telephone in the lay-by where all the taxi-drivers in the town wait, thus allowing them to form a kind of taxi answering service. No mean feat in a country where waiting for a phone to be installed can be like waiting for Godot. On the negative side is the taxi he drives, a clapped out old Polski Fiat which he has promised for years to be on the point of replacing. The car has some kind of fault, because, once started, Leszek has to keep re-turning on the ignition as he drives along, every five seconds or so. It does not inspire confidence. But there again Leszek's meter is the slowest moving in town, and for this reason he is never short of clients - curious as they are as to how his machine keeps running.

Marzena and I would often use Leszek for trips from the hill where her parents lived into the spa town - a ride of five or six minutes. On occasion, we would also travel to Cracow with him which, at a distance of 20km, probably brought Leszek's Fiat some way closer to the scrap heap. Where Leszek came into his own, however, was when I needed to get to the airport for the return trip to England, having visited my then fiancée at a time when we lived in different countries. This might have entailed booking Leszek late morning for a lunch time flight from Balice airport, just outside Cracow and only a twenty-five minute taxi ride from Marzena's house. Or maybe early afternoon for a late afternoon flight. On one occasion however I had managed to concoct a particularly unusual return journey to England. It entailed a six o'clock in the morning internal flight from Cracow to Warsaw, to catch a return flight to England.

Marzena's mother arranged Leszek, who lived practically next door, for 4-45am the next morning. Leszek did not mind, he told her when she asked if he could help: he was used to starting work at an ungodly hour on these sorts of occasions. Besides, we knew he usually charged a small premium on my airport trips, taking the return taxi journey up to a grand total of around £7-50. He told Marzena's mother we needn't worry - he would be there at 4-45 in the morning "mur-beton" - "with bells on" (literally, "solid as a concrete wall").

After one of those agonising nights in which you cannot sleep properly because you know you have got so little time in which to sleep properly, we clambered out of bed, packed me up, and took my luggage down to the hall. We stepped out into the January ice bath and went to fetch Leszek, who lived about thirty metres down the track that leads from one side of the hill. We saw Leszek's car, worryingly iced up. There was no sign of life. Nothing stirred. It was 4-40 in the morning. The plane left in one hour and twenty minutes. What should we do, I asked Marzena? There was nothing for it but to ring the bell, even if it woke the whole family. We rang the bell. The family slept.

We rang again. Nothing. It really was difficult to know what to do next. There would be no other taxi-drivers around at this hour in such a small town, and my parents-in-law did not possess a car. Getting a cab sent out from Cracow would take too long. We had to persevere with Leszek. I went up to the door and put my finger on the bell, and left it there. For around one minute. Towards the end of the minute, Marzena told me to stop. Something had stirred from behind one of the curtains. I rang again, briefly. Noise. About one minute later, Leszek's wife answered the door in her dressing gown. What did we want? We reminded her about the appointment with Leszek, to take me to the airport. My plane left in a little over an hour. Leszek's wife was stolid. She asked us to wait a minute, and returned into the house. Another minute passed, and then Leszek came to the door in his all white thermal underwear, including long johns and a white Dickensian nightcap with a bobble on the end. He was very sorry. He had slept through his alarm (I imagined a dodgy contraption that, like his car ignition, you had to bash hourly throughout the night if it was to sound in the morning). But not to worry. He would be with us shortly. We would make the airport in good time.

It seemed to take an interminably long time for Leszek to get everything together. By the time he had dressed, scraped the thick ice off his car, and started it, it was 5-15. Forty-five minutes to the flight. We ambled towards the airport, as Leszek was the only Polish taxi driver who drove *below* the speed limit (although in this respect he was rather hampered by his vehicle). After a half hour journey in which the ignition key had been turned and turned in the ignition as many times as the four wheels had spun round, we arrived at the airport, a quarter to six. Following a swift farewell to Marzena, I rushed into the airport, just in time for the flight. My heart rate eased. I had been in a hot sweat, despite the cold, due to the very real prospect of missing the flight. But now the fun was over. Or nearly. I checked in, and asked the lady at the check-in desk, who looked as bleary-eyed as me, if the plane for this short internal flight was full. No, she replied, there was plenty of room. I assumed she would therefore give me a row of seats on the jet to myself. Wrong. Firstly, it was not a jet, but a propeller plane. Secondly, when we got into the plane, which had two seats on either side of the aisle, I found that the dozen or so people who were making the journey had been seated in twos, next to each other, and spaced at equal points down the aisle, despite the ample number of spare seats available. I requested of a stewardess that I be permitted to move to a set of twin seats that was unoccupied, so I could stretch out. The stewardess asked me to wait for a moment: she would have to ask the chief steward. Why should she possibly need to ask him, I thought? She returned quickly, and all became clear. It was not possible to move me to an unoccupied set of twin seats, she explained, as *that would unbalance the plane.* In the ensuing flight I did not move a muscle the entire way, for fear of sending the plane into an irreversible downwards spin.

Though Pan Leszek's style was chaotic, I once read in the *Warsaw Business Journal* that it is just this quality of Poles that helps make them such adept entrepreneurs. In any case, such chaos, and the Poles' creativity, is channelled. In more formal business circles, Polish business cards ("wizytówki") are thrown around like confetti, and are often miniature works of art. To be handed one, and to have forgotten to bring your own to hand back in return, can be a *faux pas.* As for taxes, considered by Poles as the most heinous threat of all to business, they are avoided like the plague, with a professionalism of which even the most eminent tax consultant would be proud. Such techniques are handed down from generation to generation, and adapted to the latest of a myriad changes in the tax rules. Professional tax advisers are left to ply their trade on the larger business organisations.

No, Poles have bags of business initiative. And it is a combination in post-Communist Poland of opportunity, and an often less than level playing field, that gives them - and any foreigners willing to have a go - the possibility to use it.

11 THE POLISH CHARACTER

It was on a weekend not long after I had bought my new car, fixed the alarm, sorted out all the insurance documentation, and was simultaneously polishing and admiring my new toy, that a neighbour decided to come and take a look, and strike up a conversation.

"So, you're doing better and better", were his first words. This should have been a warning to me. This individual, generally pleasant, had always complained to Marzena and me since we moved in that the purchase of his flat had more or less broken him. I used to think: what did he want, a donation? In fact, this seemed typical behaviour for many Poles: show off if you have the money, but make it clear how short you are if you don't. In this regard, our purchase of a new car was not something he was going to let go unnoticed.

It all began with an inspection. No effort was spared. Our neighbour was here, there, and everywhere: on all fours, lying under the body of the car, head buried under the bonnet. Eventually, he gave his diagnosis:

"This car's been in an accident", he declared, challengingly. Our neighbour pointed to almost imperceptible differences between the colour of the paint on neighbouring panels, allegedly badly fitting doors, and flecks of paint where a panel had apparently been re-sprayed. Actually, he seemed to half know what he was talking about, but his motive appeared to be nothing more than to deflate us, rather than any crusade on his part to discover the truth about our new car's provenance. We had taken our neighbour-mechanic with us to check the car out before we bought it, and so I had an undisguised look of disbelief and disgust on my face when our neighbour began to attack the latest addition to our family. He saw this, and abruptly stopped. It was a fine car all the same, he said. Could he help in any way to clean it up a bit?

It turned out he could. The car was ex-company, and I was having trouble removing the last piece of gum from a prominent part of the bonnet, that had originally been attached to a large car sticker advertising the company in question. My T-cut was not really doing the trick. Did the neighbour have anything that could help? Now eager to oblige, he said he had just the thing, and returned a few seconds later holding a grotty, small tube of some kind of cream triumphantly above his head. This would get rid of anything, he assured me!

He immediately began to rub and rub the cream into the gum using a small rag he had brought along. And sure enough, it began to disperse. I was delighted. I took over the rubbing, and the neighbour stood back to watch. Five minutes later, and the gum had disappeared. Great result! Thank you very much, I told him. But he was not finished. He returned a minute later holding a spray canister. He had seen me struggling to extend and contract the metal car aerial. I should try this spray. It would loosen the thing up. He handed me the canister, which it turned out was nearly empty. The nozzle from the top of the canister fell off in my hands. I re-attached it, and tried to spray what was left of the can's contents onto the aerial. A tiny bit of liquid dribbled down the aerial. But this was sufficient for my neighbour. He vigorously extended and contracted the aerial a few times, insisting all the while it was loosening up dramatically.

"There!" he concluded, after a last manhandling of my by now tired and droopy looking antenna, "Good as new, wouldn't you say?"

I struggled to extend and contract the aerial a few times myself, and then thanked him for his kindness. I offered him the canister back.

"No-oo, no-oo", he said. "Wouldn't hear of it, old friend. Take it. It's yours!" It was as if he had just offered me the crown jewels. I thanked him as if I had just been offered the crown jewels. He returned to his flat. Moments later, the sun came out, and I discovered in the light that the cream I had been rubbing into the bonnet had stripped virtually all the paint away from where an inconsequential spot of gum had previously sat.

My neighbour's opening comment on the improvement in our lifestyle can at least partly be put down to the Poles' insatiable appetite for gossip - particularly where it concerns the neighbours. Our own neighbourhood was a good example. Within a few days of our moving in, Marzena knew the low-down on practically everyone in our block - and the surrounding blocks. This included which family lived in which flat, how many members it contained, what jobs they held, which cars they owned, and so on. Neighbours are placed into a class system only slightly less rigid than our own, stretching back in origin to the days of the szlachta and peasants. I learnt that – in wealth terms if not necessarily culturally - a person at the top is a rich businessman, followed by a successful member of the Polish Mafia (identifiable by his sports BMW, silver necklace and gold teeth) and beneath this, the bulk of the population eke out what existence they can. I was informed that most of our neighbours belonged to the first category. When, a few months after we moved in, my landlord had us round to his house for Sunday lunch, we did not have to wait until coffee to begin on the round of gossip of which Marzena was so fond. I found that my landlord, and *his* wife, were equally curious. From this I constructed a gossip league. Polish women headed it, with Polish men a close second. The Brits, as we usually do in sport, came last.

That I was not family may have explained my neighbour's minimal generosity. Polish families, as I learnt from the rituals required to enter one, are legendarily close. I remember once talking with a young colleague from work who told me earnestly that the time when his wife had gone to England to learn English on a two week course had been the worst period of his life. He was now refusing to go on a similar course even though the boss wanted him to, because he could not stand to be away from her.

The corollary of such an attitude is that families see a tremendous amount of each other (with kissing taking place on the statutory three cheeks at every meeting). Children are adored and spoilt (which for most Poles means the parents going without) and even pets are mollycoddled, if one can describe the Kraken attached to rusty old iron posts in most Polish gardens as pets.

A peculiarity I discovered in the world of the family is the astonishing number of uncles everyone seems to have. Marzena seemed to come from a vast family, judging by *her* number of uncles, until I discovered "uncle" is an affectionate term for anyone - however tenuously - connected with the family. I was an uncle to thousands of kids in Poland before I was even engaged. Indeed, the word "uncle" can be used to cover so many acquaintances, including friends of the family and more distant family members, that - almost unbelievably - a true uncle is referred to as "the brother of my father" or "the brother of my mother" in order to identify him as the real McCoy!

One unmissable characteristic of Polish families is the way they "feed up" their children from cradle to grave. They ply them with food and drink endlessly until the gossip tree remarks that maybe little Tomek could do with losing a bit of weight after all. I remember finishing one meal during a Christmas break at my in-laws' house and afterwards visiting a favourite uncle (a real one, on this occasion) and aunt's. Worryingly, they had spruced it up, which meant this was an "occasion" (again, I envisaged my father appearing). At such events, food *happens*. And sure enough, the uncle and aunt then proceeded to offer us pâté, charcuterie, stew, Polish sausage, bread, cheese, pączki, fruit, liqueur-filled sweets, tea, martini and vodka in the course of a brief afternoon. It was in vain I tried to refuse anything, or mention I had just that minute finished devouring a sizeable Christmas meal. By the time I got back to my in-laws' and rolled like a barrel through their front door, no doubt the neighbours were already starting to talk.

We have seen that Poles can be catatonic in their work, capable of either the most incredible amount of initiative, or very little. Many eminent Polish thinkers have noted this quality of extremes. Miłosz wrote of the Poles:

"An astonishingly vital people who sink easily into moronic apathy and who show their virtues only in circumstances that would crush and destroy any other human group".

In other words, Poles are at the successful end of their extremity *in extremis*. This theme came up (with endearing spelling mistakes) in the programme for an opera to which Marzena and I went, "Cracowians and Mountaineers". A prelude to the piece suggested "crushing circumstances" usually meant a fight between the Poles and someone else [*sic*]:

"We Poles, solidary in conspiration and eager to go to entrenchments
In peace-time we do envious acrobatics
And a simple lesson that history has taught us for years it is that
We are brought to harmony by a common enemy".

Surrounded by powerful states at the crossroads of Europe, the Poles have often found themselves in dire straits, and this has made them politically aware. They have had to take every opportunity they can to try to increase Poland's strength, and this has been seen in their alliances, usually achieved through the marriage of Polish Kings to the royalty of powerful neighbours. The other technique has been to back certain rulers, such as Napoleon, who achieved lasting popularity in Poland by creating the mini-state of "the Duchy of Warsaw" at a time when Poland had disappeared from the map.

Every man and woman in Poland is a politician. Well, almost. Certainly most Poles are politically aware, especially now they are permitted to hold a political view. In the past, this privilege only belonged to famous writers in exile who tried (gallantly) to bring down Communism and previous dictatorships from afar by the power of the pen. Indeed, from 1830 until relatively recently, the centre of Polish literary life was situated in the "Great Emigration", following the failure of the Polish insurrection of that year. Writers, such as Miłosz, gathered particularly in Paris to air their views.

A return to pluralism now might be said to be a return to the natural order of things for the Poles. They had a parliament as early as 1493. Soon after, in 1515, due to the passing of the law called *Nihil Novi* (literally *nothing new*, meaning no change without the common consent), the King could neither wage war nor impose new taxes without parliament's consent. By 1572, the Polish Kings were even being elected, when the "Republic of Nobles" enfranchised fully ten per cent of the population – the so-called "gentry democracy" - a result of the last Jagiellonian King being without an heir. Perhaps it was such an historic parliamentary tradition that led Mickiewicz, the most celebrated Polish writer, to declare, "The Pole is a natural democrat and republican". The intensity of the Poles' interest in politics is also demonstrated by the famous Polish saying, originally taken from the nineteenth century Polish writer Wyspiański, and nowadays uttered at will between one Pole and another:

"Co tam panie w polityce?"
"What's going on in politics?"

Even so, people view politicians with equal contempt as back home in the UK. Poles hold politicians responsible for all disasters, often justifiably so. For example, when terrible floods hit Poland in 1997, the ruling Socialist Democratic Party, the "SLD" (better known as the ex-Communist party of President Kwaśniewski[18]) failed to respond quickly to the crisis, or to promise any funds to help the victims. Some say it was as a result of such a slow reaction the SLD lost their majority in Parliament to the "AWS" (the new face of the Solidarity trade union).

Surprisingly, the most well-known Polish politician to us in the West, Lech Wałęsa, has a chequered reputation in Poland. Some of his unpopularity stems from his working class background, and his unsophisticated use of the Polish language. Personally, I can very much identify with him on this.

This is strange. Wałęsa is a true hero, who not only helped bring down Communism in Poland, but contributed in no small part to its demise in the whole of the Soviet Bloc. An electrician from a humble background, he led the striking ship workers at the port of Gdańsk, managing to mobilise the working classes who would not have followed an intelligentsia led opposition. He so increased the power and influence of the Solidarity trade union that it eventually entered the famous power sharing, "Round Table" talks of 1989. Soon after this, the controversial Polish Communist leader General Jarosław Jaruzelski, who had introduced Martial Law to Poland in 1981, stepped down in favour of Wałęsa. Jaruzelski was controversial because of this dual role he played of enforcer of the old regime and conduit for change (he was the first East European Communist leader to permit free elections). But it was for sure he was an at times brutal Communist, and it must have galled Wałęsa to know his old rival spent his retirement in a luxury villa in Anin – one of the more exclusive suburbs of Warsaw. Wałęsa was particularly remembered for the incident my father had alluded to when describing his own battles with the *ZOMO* riot police. At one point early on in the strikes, the Communist police and army surrounded a group of strikers, and no-one was permitted to enter (although strikers could leave and not come back). Somehow, so it was said, Wałęsa managed to cross the fence and join the group. Many dispute this, and say it never happened, but even the idea it might have was seen as symbolic victory for the workers.

Poland's attitude to its recent Communist past has not been without controversy. Some criticise her for taking much longer than fellow post-Communist, East European states to introduce a "Lustration" law, bringing to light which politicians collaborated with the Communists. Not surprisingly, the law, which was finally passed, was opposed at every stage of its progress by the post-Communists, but supported by the Solidarity grouping. I had first-hand experience of this dissembling attitude of some Poles to Communism. I wrote an article about a reform of Polish law for a legal publication. I mentioned that the old law had become obsolete because it had been passed under entirely different economic conditions, during Communist times in Poland. A partner at my law firm who reviewed the article before publication crossed out this sentence. "Exaggeration!" he wrote. "Poland has never been a <u>Communist</u> country. And not in 1988 for sure". This was not only inaccurate on his part; but the addition of the words, "and not in 1988 for sure" seemed an acknowledgement that Poland had been Communist at some point in its history. In any case, the Lustration law got onto the Statute Book, and found its first victim - a deputy economy minister who, having lied about his links with the Communists, became ineligible under the new law from holding public office.

As in any country, politics in Poland has produced its funnier moments. The Poles have outdone Neil Kinnock falling over on the beach, or Margaret Thatcher tripping up. At one meeting in Parliament, the Polish equivalent of the Speaker of the House was due to sum up the day's proceedings. To do this, he needed some papers, and asked his colleague sitting next to him at the head table in Parliament for them. The colleague replied he did not have them, at which point the Speaker uttered words to the effect of: "Well, fuck me, how am I going to do this speech then?" Which was fine, except he had forgotten to switch off his microphone. Murmur and then uproar in the Chamber followed the initial few seconds of disbelief. And poor Mr. Speaker, there was simply nowhere for him to hide. Soon, he was the most famous - and infamous - politician in Poland.

The Poles love learning. Most Poles are well educated, for which, for once, the Communists can be thanked. They largely lived up to their boast that education was for all, educating the previously illiterate peasant class. The Poles have broad knowledge owing to an educational system modelled on classical German schools in which pupils study a wide number of subjects to a late age. Even when they specialise, they have to have a good grip of the general area in which they are studying. Marzena told me, for example, that PhD students in the institutes of pedagogy, sociology and psychology take, towards the end of their PhD studies, an additional exam in philosophy (the faculty that contains these institutes). They have to pass such an exam before they may be awarded a PhD in their own subject.

When I asked my work colleagues whether they thought "Jan Kowalski" in Poland was better educated and more cultured than Jo Bloggs in the West they answered, perhaps inevitably, "Yes". But they went further. Two colleagues told me about when they had been studying in France along with students from a whole host of other nations. Without exception, they said, they had been able to answer questions from the teacher on general cultural matters more successfully than any other nationality. My good friend Henryk, he of *karaoke* fame, who was rapidly becoming the equivalent sounding board for my theories on Poland as Paweł had been at my first job, boasted the matters in which he had superior knowledge ranged from Greek mythology to *in vitro* fertilisation. It was no surprise, therefore, to learn that the Polish system of education involves studying a wide number of subjects right up to and including "A" level (known as "matura"), rather like the French baccalauréat.

Not everything the Communists did in Polish education was beneficial. They censored education. History, for example, was suitably cut: they never taught Poles that during the period of Soviet domination the Poles actually defeated the Soviets in the 1919-20 Polish-Soviet war. They also manipulated literature, emphasizing one pro-Russian poem of Mickiewicz, who was in fact the most patriotic of Poles. Communist ideology was also taught in "Citizens' Teaching", and the Russian language studied compulsorily. Education techniques did not develop. Pupils got into the habit of rote, not learning how to think. The Polish government must have known. From 1999, education was reformed, becoming more specialised and vocational in an effort better to prepare students for the challenges of the market place.

But despite such educational challenges – *yes* - the Poles love learning. They respect experts in any field, and will always try to better themselves in the hope they might be one day be considered such. Popular science and historical books are two of the best selling genres in Poland. Miłosz once wrote the Poles are "fascinated in the extreme with the philosophy of history". Those secretaries who could afford it - in both the jobs I had in Poland – would enrol on business English courses or take degrees, and lawyers took MBAs at night school.

Whilst we in the West may have become blasé about such opportunities, to the Poles, these were life chances many of them did not have in the past. No doubt the older generation emphasise this when encouraging their kids to keep up with their learning.

And encourage their children they do, in more ways than one. Paternalism is practised on a grand scale in Poland. The first time I noticed was when Marzena bumped into an old school friend at a bus stop in Cracow during one of my early trips to Poland. It was summer, and they were chatting away when an old lady, with a stick, grabbed Marzena's friend by the elbow and dragged her under the bus shelter, muttering something. I was just on the point of defending Marzena's friend from this unpleasant old codger when I realised she was the mother, telling her fit and healthy young daughter to get into the shade.

Perhaps Polish parents like to tell their children what to do because they have been told what to do all of *their* lives, something which has fostered the browbeaten nature of the Poles. They have been under the domination of one people or another for much of their past. The history books tell you this is because Poland is a flat land (Tatra mountains notwithstanding) made for invading armies to roll across. Indeed, the "Polonians" who settled Poland were the "People of the Open Field". But it has also invariably been surrounded by powerful neighbours – in particular Prussia (later Germany) to the West, and the Russian Bear to the East. Furthermore, at one time or another, Poland has been attacked by, in addition to the Russians, Prussians and Germans - Swedes, Lithuanians, Turks, Austrians, Ukrainians, Cossacks, Tartars and the Teutonic Knights. Between 1795 and 1918, following a period of ungovernability caused by excessive use of the *liberum veto* (a measure allowing a single vote against a proposal in the Polish parliament to defeat it) Poland went off the map of Europe altogether. It was divided up between the Russians, Prussians and Austrians. During that period, Austria took the province of Galicia, in the south-east of Poland and nearest to their Empire, Russia the east of Poland, nearest to their territory, including Warsaw, and Prussia the West of Poland, including the prize of Gdańsk (then Danzig). Although the Poles attempted various insurrections and rebellions during these 120 years of partition, they all failed. The 1830 insurrection provoked a Russian backlash. Within one year the Poles were defeated, Russian repression set in, and the first wave of Polish emigration, chiefly to America, began.

This history has been vital in the formation of the character of the Poles. Having had true independence only between 1918-39 and since 1989 (after Communism) in the last 200 years, they are intensely proud and nationalistic. They also adore their heroes (the more romantic the better) even those that ultimately failed in their plots against the oppressor, because they are seen as preserving the Polish spirit and identity at a time when it was so endangered. We have already seen how Napoleon is worshipped by Poles to this day. The lyrics of Poland's national anthem glorify his exploits, and his legal system, as I noted daily, still forms the basis of Poland's jurisprudence. Polish poets are just as much regarded as heroes as soldiers on the battlefield, as they encouraged Poles to struggle for their freedom. Indeed, Polish literature over the centuries has revealed an almost non-stop obsession with the need to throw off Poland's oppressors. Jasiński's *To the Nation*, written in 1794, is a typical example:

"Pay no heed that you are bound by heavy chains.
Wherever people have said "I want to be free" they have always become free!
Keep in mind examples of the West,
What the forces of tyrants are, and the power of a nation".

Not content to honour their heroes in stone or bronze, or by naming streets after them, the Poles have immortalised three heroes (Kościuszko, Piłsudski and Wanda) by building giant mounds of earth for them on the outskirts of Cracow. Tadeusz Kościuszko's heroic act was to defeat the Russians at the Battle of Racławice with an army consisting largely of peasants armed with scythes. This was in 1794, a last ditch attempt to rescue Poland before it was partitioned off the map a year later. Kościuszko was also a former hero of the American War of Independence. Piłsudski was a huge military and political figure in Polish history, sworn in as first head of state when Poland was put back on the map after the First World War. He also defeated the Russians in 1919-20, and ruled Poland with a firm hand in the late 1920s and early 1930s following a series of weak governments. The eighth century Polish princess Wanda reached her esteemed position by committing suicide – supposedly jumping into the Vistula river and drowning rather than marry a German prince! No doubt she appeals to anti-German sentiment to this day. As for the mounds that commemorate these deeds and personalities, they are quite something to see, producing a peculiar effect that has - simultaneously - a natural and artificial feel to it.

Such a history of invasion and destruction has left the Poles wary. When asked how he is in the morning, a Pole will invariably answer "tak sobie" – the famous "so-so", or even - "może być", "could be" - as opposed to the typically English "fine - how are you?" Connected with this is a certain resignation and fatalism about the Poles. Many of their sayings take the form, "it doesn't matter whether you do this or that – you still get the same result". We have already seen this in relation to work ("it doesn't matter what you do / you get the same reward"). It can even be applied to the common cold (something *very* common in the Polish winter) in the following form:

"Katar leczony, trwa jeden tydzień,
Katar nie leczony, trwa siedem dni",
"A cold that is treated gets better in one week,
A cold that is not treated gets better in seven days".

One characteristic the Poles do reveal in this regard is self-pity – and such self-pity goes back a long way. Our old friend Opaliński wrote about it, although, unusually for him, on this occasion, his words seem more a defence of Poland than an attack:

"God keeps us as fools. And this comes close to the saying that, among people, a Pole is God's plaything. If the Divine Hand of the Almighty did not hold us up, long ago we would not have escaped from our foes and, I will add, from utter destruction… God has grown used to treating us as a lord treats his fool. When a crowd of young boys closes in around a fool – one pinches his bottom, one pokes him where it hurts; the fool defends himself and shouts, once, twice, and the lord listens patiently, while the boys maul the fool without a respite and he begins to yell at the top of his voice, mouth wide open, so that he annoys the lord with it, and finally the lord calls to the boys: 'Quiet down! How much more of that?' And the boys dive into the bushes away from the fool and playing. Thus God sometimes waits till our enemies have had their fill of swarming all over our miserable Poland. And only when they annoy her too much and Himself, He calls: 'Be quiet Turks! Be quiet, Tartars!' And the Turks take to the bushes together with the other infidels."

No, the Poles have not been able to rely on the course of history. This may explain why so many are superstitious. Take my landlord Jan, for example. Not only does he beep his horn vigorously every time he enters or leaves Warsaw for good luck, but he will never shake hands with me over the threshold of our flat. It is bad luck. As for my colleagues at work, many of whom were taking exams to qualify as lawyers, they would religiously reply to my wishes of good luck before every exam with the words "No thank you". It's a tradition. Almost as if to say, "Luck - I don't need it!" I gave up wishing it them long ago.

But subjugation and superstition have not in any way blunted the Poles' outgoing sense of style and the aesthetic. In addition to their modern architecture, Poles are well known for their love of art. Whilst living in Poland I saw an exhibition of the brilliant Polish oil-painter and impressionist, Jan Cybis, as well as an exhibition by the marvellous Chagall, whose paintings include evocative representations of past Jewish life in Poland. The turnover of exhibitions in Poland was frequent, and pleased Marzena, who has an artistic eye. Personally, I was equally pleased by the considerable number of seats dotted around the galleries at strategic points. Poland's love of art goes back a long way. The nineteenth century painter Jan Matejko, who famously painted the Battle of Grunwald (a stupendous canvas painted in brilliant colours showing the combined Polish and Lithuanian armies defeating the Teutonic Knights in 1410) is to this day something of a national hero. Streets and squares are named after him, and statues of him proliferate in Poland. But Poles do not just look back to past artistic glories. Modern day Polish painters are successful throughout the world. Wojtek Fibak, the former Polish tennis player, saw the potential for Polish art, and was instrumental in promoting it globally. He is said to have picked up a large number of paintings cheaply, before the recognition arrived, and now has one of the most valuable collections of Polish paintings. Marzena and I saw a good selection of modern Polish art at the Modern Art Gallery in Łódź. Although taken with the more worthy artists we saw represented, including the abstract painters Brzozowszki, Nowosielski, Pankiewicz and Witkiewicz (also a playwright) it was a Socialist Realist piece from 1950 which most caught our eye. It showed two ruddy-cheeked workers, a woman and a man, standing arm in arm, next to a peroxide blond wearing sunglasses and carrying a shiny handbag. The labourers appeared serious and humble - as if they valued only the worthy things in life. The blond appeared superficial and materialistic. But most fascinating of all the blond had emblazoned on her dress a series of stickers meant to represent Western material excess, including the words "Coca-cola", "Wall Street" and "London". We had to chuckle at the blatancy of the propaganda: surely it preached only to the converted, didn't actually convert anyone to the *New Faith,* Communism?

Poles seem to love all forms of culture, not just art. In terms of music, there is the opera, annual rock and jazz festivals, Mozart and Beethoven festivals, the Chopin piano-playing competition every five years – and even the occasional visiting folk orchestra from the Star Ship Enterprise. These are all worth attending, but I confess to having given a miss so far to the annual "Competition with Polish Traditional Herdsmen's Instruments". In addition, Poles boast (legitimately) that Krzysztof Penderecki, multiple Grammy award winner, is one of the greatest living composers.

Polish literature, too, as we have seen, is popular, and, according to Miłosz, has only failed to generate the interest it deserves abroad because it has been oriented more toward poetry and the theatre than toward fiction. As a brilliant poet himself, who won the Nobel Prize for literature, Miłosz was living proof of his own theory. But it is his book of essays "The Captive Mind" that is a must for anyone trying to understand the insidious spread of Communist thought through an occupied society. Again, it is that Polish sense of style that has imbued their literature, for even to this day it is the three great *romantic* poets (Mickiewicz, Słowacki and Krasiński) who are regarded as the leading figures in Polish literary history.

Polish theatre has been particularly avant-garde. Stanisław Witkiewicz was the true founder of the theatre of the absurd long before Ionesco and crew came along. He apotheosised style, seeking "Pure Form" ahead of substance in his works. But it is the lack of style and minimalism of Jerzy Grotowski that has had the most impact. He has been a key mover in experimental theatre, creating the "Polish Laboratory Theatre" that performs on bare stages and without costumes to small audiences to try to bring actors and audience closer together. This includes asking members of the audience to participate in the performance. Grotowski's productions have been admired and adapted by theatre groups throughout Europe and America.

Poles also have a sense of style in the way they dress, though this seems to have permeated more the female half of the population. The girls who – the policeman's wife aside - are exquisite, wear striking clothes: flamboyant black or white furs in the winter, and in the summer, mini-skirts of super short length. Add to this bright red lipstick and plenty of dark eye shadow (no wonder Max Factor[19] came from Poland) and you can see why traffic practically stops in the streets. I remember at my wedding the male contingent in the English wedding party being in a daze for most of the weekend - and this included my father and his cronies.

Like every nation, of course, the Poles have their faults. One character feature that grates is their excessive bureaucracy. This may be a throwback to past domination, and not a Polish trait since time immemorial. The bureaucratic tendencies of the Communists are legendary, but even before then, Poles were ruled by bureaucrats. The Austrian partition of Poland was well known for its red tape. Bureaucracy is something the average Pole himself cannot abide, and one part of the country - the Cracowians - have gained an unwelcome reputation for being bureaucratic. This is no surprise, as Cracow was in the part of Poland that came under Austrian rule. As for how these things appeared to an Englishman, the answer is that, having had to obtain in the course of his time in Poland the following: to reside and work, an interim work certificate, visa, full work permit, and certificate of temporary residence (known as "zameldovania", and necessary almost for drawing breath); to drive a Polish car, registration certificate, purchase tax, translation of English no-claims bonus, car alarm, two types of insurance, new Polish number plates, and regional MOT; and to set up a bank account, *just ask security cards* - there really was only one conclusion to draw.

Perhaps a more serious character flaw is the conservatism in Polish society, which to us in the West can look more like intolerance. I got thinking about gender equality when, one day, the secretary at my first law job in Warsaw – Anna - came into the office bruised and scratched about the face. As most violent crime usually happens within the home, and as I had not heard any rumour about the office she had been mugged on the streets of Praga[20] where she lived – a reputedly rough part of Warsaw - I made an assumption this had been inflicted on Anna by her father or boyfriend. A government awareness campaign supported my theory. A ubiquitous hoarding around Warsaw depicted a beaten up mother and child, and underneath them the words, "And all because the soup was too salty". In Poland, many women suffer domestic violence, caused as much as anything by the high alcohol intake of Polish males. Women lack effective representation and support groups - ironic in a country that adheres to the cult of the Virgin Mary, and is supposed to place women on a pedestal. Indeed, it was the pro-Catholic, right-wing dominated Polish Parliament that threw out a draft bill in April 1999 which would have equalised the rights of men and women in family, political, social and economic life[21].

As for the attitude of the Poles towards minorities, there are few blacks in Poland. One black girl I knew in Poland claimed she was spat at on the street. What I witnessed first hand, when I was watching a football match between England and Poland with a number of Polish work colleagues, was their amusement every time a black player on the English team received the ball. Their mockery did not seem to be malicious, but it would have been offensive if any blacks had happened to be in the room – especially as the Poles referred to every black

English player as "Toby Nairobi". I heard of a black person who sued a Polish magazine for a tasteless black joke. With regard to homosexuals, I suspect it is not always easy being gay in Poland, even if they are served by a substantial number of widely distributed magazines. Most young Polish males I met did not exactly castigate homosexuals, but there was a tone of disapproval in their speech that was unmistakable (they often used the pejorative Polish word "pedał" or "fag" to describe a gay person[22]). Possibly the most controversial question of all on the subject of minorities – Polish anti-Semitism – we'll consider later.

This conservatism may partly be attributable to the immense influence of the Catholic church in Poland. Gay activists criticise the church for its attitude to homosexuality. Its radio station "Radio Maryja" has something of a reputation for making anti-Semitic pronouncements. And we have seen its approach to gender equality. Time will tell if the opening of Poland to the West changes things in a country that is ninety per cent Catholic and lacking in any significant ethnic minority.

Something more difficult to relate to the specific example of the Poles, that simply may be more characteristic of human behaviour in general, is the high level of adultery committed in Poland. I first noticed this when young male colleagues at work asked me if I wished to come out with them for a "good time". A good time, it transpired, meant laddish behaviour: vodka, a strip club, and women. The general idea seemed to be that a good bit of extra-marital sex could do one wonders. Those partaking included a preponderance of Polish men already married with children by their early twenties, which I attributed in part to the Catholic distaste for contraception, and felt must have contributed to this tendency for infidelity.

But no nation is perfect, and in my time I have found much more to admire than criticise in Poles, and have really appreciated their sense of style, exciting zeitgeist and other attributes. This has changed *me*: many's the time I have used my Polish X-ray vision to question all sorts of aspects of English life I'd previously accepted without hesitation. All of which begs the question: what do the Poles think of the rest of us?

12 WHAT THE POLES THINK ABOUT US

As I bumped along the unmade road that led to the narrow courtyard in front of our flat, on my way home from work, I noticed in my rear view mirror that a car was right on my tail. Typical, I thought, and vowed once more to go on a one-man mission to change the driving habits of the Poles. Too close to the car in front. As it turned out, I should not have been complaining about the driving of others. It was early June, and having only bought my new car, with left-hand drive, a couple of weeks earlier, I was still having trouble getting used to changing gear with my right hand. Occasionally, I would attempt to change gear with my left, either crashing it painfully against the driver door or swishing it silently in the air with all the skill of a Marcel Marceau.

I turned into the pebble courtyard and deliberately drove five or six metres past my garage. I would back up to it in order to make leaving easier when I went to work the next day. The practice at reversing would be less difficult now than at eight o'clock the next morning with sleep still in my eyes. Having stopped the car, I pushed the gear stick slowly but deliberately into reverse, and let out the clutch gently. The car rocked a little, but would not move. I noticed in my rear view mirror that the driver in the car behind had left me little room in which to go back. He was also looking at me askance, as if to say, "What's happening?" I put the car into neutral, and then back into reverse, ready to back up again. Again, I let up the clutch, a little further this time, but the car still seemed caught up in some kind of invisible swamp. I glanced in my rear view mirror again. The driver's mouth was agape. What could be wrong? Suddenly, I remembered something. All week, workmen had been digging a hole in the courtyard because some drains in the opposite building had become blocked. It had been a messy affair, and when it was finished, they had

147

filled the hole back in and covered it with large pebbles and stones. If I was not mistaken, I was caught up in these!

I poked my head out of the window and noticed I was right in the middle of where the hole had been. Nothing for it, then. I had to take my courage in my hands and lift the clutch fully on my precious new car, even if this risked rocketing backwards. Still in reverse, I began to lift the clutch. As I did so, the driver of the car behind me sped past, narrowly missing my off side, and ground to a halt in the parking spaces ahead of me. I released the clutch fully, and after a brief crunching sound as the car struggled for grip, I was away. I got the thing under control, and backed slowly up to the garage.

I put on my Mul-T-Lock, got out of my car, locked the car doors, and switched on the alarm. No one was going to steal *my* car. As I walked to the communal entrance to the block, I noticed the driver of the car that had been right behind me locking his car, and about to make his way over to the block, too. He was not a resident, so probably a friend of one of the neighbours. I suddenly saw red, and though it would have been simpler to have gone directly into the block and entered my flat, for some reason (that old *ZOMO*-fighting truculence?) I called to him: "You know, when someone's trying to back up, you might leave him some room!" It didn't occur to me he might not have spoken English.

A young man in fashionable, baggy shorts, with a long ponytail and John Lennon glasses, strolled over to me. In a Polish accent, but with some American influence, he said to me in English: "if you can't drive properly, you should find somewhere to practise". I was taken aback, really had no reply. But I had to say something.

"Actually", I began, "it just so happens I'm learning to drive a left-hand drive car. So you might have some understanding of the situation."

"I learnt to drive in England, and I've never had any trouble switching between the two", was his reply.

"Well you must be some kind of genius, then" I argued, sulkily.

"Everybody tells me so", he countered.

I had met my match. As I opened the door to the block, and spitting blood, all I could say was:

"Well, that's funny - that they call you a genius, I mean - because I was only joking".

I made my way inside. I nervously stuck the key in the door to my flat. Suddenly, apparently riled by my last, weak comment, my opponent, viewing my ample figure, yelled, "We'll talk again when you've lost some weight!"

"We'll talk again when you've lost some hair!" I retorted.

Touché.

After I had calmed down in my flat for a few minutes following this encounter, I reflected on the irony that my combatant, who was arguing with an Englishman, had himself spent some time in England. And, presumably, a fair amount of time, if he had learnt to drive there. I should not have been so surprised, for the answer lies in the fact the English are one of the more popular peoples with the Poles. Indeed, if one survey I read in a Polish sociology journal is to be believed, precisely the fourth most popular. The popularity of the English is made up of several components. Englishmen, for example, are seen as gentlemen. This I find ironic considering I have seen more seats given up by the young for the elderly on one journey on a Warsaw tram than on a lifetime in the tube in London. I have also seen more ladies' hands kissed and more doors chivalrously opened in Poland. The Poles - famously romantic - knock spots off the English in this respect. The English are also seen as hardworking, and respected for their sang-froid and orderliness. However, this can work the other way, and it is generally thought English families are not close, and the English not demonstrative enough. Poles consider the English have a superiority complex, related to their days of empire, continuing through to this day in many guises. These include the belief of the English (as the Poles see it) that they do not need to learn any other language because everyone should speak their own, and the idea they have the best television in the world, the most famous rock groups, the most prestigious parliament, and so on (the list is endless).

While the English score highly for the war, even this is not all kudos. The Poles believe the British let them down by not defending them, as they (the British) had promised to do, when the Germans invaded. I once got into a debate with my colleague Paweł about this, and drew a simple map of Europe for him, dated 1940, showing that the Nazis controlled most of Europe except for Britain early in the war. Surely Paweł, one of the most intelligent Poles I had ever met, would acknowledge the dilemma of the British position? Paweł replied, however, that the British let the Poles down, and then drew his own map of Europe dated "end of the sixteenth century". He showed Poland controlling a swathe of territory from central Europe all the way through to the Black Sea. Surely he was wrong, I questioned? But it turned out he was right. At this time, Poland controlled over a million square kilometres of territory, and the Polish ducat was the strongest monetary unit in Europe. A true Pole, Paweł had turned the clock back four hundred years and regained his pride. The Second World War now seemed irrelevant.

But it was in the Second World War that the Poles and British came together. Famously, Polish pilots flew and fought bravely and brilliantly in the Battle of Britain (one of their squadrons had the highest number of kills of any allied squadron in the Battle) and the Polish government in exile was based in London. These two facts have formed the topic of conversation between me and almost every taxi driver in Poland who discovers I am British. Our understanding soon relaxes us both: the driver thinks he is going to get a big tip for our past collaborations, and I that I'm not going to get ripped off. In this respect, we both end up disappointed, but the spirit of '40 lives on.

I guess the English in Poland are doing their best to dispel their positive stereotypes. In addition to arguing in shops, banks and restaurants, I have even single-handedly destroyed our most prized asset of all - our gentlemanliness. It happened one day when we were waiting in a long queue for the car wash. As our turn approached, I got out of the car and in halting Polish asked the gentleman whose car was currently being washed how I operated the machine using the card I had been given. He looked at me as if studying a monkey at the zoo - up and down - and said nothing. Strange bloke, I thought. So, I asked the driver in the car behind, who performed the same ritual. What was wrong with them all? It was only after Marzena and I arrived home, having had to work out the car wash for ourselves, that Marzena noticed something on my sweater. It looked, inexplicably, like faeces; in fact, it was the remains of my Almond Magnum ice cream. The flaky chocolate, as flaky chocolate tends to do, had fallen onto my sweater and melted all over it - in frighteningly large quantities. I felt a sudden desire to rush back to the car wash, in the hope the two drivers were still there, post-wash, carefully checking the shine on their cars. I could then explain to them I was not recently escaped from the loony bin - just a sloppy eater. But too late. The reputation of the English tarnished forever. Let's hope they thought I was American.

But I was not alone in my boorish behaviour. Another Englishman, with whom I worked at my first job in Poland, did worse. He was known for telling the same joke to Polish girls in the office. He would sneak up, every Friday, to whichever one of them was wearing the shortest skirt, and ask, unctuously:

"Did you know, that today is "POET's" day?"

"No", they would answer, in the sweet accent of a Brigitte Bardot.

Excited, the Englishman would capitalise.

"Yes: "Piss Off Early Tomorrow's Saturday". What are you doing Saturday?"

Fortunately, even young Polish girls learning English can tell a bad joke when they hear one, and a creep when they see one, and I think the Englishman spent most of his weekends alone.

The Polish sociology journal places the Americans as the most popular people with the Poles. This can be explained in part, of course, by the huge number of Poles living in America or related to Polish Americans (around fifteen million). There are said to be more people of Polish origin living in or around Chicago, for example, than any other city in the world except Warsaw. But the Poles also admire Americans for their successful economy and pursuit of wealth. The young Poles of the street imitate their youth culture. Lads with bright white Nike sneakers and baggy jeans hanging halfway down their backsides are a common sight. In sharp contrast, many Polish intellectuals see the Americans as "nie kulturalni" - uncultured.

The French come next in the popularity stakes. Here, there are strong historical links, such as royal marriages between Poles and the French over the centuries. Also, some of Poland's most illustrious sons and daughters have spent time in France, including Chopin, who spent his life in exile there, Marie Curie (or, as the Poles call her, Marie Curie Skłodowska) and more recently Nobel Prize winning author Czesław Miłosz. French style has always been much admired, and the Polish nobility often imitated French architecture in Poland when building their palaces. So close was the link with France that French was Poland's second language right up until the Second World War.

To this day, the Poles keep an eye on their chic friends, and now hope to imitate France again by turning their own country into an equally successful tourist trap.

The Italians are next. The Poles seem to have an affinity with the Italians' warm and lively nature. Both countries are extremely hot in the summer, and both peoples live a similarly catatonic life during this time, the Poles finishing work early and then keeping out of the sun, and the Italians taking a siesta. Many Poles now go for holidays in Italy, because it is good value, and they like the facilities on offer (especially the food) and the people. Historically, the Poles and Italians were also drawn together by the many Italian artists who came to work in Poland (including, as we have seen, the Italian Renaissance architects). And both countries are staunchly Catholic.

There is also a blacklist of nations the Poles dislike. Top of this list are the Gypsies, who have entered Poland in significant numbers. Romanian gypsies can be found begging at almost every street corner. Some, kneeling perfectly still like mime artists, simply hold a cup out and have a begging note scrawled in Polish and hung around their neck. Others, however, are more "active" beggars. They accost you in the street, sitting in a restaurant, or when you are stopped in your car at traffic lights. The Poles generally dislike them, and often shout at them and tell them to go get a job, and seem rarely to give them money.

There was, however, one group of gypsies that people had a lot of time for. They were a musical troupe who entertained the passers-by in Cracow's atmospheric old streets. Their most singular member was an old man who played the violin. He was a tiny, shrivelled figure who sat curled up in a wheelchair the others pushed along. He was totally blind, had only one leg, and held the bow of the violin with a hand snaked back over itself. But he made the violin sing. Sometimes, I would stand for half an hour at a time listening to them play. When I learnt they had even recorded an album, my enthusiasm redoubled. I gave them generous tips. I even had an idea to get the group to play at our wedding. I invariably caught them on trips to Cracow, for in the summer they seemed to play everywhere around the old town. Then one day I learnt the old man had died. I felt a peculiarly deep sorrow, picturing his crumpled face as his violin strained to the sound of melancholic, East European tunes.

Next on the black list come the Germans. They are, of course, disliked most for the war, in which one quarter of the Polish population perished. As Slavs, the Poles were considered an inferior race to the Aryans, and were destined to become slaves of the German Thousand Year Reich. What was inflicted on Warsaw was particularly dreadful. One guidebook shows a picture of the Warsaw ghetto just after its destruction in 1944, following the "ghetto uprising" by Warsaw's Jews in 1943. It is only a picture of land, not humanity, but is nevertheless harrowing. Not one building or stone has been left in place. Utter flatness and rubble. Here, however, the Poles are careful also to blame the Russians – another of the nations high up on the Poles' black list. It was, of course, the Nazis who razed Warsaw in response to the Warsaw uprising carried out by the Polish underground army in 1944, a year after the ghetto uprising. But as the Poles slowly lost the battle, and the Nazis began their destruction of Warsaw, a well-equipped Red Army stood and watched from the eastern bank of the Vistula, without coming to the aid of the Poles. The reason was obvious: an independent-minded Warsaw, liberated with the help of the Russians – but chiefly by the Polish underground army - may adversely have affected Stalin's plan to suppress Poland and make it a part of the Soviet Bloc. So it was preferable for the Russians to wait for the Nazis to eliminate the Poles, and then move in themselves.

Latterly the Polish government has been more pro-German, appreciating the importance of trade with Germany. Professor Norman Davies, an eminent English historian of Poland, also believes the young are pro-German, because they have not witnessed the two World Wars. Although this matches my theory about the openness of young Poles, I was not so sure. When I asked Henryk at work about the matter, and gave Davies' view, he disagreed with the Professor. Yes, he said, we now fawn to some extent to the Germans. But this is more a question of *realpolitik*, of wariness towards the traditional powerful neighbour to our west, rather than any degree of sympathy - the same wariness we still display towards the powerful neighbour to our east, he added, with a stoical wink.

Next among the unfavourites come the Ukrainians. Their crime is to have taken a swathe of Polish territory to the east following the end of the Second World War. Many Poles found themselves to be "Ukrainians" all of a sudden. Lwów in the south-east of Poland, which had been a Polish city for centuries, was lost. Many of the Lwów Poles were then re-settled in Western Poland, formerly Eastern Germany, in land given to the Poles as compensation for land they lost to the Ukrainians. Wrocław, formerly the German town of Breslau, developed a strong university from this time consisting to a large degree of resettled inhabitants from Lwów. However, and as with most history in this part of the world, the situation is more complex than it appears. For at about the same time as the Poles were being expelled from Western Ukraine, Ukrainians from the south-eastern corner of Poland were having the same fate inflicted on them.

Like any other nation, then, Poles have their likes and dislikes with regard to other peoples. Only that, with their history, they generally have had more cause to dislike. But whatever the rights and wrongs of these preferences, and however many enemies Poland has had over the centuries, there is one thing Poles, including Miłosz himself, have never understood with regard to their *friends*: why have they never regarded the Poles more importantly?

The Poles, by any standard, have been a visionary people. Was it not the Poles who began a Parliamentary tradition as early as the fifteenth century, and began electing their Kings in the sixteenth century? Did Poland not introduce the first Constitution in Europe, and the second in the modern world, on 3 May 1791? Was Poland not the traditional bulwark against invaders from the East, and other heathen, *the antemurale Christianitatis* (rampart of Christendom)? In 1410, at the Battle of Grunwald, did Poland not defeat the Teutonic Knights, thus beginning the decline of that most ruthless and unpleasant of orders? In 1683, at the Relief of Vienna, did the Polish knights not rescue Europe from an encroaching wave of Ottoman Turks, finally repulsing them from the Continent for good? And in 1920, scarcely having recovered its independence, did Poland not halt the westward spread of the Bolshevik revolution, turning back the Red army almost at the gates of Warsaw, in the "Miracle on the Vistula"? And when Communism did take root further west, did Poland not almost single-handedly overthrow it, thanks to Solidarity and Mr. Wałęsa? Is Poland not still a bulwark, this time for NATO against the instability of the former Soviet Union? And by joining the EU, would it not - a country of some 40 million people, and at the precise geographical heart of the Continent - be by far the most significant new member of the club? In a world in which travel and tourism constitutes the world's largest industry, is it not already, as one of the most visited countries in the world, an important player? Was not the Pope Polish, and are not Penderecki, Roman Polański… and Boniek!?

But all that seems to be remembered about the Poles are some comments of the late Sir Winston Churchill about Polish mistakes...[23]

To the eternal chagrin of the Poles, it is in Russia the West has traditionally taken interest, no doubt awe-struck by the size and power of that country, and equally, its potential for self-destruction. This is galling given the Russians are another nation on the Poles' blacklist, not just for doing nothing while the Nazis laid waste to Warsaw, but because of their historical penchant for attacking and occupying Poland. However, maybe the Poles share the blame for the West's traditional lack of interest in them. A little like the self-effacing guide who showed us around the palace at Wilanów, the Poles have sometimes been reluctant to promote themselves. For example, there was a powerful movement in Poland against joining the EU, even though accession would clearly be an opportunity for the Poles to show themselves off a bit. It made me wonder if they nourished such ambition in their hearts, as they clearly did in the past, when Maciej Kazimierz Sarbiewski, a poet and theoretician of the early seventeenth century, wrote of Poland:

"No nation knows the world better and none is known better throughout the world. The Poles travel everywhere and similarly allow everyone to visit their native land",

and Kochanowski himself, father of Polish literature, declaimed:

"About me Moscow will know and the Tartars
And Englishman, inhabitants of diverse worlds.
The German and the valiant Spaniard will be acquainted with me
And those who drink from the deep Tiber stream".

Perhaps as a reaction to the indifference of the West, the Poles are proud of themselves, anyway. Having established their identity again after their incredible shifting borders, they are extremely patriotic. On November 11 each year, instead of remembering with sobriety the end of the Great War, Poles instead celebrate the independence they won again in 1918 having been partitioned off the map for over one hundred years. The importance of this date never became more apparent to me than when, just before one such November day, I was walking through the sprawling, shabby market that occupies part of the main square surrounding the Palace of Culture in the centre of Warsaw. It was bitterly cold - minus 10 and dropping – at the end of the day. And yet, despite this, I saw an incredible thing as I passed through the now mostly deserted stalls at around 6 o'clock in the evening. There, outside one stall, standing on a chair, was a stall owner reaching above him, struggling to slot a small Polish flag into a flag pole holder. He was having trouble making it, because the snow fell on him, and his hands, without gloves, were shaking in the bitterness. It seemed like madness to persevere – I was cold despite being wrapped up like a hot water boiler – but tomorrow was independence day, and the man was not to be beaten.

I could not myself be accused of indifference - mainly due to my upbringing. My father, other than for his contretemps with the *ZOMO*, has always been avidly pro-Eastern Europe. He used to be head of a team in a government laboratory investigating alternative energy sources – an international subject. He would make it his business to invite East Europeans over for secondments to his team, and would look after them during their stay. Many an evening meal in our household was spent learning from these temporary émigrés about life under the Communists, and after. I remember one young Russian describing conditions in Moscow after '89 as like life in the Wild West. And we heard from others, too - Romanians, Bulgarians, Yugoslavians, and of course Poles. Wide-ranging discussions would take place on the evils of totalitarianism, on Communism, back to Marx and Engels, and upon hopes for the future. My father's house resembled one of the nineteenth century Parisian salons.

He was aided in his insight by his membership of PUGWASH, the international group of scientists striving for world peace. In this guise he visited almost all the countries of Eastern Europe when they still lay behind the Iron Curtain. Later, when the Cold War was over, Joseph Rotblatt, octogenarian founder and head of PUGWASH, would receive the Nobel Peace Prize for his contribution to the organisation, along with the PUGWASH members. As a young Polish Jewish immigrant into Liverpool just before the war, whose wife soon perished in the Holocaust, Rotblatt had been welcomed into the family home of my father's parents - an eminent Freudian and his wife. Their discussions must have influenced Rotblatt's development. My dinners with my father and his guests influenced mine. Even before I met and fell in love with a beautiful Polish girl, I did not need to be convinced of the importance of Eastern Europe.

13 THE JEWISH QUESTION

"The Jewish Question - ah, the Jewish Question."

Our landlord Jan sighed.

"The Jewish Question is a very complex issue", he continued, then paused.

Jan glanced around at the comfortable, stylish houses and flats neighbouring our garden, in which we were all standing. It was eight o'clock in the evening on a late August day in 1998. We were all - that is, Marzena, Jan and I - having a beer to celebrate Marzena's and my first year in his flat, and to mark the end of the summer. But it was already getting chilly, as it did in Poland at that time of the evening at that time of the year. Jan quickly rubbed his shoulder to keep out the cold, holding a beer in his other hand.

"Let me tell you a story before it gets too cold out here", he continued. "It was 1942. My family was quite poor. I was living with my brothers and sisters and my parents in my aunt and uncle's house. They - my aunt and uncle - had children too, my cousins. It was a crowded house. Suddenly, one evening in February 1942, just before the Nazis started their most ruthless stage in the process of rounding up and exterminating Jews, there was a knock at the door. It was eleven o'clock at night. My uncle opened the door, cautiously, and there, standing before him, were four figures: two parents, and their son and daughter. They were Jews. There were a lot of Jews in Poland at that time, because they had found peace here before the war. They asked for shelter. My uncle and aunt took them in. We harboured them, even though to be found harbouring Jews meant certain death to those protecting them. My aunt and uncle looked after those four Jews until the end of the war. They survived. Now, every year, the surviving members of our family and the Jewish family meet on the annual march between Auschwitz and Birkenau - you know, the one

Netenyahu went on this year. My family has been officially recognised by the state of Israel for what it did. We are righteous gentiles."

Jan had always been a favourite of Marzena and mine. But when we learnt of what his family had done, Marzena, as a doctoral student in Jewish studies, and I, as a Jew, took him closer to our hearts. He continued, proceeding to summarise the Jewish Question more simply and eloquently than his earlier assessment might have promised:

"No one is saying there is no anti-Semitism in Poland. Of course there is, just as in many other countries. For instance, a Pole may have a particular cause to hate Jews - maybe if a Jewish Communist, a member of the "SB", the Polish equivalent of the KGB, was responsible for the death of someone in his family. And it's possible - believe me – because there were many Jewish members of the Communist party and the SB. But anti-Semitism in Poland is not the disease that everyone says it is. It is probably no worse than in any other country."

"And then there are people like you", I said.

"And then there are people like me".

The Poles must have the worst reputation of any people for being anti-Semitic. It appears they must share guilt for the Holocaust with its Nazi perpetrators. The theories, particularly on the part of my fellow Jews, abound, but may be capable of summary like this: either the Poles helped the Nazis in their crime, or turned a blind eye. Hardly any of them helped the Jews. But would you have done, under pain of death? And does this make the Poles as responsible as the Germans? Whilst this debate rages on, I'm better placed to recount the pre-war history of Polish Jews, and what it is like to be a Jew in Poland in modern times.

I was sympathetic to my landlord Jan's view, for it is all too easily forgotten that it was in Poland the Jews found solace from an early time, and for a long time. I learnt about the history of the Jews in Poland from a course on that subject during my Jewish Studies year at Oxford in 1994, the time when I first met Marzena. It was given by an accomplished American-born professor, who has since passed away much too young. The professor took us back in time to the thirteenth century, when King Bolesław the Pious of Poland gave certain privileges to the Jews in a Charter; now they were allowed to trade, and also open synagogues and schools - very important to the People of the

Book. In the next century, Casimir the Great, who it was said turned Poland "from wood into stone" - by strengthening Poland politically, economically and legally, as well as erecting magnificent buildings - still found time to help the Jews. He allowed them more privileges in another Charter, including permission to lend money for interest, freedom of movement, and freedom to settle anywhere in Poland. Then, in 1551, Sigismund Augustus, who was known for being favourable to the Jews, issued yet another Charter, granting Jews the right to set up "Kahals" (administratively independent Polish Jewish ghettos). The King also took all power over the Jews into his own hands, which meant they were better protected. All of this culminated in the Council of the Four Lands, a governing body over all the Jews of Poland and Lithuania, set up around 1575. It was like a Jewish Parliament, which existed in no other country in Europe. Two years earlier, the Compact of Warsaw had guaranteed the constitutional equality of all religions in Poland.

The sixteenth and seventeenth centuries thus became known as the "Golden Age of Polish Jewry". The Jews enjoyed prosperity and security, were favoured by the Polish nobility, and even became nobility themselves. At this time, they were merchants, diplomats, doctors, jewellery-makers, tax gatherers, moneylenders and businessman. The Jews were the middle class of Poland. They continued to live in ghettos, and spoke their own language – Yiddish – a German dialect with Hebrew and Slavonic additions. Not so long after Spain expelled its Jews, in 1492, the Jews of Poland rested. They even said so themselves, making a play on words of the name "Poland", and corrupting it to "Po-Lin" - Hebrew for, "Here, one rests".

Their security continued on until the Nazis almost entirely exterminated them. As this was taking place, many Poles, including the Polish nobility, traditional supporters of the Jews, were concerned about the dark turn of events. Along with the rest of Poland, they had harboured the Jews over the centuries, employing them as stewards on their estates. On the eve of their genocide, there were three and a half million Jews in Poland, more than in any other European country. One of the Polish underground, the spy "Karski"[24] (a pseudonym), even investigated claims a holocaust was taking place – at great personal risk. Karski saw the evidence with his own eyes, escaped to the West, and alerted the allies to what was happening to the Jews of

Poland. But people were sceptical of him. And more's the pity, because after the war, only 300,000 Polish Jews remained.

No one can say the presence of the Jews in Poland was not an ongoing conundrum. "The Jewish Question" was the traditional term for the question of what to do with this nation of three million and more people living without a land. This would lead to the Zionist movement and eventually the creation of the state of Israel in 1948. Until then, Jews were the victims of Polish pogroms, both before and even immediately after the war, many of them very serious, involving the deaths of many Jews. The pogroms are a source of poor Polish-Jewish relations to this day.

I saw the evidence of Polish Jewry's rich and successful past when I went on a field-trip to view the Jewish remains in Galicia - the former Austrian partition in the south-east of Poland. It was summer 1994. My diploma year in Jewish studies had just ended. Marzena had returned to Poland. As well as seeing her again, I would, in travelling to Poland for the first time, see first hand what until now I had only read about the Jews of Poland.

The field trip started in Kazimierz, the suburb of Cracow where 65,000 Jews lived until their murder during the war. Jews had been living in the centre of Cracow since the twelfth and thirteenth centuries, often occupying some of the most expensive homes. But in 1494, the Jews were blamed for a devastating fire and banned from the city. They settled in Kazimierz, which was then a nearby town.

Kazimierz today is a strange mix. Like much of Cracow, the architecture is preserved and glorious, though in need of renovation. After the war, when all the Jews had gone, criminals and needy types were housed in the Jews' former homes. Consequently, Kazimierz today is a somewhat rough area, though more so at night. Right in the centre of this town stands "ulica Szeroka", the central square of the Jewish ghetto. It is a priceless throwback to the past. Although the centre of the square, which is more a rectangle, is these days lined with parked cars, it retains an ambience of the past that is almost indescribable. This is in no small part due to the presence of several hotel-cafés with Jewish themes, in which one can eat Jewish food, sit amongst Jewish artefacts and listen to Jewish music. To sit in these cafés with the traditional Jewish dish chopped liver and a beer is an experience wholly different to that of sitting in Cracow's rynek. It is equally apropos for relaxing and watching the world go by, and maybe better, for the square is more tranquil than its big brother in the city. But the other feeling - that of reminiscence and loss, is immense for an Ashkenazi Jew like myself who originated from these parts. You look up at the sepia postcards in the cafés, showing hordes of long-bearded Jews, parading little boys with cute ringlets, and Jewish mothers pushing big-wheeled prams - in this very same square before the war - and the tears well in your eyes. They are all gone. To sit in ulica Szeroka and imagine in this way is something you can only do so often. It is both very good and very bad for the soul.

Also evoking the past is the "Remuh" synagogue, so named after a rabbinical sage, which his father built. It is the only synagogue in Cracow that remains active, with a dwindling, ageing population. Religious Hasidic Jews ("Hasidim") visit the synagogue in numbers, and leave pebbles on the Remuh's grave to remember him. Situated on one edge of the extensive cemetery, there is also the grave of a renowned "Rabbi Lipman-Heller" (1579-1654), the rabbi of Cracow from 1643, as if to emphasise my proximity to this place. A relation of Joseph's and mine? To the other side, one wall of the cemetery has been made into a spectacular and moving collage of Jewish headstones, ransacked by the Nazis. Inside, the synagogue is cramped. It is usually either almost empty, or too small to house the large number of genuflecting Hasidim who have all tried to shuffle in. As for the attendants at the synagogue, they are always happy to take a tip, but you can't exactly blame them. One of them showed me his Auschwitz number tattooed on his wrist, still visible fifty years on. Marked for life.

At the opposite end of the square lies the fittingly named "Old Synagogue" (the oldest in Cracow, and one of many no longer used) built by Polish Jews, on the site of a synagogue established by Jews of Czech origin in the eleventh century. It is a dull red brick building, of Renaissance style, again strangely melancholic, containing the usual arched windows that make such buildings recognisably Jewish. In front of it lies a small courtyard, perfectly proportioned and with a pleasant aspect, and I am just waiting for someone to set up a café there. The rest of the square contains more buildings with a Jewish theme, including a well stocked Jewish bookshop, and a small park surrounded by railings made out of Menorah - or Jewish candlesticks. Outside the square are at least half a dozen more synagogues. The neo-Romanesque Tempel synagogue, a progressive synagogue where a more liberal form of Jewish worship was conducted, has been magnificently and painstakingly preserved outside and in, right down to its stain-glassed windows. The Ajzyk synagogue, built in the Baroque style, and which used to be the wealthiest synagogue, is painted a rich cream colour. It is a towering structure, the size of a sports hall. At the time it was built, in 1638, the Jewish town of Kazimierz was one of the largest and most resilient Jewish communities in Europe.

On a blazing hot summer's day, the first day proper of our field trip, our energetic guide - an eminent academic from Oxford University - marched us from Kazimierz to Płaszów, a small concentration camp near to Cracow. If we wilted in the heat, I wondered how the thousands of Jews had managed there, or in the cramped ghetto in which they had lived before being taken to Płaszów. The ghetto wall still stands in a part of the town not far from Kazimierz. The camp is now just green hills and fields, although our guide showed us the one Jew who had unwittingly gained immortality. His name was Chaim

Abrahamer (d.1932) and his gravestone remains on a part of one hill because the Nazis missed it when pulling all the others up. There also stands the house said to be that from which Amon Göth, head of Płaszów, shot randomly at Jews as they scuttled about the camp, now immortalised in *Schindler's List*. Tacky *Schindler's List* tours leave from Kazimierz by the hour.

After a couple of days in Kazimierz, we spent a week touring further afield in Galicia. In Tarnów, an important market town in the past, we saw the remains of a spectacular "bima" - the elevated platform at the centre of the synagogue from where the prayers are sung. It was immensely high, and was all that remained of the whole synagogue. It would have stood open to the elements, except the town council had paid for a smart wooden ceiling supported by four brick pillars, that sheltered it. The bima was situated right near the centre of town. Again, the evident wealth of these Jews was what struck one. But the Jews of Tarnów stood very little chance: they were the first to be housed in Auschwitz, along with "troublesome" Poles.

Outside Tarnów, at Zbylitowska Góra, we visited a spot in a forest where several thousand of the Tarnów Jews had been rounded up and massacred in one event. Here, our guide suddenly became sapped of his energy. He explained that this part of the tour was the hardest for him, as his Polish Jewish relatives had been rounded up and shot like this, in a carbon copy of the same event in another part of Poland. He read us an account of the Tarnów massacre from someone who had survived it. It was horrific. The perpetrators acted like animals. Half the Jews who died in the Holocaust were shot in the woods in this way.

We visited graveyards and ruined synagogues throughout Galicia, invariably situated right in the centre of the towns, again indicating past glories. But often the only way in was via a janitor who would have to be found to unlock the chained gates that barred entry to the ruins. Once inside, most of the synagogues resembled building sites. We would walk over boulders and along planks to see what we could see. Our guide would bring the remaining statues and frescoes to life for us: this carved lion's head indicated strength; that bearded figure depicted was Noah. But it was all sad. In the graveyards, often headstones would be scattered in broken pieces all around. The Nazis broke them, and no one had tried to bring them to any order since. Only in Łańcut, actually famous for a palace of the former Polish aristocracy, was there a fully restored synagogue where you could easily picture yourself attending the Sabbath service.

In the town of Dąbrowa Tarnowska, we met an aged Holocaust survivor, who took us to his Bet-Hamidrash - a small synagogue situated in a private house, and one of only a handful remaining in Poland. This one was in his garden. When the twenty-five or so of us had crowded in, and were squeezed around the bima that itself almost filled the tiny room, it all became too much for the old man. He began to cry, howling and wailing. *They made a pigsty of my synagogue*, he shrieked. *Oh, what they have done to it!* It turned out the building had been soiled over the years by being used as a public convenience. After surviving the Holocaust, it was not surprising this was too much for him. Suddenly, the old man beckoned us all. *Come this way, come this way*, he entreated us. We filed out of the Bet-Hamidrash and through into his house, and there he confronted us with his equally aged sister. *Two years and four months! Two years and four months!* he shouted. We didn't understand. *Two years and four months! Two years and four months!* he shouted again. *My sister survived the Holocaust by hiding under the floorboards of this house for two years and four months!*

Most harrowing of all on this week's tour was the trip to Bełżec concentration camp in the far east of Poland. Unlike in Auschwitz, the Nazis had time to flatten Bełżec, and now it is just fields, with the ubiquitous and eerie railway track entering the camp, and the equally ubiquitous and unfitting Communist memorial to the dead. There were two particularly remarkable things about Bełżec for me.

The first related to a fellow member of the trip, who was about to retire as a guide at Auschwitz. He was a prickly man, who had failed to impress during the trip, offering fewer insights than our English academic friend. He also got lost in one of the Polish towns we stopped in and had to catch us up later by train, causing momentary panic until we decided to move on and let him fend for himself. At one point, during my wander around Bełżec, as I was standing some way behind the Communist memorial, I suddenly found myself alone with him. He addressed me, as he had taken a liking to me. I think I was one of the few who gave him the time of day.

"Look here!" he said, and bent down, scooping up the loose soil, stones and twigs of Bełżec in his hand. He let the soil drain away, and then began to flick out stones and twigs. Finally, what looked like two white fossils remained in his palm.

"Bones!" he said. "They might have been able to hide most of the evidence, the Nazis, but they couldn't hide all of the evidence", he went on. "These are bones of the Jews".

This was one of the most surreal experiences of my life. It happened in a flash, and I wanted there to be the rest of the group witnessing the moment with me, so that we could all debate together whether this strange man, a guide at Auschwitz, was right. I wanted our Oxford academic friend to be with us. But there was only me. I scooped my hand in the soil, too. The stones, twigs and soil drained away. And I, too, was left with "bones".

The second unusual event was the reading by our guide of an extract from an account of life in Bełżec. Incredibly disturbing, it chronicled the Nazi experiments on living humans, the food rationing, the forced labour, the beatings, the plotting by the prisoners, the deaths. At the end of the reading, our guide explained there was currently a dispute as to copyright in this account. Why? someone asked. Because the account was priceless, written by one of only three Jews who escaped from Bełżec during the entire war. Total Jewish dead in Bełżec: 600,000.

Our second week was spent in the Auschwitz-Birkenau complex, where 1.1 million Jews met their deaths. One hour from Cracow, it has now regained its Polish name of Oświęcim, though the Germanisation of the name to "Auschwitz" will forever be associated with the place. We stayed in the "Guest-house". The Guest-house in Auschwitz consists of a small rectangular room, with two beds crammed together except for a narrow gap between them. There is one small window. The view is of the barbed wire of the camp.

Unlike Bełżec, Auschwitz remains preserved almost in its entirety. To all intents and purposes, it is as it was. The Nazis left in a hurry, as the Russians approached and eventually liberated the camp. As *you* approach, the watchtowers and barbed wire are everything you ever expected: harrowing and nauseating. As you walk into Auschwitz, which is more built up than Birkenau, the sign in twisty black metal over the entrance, "Arbeit macht frei" (work sets you free) reminds you of the Nazis' sick sense of humour[25]. The camp consists of a number of faded red brick buildings, originally pre-war barracks for Polish soldiers. Inside one such building are the spectacles, false limbs, preserved *hair* and suitcases of the dead Jews. The suitcases, somehow, are the most depressing. Most have painted on them the names of the towns from which the Jews, when they were piled into the cattle trucks, were "resettled". Cologne, Frankfurt, Thessaloniki, Amsterdam, Prague, Vienna - Jews from all over Europe, who had been living full lives in large communities, met their deaths here.

Further along, to one edge of the camp, is the wall of death, against which 20,000 prisoners were shot throughout the duration of the war. Myriad candles now mark the spot. The prison block, next to the wall of death, contains cells into which prisoners were, presumably, *pushed* before being neglected. They are so small that standing up is impossible; the inmates must have died within hours or at the most days from the cramped conditions. The trolleys on small rails which ran gassed Jews into the crematoria incinerators remain perfectly preserved. They are horrific in their efficiency.

Birkenau lies about three kilometres from Auschwitz. You take a bus there. As you approach, you see perhaps the most famous and eerie concentration camp sight of them all: the central watch tower at Birkenau, containing a high, arched entrance, through which trains took Jews right into the camp itself. There, a false arrival sign made them think they had arrived at some salubrious destination. Many were already dead after up to 10 days in intense heat or freezing cold with no food, no water, and no sanitation, crammed into sealed goods wagons like sardines. The remainder would be greeted by the chief SS officer on duty who, with a flick of his hand, would assign the weaker, on one side, to instant death in the crematoria, and the stronger, on the other, to slow death by working until they dropped. The latter was preferable, or was it? Here, whole families saw each other for the last time. Girls ran to the "wrong side" in order they could be with their mother and sisters at the final moment. Mel Mermelstein gives a nightmare-inducing account of these moments in "By Bread Alone". Read Ka-Tzetnik 135633 (the author's name is a pseudonym, "Ka-Tzetnik" being a Yiddish abbreviation for "concentration camper", and 135633 being his Auschwitz tattoo number) and you began to question the point of everything. Only Primo Levi's detached prose offers you the lifeline to go on living that Levi himself could not grab.

Birkenau consisted of hundreds of long wooden shacks housing prisoners. A few of these shacks remain complete. Inside are the images we have all seen. The cubic, wooden bed structures, 3-tiers high, made up of a series of planks, on which eight or more prisoners on each tier would have to try to find sleep. One's nerves snap at the sight. A thousand to a hut. Such squalor. And then, in the next shack, an empty space other than a low, open latrine running down the centre: thirty or more toilet bowls, two deep, on which one had only a few seconds every day to do what one had to do. Outside these preserved shacks, that show all too clearly how life was in Birkenau, all that remains of the rest of the buildings are their heating devices, consisting of the body of an oven and a narrow chimney extending ten feet up into the air. These chimneys - hundreds of them - litter the vast expanse of fields that is Birkenau. They look odd, like man-made giraffes or a Dali sculpture. They also show how many prisoners were held in Birkenau – up to 100,000 at any one time.

At the far end of Birkenau is a wide area of smooth paving, a memorial to the people of all the different nationalities who died here. Controversy reigns over everything concerning Auschwitz-Birkenau, not least the lack of precedence given at this memorial site to the Jewish victims of the camp, who at 1.1 million, made up 90% of the dead. This was a legacy of the Communists who characterised the Second World War more as an ideological struggle against fascism than a battle involving soldiers or creating victims of specific nationalities or religions. To this day the memorial at Birkenau is referred to in the Auschwitz-Birkenau guidebook as "The International Monument to the Victims of Fascism". Many Jews feel not enough has been done, since the fall of Communism, to remedy this deliberate oversight.

The remains of the gas chambers and crematoria at Birkenau are still visible, though not preserved to anything like at Auschwitz. Nothing remains above ground level, but the pits into which the Jews were crowded are still there. They are huge, and inspire fear even now. Two thousand could be gassed at any one time. The Nazis threw asphyxiating zyklon B pellets down through holes in the gas chamber roof. It took just fifteen to twenty minutes for all to die. Doors were barred shut and there was no escape.

Afterwards, the bodies were wheeled into incinerators on the same type of small wagons as at Auschwitz. The tracks on which these wagons ran can still be seen in the concrete. An East Germany company churned out the incinerators, knowing full well their purpose. It calculated that one incinerator could burn two bodies in thirty minutes. There were 15 incinerators per crematoria and therefore the system was capable of turning 1,440 bodies to ash every day. Yet there were times when the death parade grew so gruesome that even this apparatus could not meet demand, such as when the Nazis were liquidating hundreds of thousands of Hungarian Jews in 1944.

As for the gas chambers, they were well below ground level, and the victims had to walk down steps into them. After they had been gassed, they were taken by lift up to the incinerators, still below ground level. However, in crematorium III only, there was a separate entrance at ground level which can still be seen. It consists of a ramp with steps on either side. Down this ramp, dead prisoners from the camp, who had perhaps died from disease or overwork - as opposed to newly-arrived wagon loads of Jews who were marched straight into the gas chamber - could be rolled downwards, either to be burnt in the incinerators, or further down to be stored in the gas chambers during, for example, exceptionally hot weather. It seems everything was thought of.

Crematorium 4, a little further away, was blown apart by the Jews in a brave internal plot in the autumn of 1944, in an act that somehow fills me with vicarious pride. Its destroyed remains can still be seen.

Birkenau, from the moment you pass through its watchtower, is more eerie than Auschwitz. It extends endlessly, through forests, tracks and fields. It reminds me of an area behind the village I grew up in known as "The Rec", where all sorts of illicit goings on occurred, and where a young boy was one day murdered after my family had left the village. The shudders I got walking around Auschwitz were all the deeper for this curious personal association I felt with the place. My state was not eased by the cesspools which exist in one part of the camp, into which the ashes of Jews were thrown, so hopeless was the Nazi's task of eradicating the evidence when so many had been slaughtered. If this could be so, then perhaps the Auschwitz guide was telling the truth in Bełżec, after all?

Marzena and I joke blackly that I was lucky enough to escape from Auschwitz. I could not face another night in those dingy guestrooms. Leaving the trip early, if naughty, had the added advantage of allowing me to see Marzena - who had not been on the trip - a little sooner. I talked and talked to her about my experiences of Auschwitz. I did not know if she would understand, but she did. She had been there many times, she said. She did not go any more because it upset her too much. But every Polish child in the vicinity was made to go to the Auschwitz-Birkenau complex before they finished their education, although, in her day, the Communists had not told them that most of the victims were Jews and other ethnic minorities.

Four years later, during our rediscovery of Warsaw, we saw some of the Jewish remains there, as well. These included the Nożyk synagogue, which still functions as an active house of worship, a good-looking building even though someone has slapped a concrete block on its side. I also discovered that the modern office tower in which I worked was situated right in the heart of the Warsaw Jewish ghetto. A part of the ghetto wall was still visible five minutes' walk from my office, noteworthy for its history but not to look at. And IB Singer, the Nobel Prize winning Polish Jewish author who wrote in Yiddish, lived for many years on the street that adjoined my office (which gave me a small thrill every time I parked my car there).

Some of the most interesting remains are at the Jewish cemetery at Powązki, which remarkably was left unscathed during the war. Here, the disorder and mess is the same as at the Jewish cemeteries in Galicia, but with one difference: Powązki's Jewish cemetery is massive, with a large number of Jews buried there. They include Ludwig Zamenhof, the creator of the international language Esperanto, whose gravestone is accordingly worded in his language, and Janusz Korczak, a Polish-Jewish doctor and children's author who refused the Polish underground's offers of safe passage and accompanied the orphans in his care to death in a Nazi death camp. Many of the headstones are broken, toppled, illegible or covered with stinging nettles. We gazed in vain at one section where damaged but still sublime Greek pillars reached up towards the roof of leaves that covered the cemetery. We wanted to get closer, but couldn't because the path was just too overgrown. Only the part of the cemetery filled with more recent gravestones was reasonably kept. I remarked to Marzena it was sad, and she replied, yes, it was, but these were the lucky ones: think of the millions of Jews who disappeared during the Holocaust without a trace.

Further along our journey, the city of Łódź featured plenty of interesting Jewish legacy. Here, it was not so much places of worship that struck one, but the evident wealth of the Jews who lived in Łódź before the war. And if the presence of synagogues and Jewish cemeteries in the centre of small Galician towns had impressed in this respect, then the Jewish remains in Łódź would do so even more.

Łódź used to be a thriving textile centre, and was once known as the "Polish Manchester". It still hosts a number of textile fairs. During its zenith, the Jewish textile manufacturer Izrael Poznański was one of the wealthiest businessmen in Łódź. He built a mighty textile factory housing weaving and spinning mills, and also constructed warehouses, tenement blocks for the workers and a palace for himself, all adjacent to each other in an enormous complex in the city centre. The complex remains to this day, supposedly one of the best preserved Industrial Revolution factory sites in Europe. The buildings are now badly in need of repair –windows broken, brickwork falling apart, and the high entrance gates to the factory remain padlocked[26]. But despite such dilapidation, the sheer size and beauty of these constructions is awe-inspiring. Strangely enough, the factory buildings outshine the more picturesque Poznański Palace, the family's private residence which sits adjacent, not so much in appearance (though their mock-Gothic look is attractive) but in the images they conjure up of the past, of this factory as a noisy, vibrating hub of industrial activity.

The story of the Jews of Łódź during the war is the usual horror story, involving the usual controversial Jewish figure who half-sided with the Nazis supposedly in order to save as many of his fellow Jews as possible. What is less controversial is that the Jewish community in Łódź before the war, as represented by Izrael Poznański, was one of the most thriving in Poland. To this day, the Jewish cemetery on the edge of town, padlocked like Poznański's factory, is the largest in Europe, containing some 180,000 headstones.

I rarely, on a personal level, encountered anti-Semitism in Poland during my various stays in the country. This is one reason I try to take a measured view on the thorny question of Polish anti-Semitism. Or perhaps it is my awareness of the awarding to many Poles, including my landlord, of the title "righteous gentile". Or the new citation made by Israel to many Poles (including a friend of ours) for carrying out acts to "preserve Jewish memory", such as tending Jewish cemeteries. Both of these are little known honours. It could even just be the surprising amount of coverage I see given to Jewish matters and Israel on the Polish television - certainly more air time than in UK.

That said, it is still the practice of some Polish politicians to try to smear their opponents by referring to their (allegedly) Jewish roots. The political right has led much of the anti-Semitism. Lech Wałęsa, when President of Poland, was once accused of not denouncing anti-Semitic statements made by a well-known priest who was also an old friend. And Jewish cemeteries in Warsaw have been desecrated. The longer I stayed in Poland, the more I became privy to small acts of anti-Semitism that have, as it were, become part of the wallpaper. So, Poles tell the same sort of jokes about Jews as the English do about the Irish. If ever there was a scandal in the newspapers, the view of the average man in the street might be that the cause was a "Jewish conspiracy"[27]. It was also possible to find anti-Semitic graffiti in Poland – I once saw the words "Żydzy Świnie" (Jewish Swine) daubed on the walls of a bus shelter.

But if my personal experience of anti-Semitism in Poland is taken as the paradigm, my landlord Jan's view that anti-Semitism here is not rampant may be right. President Kwaśniewski on many occasions declared his mystification at the stereotyping of his people as anti-Semitic, and stated categorically they were not and his nation welcomed the Jews unreservedly.

My good friend from work, Paweł, put it well. He was not at all anti-Semitic, he said. Our own friendship was proof of that. But this unremitting stereotyping of his nation as anti-Semitic got him down. Why did people insist on perpetuating such a stereotype, he asked?

The attitude of the Poles may be best encapsulated by a Jewish joke I once heard. It concerns a number of people waiting in a long bread queue in Poland during Communist times, when food was in woefully short supply. Suddenly, the owner of the bread shop comes out to address the queue. Because of an even greater shortage of bread than normal, he says, he's going to have to ask all the Jews in the queue to leave. They leave. Three hours later, he comes out to make a similar announcement, but this time it is the gypsies who have to leave. Finally, three hours after this, the remaining queue hardly having moved, the owner comes out, head hung in shame, and declares there is going to be no more bread at all today, and they should all go home. At which point, one Pole says to his compatriot, "You see: the Jews always get the best deal".

Jan's view was that such jokes are a subtle way of complimenting the Jews. He said they usually made the Jews out to be clever and canny. He gave as an example the joke about the pregnant Jewish mother before the war who asked the local rabbi whether she would have a boy or a girl. The rabbi deliberates for a short while, looking very serious, and then reveals the woman will have a girl. After she leaves, however, he writes down in his diary the woman's name, and the date of her visit, and next to this information, the word, "Boy". The idea was that the rabbi could not lose. If the woman had a girl, she would be satisfied with the rabbi's prediction, and if she had a boy and came to the rabbi to complain – he was covered. I heard what my landlord had to say, but told him I did not totally agree. Such jokes could still be offensive and I doubted anyway all Jewish jokes told by Poles were so mild. For example, I remembered being told by a colleague at work about the Polish expression for someone who looks shifty, and is forever spinning his head around nervously. "Like a Jew in an empty shop", was the expression, he said - I think momentarily forgetting who I was.

I leave the final word on the Jewish Question to the Englishman - now honorary Pole - Professor Norman Davies. Professor Davies has reached his esteemed position by writing brilliant accounts of Polish history. In these accounts, he often touched on the Jewish Question – the question of what to do with this nation of European Jews who, lacking a homeland, settled largely in Poland before the war. I encountered Professor Davies at a meeting to develop business links between Poland and the UK, held in London. On this occasion, I shuffled up to the Professor, and put forward my simplistic thesis that the "Jewish Question" nowadays really meant the present-day relationship between Jews and Poles. On which subject, I added, was the Professor aware he himself had been accused of being anti-Semitic, of giving a favourable historical interpretation to the Polish treatment of the Jews? Oh, he was aware, all right, he said. And what did he think of this latter-day "Jewish Question", I asked?

"Ah", the Professor said. He stroked his chin. Opened his mouth, as if to speak, and then, thinking better of it, shut it again. Perhaps he was nervous I too would brand him anti-Semitic? More stroking of the chin. Very professorial. Finally, he glanced about, as if to check nobody else could hear, beckoned me closer, and spoke.

"The Jewish Question", he began, and then paused. "The Jewish Question", he stopped again. "Let me tell you", he continued, finally on a roll, "The Jewish Question, without any - without *any,* shadow of a doubt, is a very, *very* complex issue".

14 POLISH GOLDEN AUTUMN (AKA TATRAS REVISITED)

It was a time that encapsulated so many of the things I had learnt about Poland, all wrapped up into one short period. It was the beginning of September, 1998. One year on. I had worked throughout the at times bitingly hot summer, and now I was having two weeks off to relax. Marzena and I would spend the time in Poland, learning more about the place as we holidayed - rather than jetting abroad as most of my Polish colleagues at work had done for their breaks. They went with their families mostly to Greece or Italy, telling me all they wanted to do was spend two weeks on the beach. Given the opportunity and means to travel, the Poles display the same appetite for sun, sea and sand as we in the West. Of course, this may also have something to do with their anticipation of the Polish winter that lies ahead.

Cracow, as usual, was our starting-point, staying with my in-laws. We spent several days in and around the old royal town, sipping beer or hot chocolate (when it was a mite cooler) on the rynek, visiting the old Jewish town, shopping. We even re-visited Auschwitz, though Marzena rightly complained it was not the best place to go for a holiday. In return, therefore, I promised to take her back to Zakopane and the Tatra mountains, even though our first visit, the previous icy October, had not been auspicious.

We set off for Zakopane early on a raw September morning - but the skies were blue, and we reckoned it would warm up. The journey took a little under two hours, which was quicker than normal because we followed the Cracow to Zakopane coach all the way as it veritably rocketed up the mountain, overtaking car, fellow coach and lorry, including on hairpins where one had no idea what was around the corner. It was all I could do to stay in the coach's slipstream. It seems coach drivers in Poland attend the same training school as the taxi-drivers.

Before reaching Zakopane, we headed off for the beauty spot "Morskie Oko", or "Eye of the Sea", which takes its name from the legend that says this lake was formed from the Baltic Sea aeons ago. Marzena had not visited the lake for a long time, and spoke longingly of its beauty. We parked the car in a gravel car park, and paid our 1½ złoty each to enter the tarmac track that leads to it. In days gone by, Marzena said, you had been able to drive right to the lake, but now the last bit was a short walk uphill - maximum half an hour. I decided my dodgy knee was up to it but, for safety's sake, and as much to practise my Polish as anything else, I asked the attendant how many minutes' walk it was to the lake.

"Minutes?" she questioned, eyebrows raised. "It's two hours walk each way - *nine kilometres* each way".

Marzena succumbed to a fit of hysterics. She had thought it was only a kilometre or two, and the thought of me dragging my dodgy knee up the mountain was too much for her. Ahead of us we saw two horses attached to a long cart, with seats on, which was almost full up with passengers. There was hope. We rushed up to the driver, who was preparing to leave, and asked if he was going to the lake. Yes he was, and it cost around 40 złoty (£7) return per person. We paid our money, and clambered aboard. The horse and cart set off.

The journey was through evergreen forest, past mountain streams and waterfalls, all the more pleasurable as by now, as predicted, the September sun was shining through. The journey took an hour as the horses climbed slowly up the steep bends. But it passed by quickly for us, as we got talking to a friendly "Polonian" (ex-pat Pole) from America who was visiting his family in the area. As a native of the Tatras, this gentleman was the quintessential Polonian, for it was from this region, where poverty was endemic in the past, that many Poles emigrated to the US and elsewhere. Our friend's main cause, which could be characterised as a gripe, was environmental contamination in Poland. We got talking about this when I said it was a pity we could not drive a little closer to the lake above. Our friend demurred: prohibiting cars was just the sort of forward thinking that preserved the natural beauty through which we were now passing. Poland needed more of this radical attitude with regard to the environment. The pollution in Poland was "fatalny", he explained – "disastrous" – citing Warsaw, where he had lived for some years, and where he said (rightly) you had to take a bath in yellowish water. Even living in the Tatra mountains, he went on, his brother was now ill with his lungs, and many died young in Poland of such diseases. There were too many cars everywhere, too many smokers (the US had the right attitude on this) and the Baltic was the most polluted sea in Europe. Our friend continued so persuasively, yet in such a gentle manner, that he soon convinced Marzena and me.

Having exchanged more views to the metronomic clip-clopping of the horses pulling us up, we discovered that the last one and a half kilometres were on foot, to protect the forest even more. I don't know who was happier: our friend, or Marzena and I – his new converts. We left him and skipped up the hill, eager to stretch our legs, whereupon we came to the lake itself: Morskie Oko. It reminded me of a Lake District tarn: an expanse of water, glittering in the sun, surrounded by angular spruces and spectacular, snow-peaked mountains. It was idyllic. We stared in amazement for about twenty minutes, but decided not to walk around the lake, which though it looked like a half-hour skip, was apparently a two-hour hike.

We returned down the mountain path to where the horse and cart had left us - an area of concrete and stones, looking a little like a school playground. About ten horses and carts were stationed there, but only one looked anything like ready to leave. There were about five or six potential customers milling around it, but we soon found out the problem. The driver, dressed in traditional mountain dress – magnificently embroidered heavy woollen pants, peasant's hat and slippers - would only leave when he had a full complement, and not a moment sooner. We were trapped. Marzena and I, and the other potential passengers, began to banter with the driver, who, it turned out, was a character. We tried to persuade him to go, but he had a response (usually a quip) for everything. At one point, the driver even told us you had to wait for planes, too: he knew, because he'd been on one once. I took a look at the decrepit old cart and ageing horses, compared them to a 747, and realised I could not win with such reasoning. Instead, we all decided to climb up onto the cart, take our seats, and try to persuade passing pedestrians to join us.

The cart filled up slowly, the driver joking all the while. A passing drunk asked if he could approach the driver's horses, whereupon the driver replied: "you can, but remember: always approach a horse from the back, a dog from the front, and a woman... from any side!" A wink and a chuckle to us - his audience on the cart. Finally, the opportunity the driver had been waiting for. As the cart neared full, a rotund gentleman approached. His huge belly, which wobbled slowly from left to right in front of him as he walked, protruded from under his inadequate T-shirt. I couldn't see him making it down the mountain - unless he rolled all the way. As he neared the cart, he shouted abruptly to the driver, "How many more passengers before this contraption gets going?" The driver, eyeing the man's ample figure, paused for dramatic effect, cleared his throat, and replied: "Well, like you sir - *not too many*", waited for the big guy to get on, then himself jumped up onto the cart, which was rocking with laughter, and we were off.

The journey down terminated with a farewell joke by the driver, who compared Marzena's legs to those of some strange mountain animal, which Marzena could not directly translate. I assume the comparison was not entirely unflattering as she didn't complain too much. We set off for Zakopane, which we reached after driving through more delightful forest, sometimes shading the road, sometimes allowing the sun to creep through. I realised as we entered Zakopane how lovely it was, and how wrong I had been about it in gloomy October. The architecture of the chalets on the outskirts of town, where we had not been the previous winter, was characterised by steep roofs (presumably to facilitate snowfall) and the plentiful use of wood. At one point, we came upon an exquisite, tiny church on the bend of a road, its towers, balconies and spires all carved from wood. We parked in the centre of town, and walked the main street as we had done the previous autumn. This time we were more impressed. The street itself was laid with new, light pink paving stones, and marked out by old-fashioned, black, twisty lampposts. On either side, open-air restaurants gave off alluring smells, mostly of meat roasting on spits, but also the smouldering aroma of a waffle stall I already had my eye on. Crowds of people milled around, popping in and out of the expensive jewellery, clothes and other shops selling furs, thick woollen sweaters, amber and carved wooden products like walking sticks, sculpture and furniture. We both ate a tasty mountain stew on the terrace of a restaurant giving onto the main street, and watched the people go by. It was clear from their passing conversation that many were foreigners who presumably came to the Tatras for their combination of unspoilt beauty and value for money.

After lunch, we grabbed a waffle and walked to the cog railway that would take us to the top of Gubałówka, a ski resort in the winter. The railway was incredibly steep, and took around six or seven minutes to reach the top. There, we had spectacular views of the Tatras and surrounding valleys, and in temperatures somewhat preferable to those we had encountered at the top of the same mountain range the previous October. Marzena, who used to ski here in the winter, pointed out notable landmarks, including a high peak onto which someone had managed to erect a cross.

We spent the night in a quaint chalet on the edge of Zakopane, in a nook just below a mountain. It was typical of its kind, with the host and hostess living in the basement, and the guests on the two or three floors above. The food was delightful, and our host couple warm and attentive. They displayed that same mountain humour that had been characteristic of the mountain driver, and which, as Marzena told me, could sometimes transform quickly into a fiery, argumentative side,

which they were not embarrassed to show off in front of guests -
though which mercifully was usually directed at one another. Their
humour was generally mocked by the rest of the Poles, but Marzena
told me it was wise and replete with aphorism. She told me the culture
of the mountain people was a rich one, and they were proud of it.
They displayed a strong regionalism (the people of the Tatras refer to
their part of Poland as "Podhale" – under the mountain pasture). They
taught their different dialect at school, kept up age old skills such as
wood carving, continued their musical tradition, and dressed up in the
sort of clothes we had seen on the mountain driver - particularly on
special occasions, such as at weddings, church and on local and
national celebrations. They preserved these traditions not only because
they went back a long way, but because they reflected a characteristic
feature of this people - their closeness to nature.

I would later discover more of the tradition of the mountain
people when, once back in Warsaw, Marzena took me to see the Polish
opera "Cracowians and Mountaineers" at the Polish National Opera.
The piece, written by the father of Polish theatre Wojciech
Bogusławski, is an amusing tale of the rivalry between the two
eponymous groups. It reminded me a little of a Polish "Fiddler on the
Roof" (there is even a Jewish innkeeper who plays a big role). The
most noticeable aspect was the costumes that put that of the mountain
driver to shame. Having said that, it was the Cracowians' clothes that
impressed most: they wore red felt four-cornered hats, long velvet
sequined waistcoats in blacks, browns and deep blues, gold belts and
black boots. But for much of the show they were on the back foot to
the rowdy mountaineers, who mostly wore simple white collarless
shirts, short brown waistcoats and thick brown belts. In terms of
dress, myself, I would have given it to the Cracowians on points, but
then I am biased, as I married one. My close observation of the
costumes had something to do with my inability to understand most of
the words, songs and jokes. This was a shame, because it is evidently a
crowd-pleasing opera, particularly so at the end of the performance
when the main characters come amongst the audience. They sign
vignettes to which the author deliberately gave political overtones at a
time when Poland was on the cusp of its third and final partition.
Nowadays, the performers update the lyrics to satirise current political
developments. But at least I was able to take in the tunes and the

dancing, interspersed with high pitched yelps and cries. And I came to understand that the people of this region of Poland and their traditions are a popular (we had never seen the opera so packed, including plenty of children) and vital part of the fabric of Polish society, of which the Poles are rightly proud.

The next day, in Zakopane, we set off for more sightseeing, and wandered again along the main street nibbling the smoky mountain cheese ("oscypek") that we bought from a street-vendor. We returned late that night to Cracow. We had only spent two days in the Tatras, but now I could see why the Poles adore them so. They are a reasonably priced alternative to the Alps, and other than for a lack of refinement in some of the resorts, a good match for their more famous rivals.

On our way back to Warsaw, after spending just over one week in the south, we stopped off at the mediaeval town of Kazimierz-Dolny. This grain town, still home to granaries, was so successful in mercantile times that by the end of the fourteenth century it was known as "Little Danzig" (Danzig would become Gdańsk). A guide book describes the town as "simply beautiful" - almost as if no other words could hope to describe a town of such outstanding attraction. Certainly, Kazimierz-Dolny has exceptional features, particularly its market square, overlooked by small mountains and situated adjacent to the Vistula River. The square itself has a well in the middle, and is lined by old burghers' houses in various styles, including Renaissance and Gothic, emphasising the town's successful past. Most arresting of all are the adjoined Przybyła brothers' houses, the joint facade of which features a cascade of friezes, including dragons and figures of saints carved into the clear grey stone, topped by small statues and spires.

At the top of the square, which extends up a small, steep hill, there are a few shops, including a bookshop. We popped in and, having browsed a few books, asked the lady serving whether the simply beautiful main square in Kazimierz-Dolny (we were careful to use the words "simply beautiful") was its main feature.

"Oh, no!" she replied, "there's much much more to Kazimierz-Dolny: for example, walk further up the hill, to the lovely Parish church and the castle!"

"How far is that?" we asked.

"Thirty metres", she replied.

We walked the thirty metres, admired the church, and took in a pleasant view of the surrounding countryside from the castle ruins. But that was it. We were now on the edge of town. So we returned to the main square. There were other sites to see, including a smaller market square, and some Jewish remains (Kazimierz-Dolny was once eighty per cent Jewish) - but not too many. Kazimierz-Dolny is pleasing but not extensive, and to enjoy it, it's best just to sit in the main square with a beer, wandering off now and then to purchase a wood basket or magazine rack made from the reeds that grow in the nearby Vistula. Then, you might amble over to the Zielona Tawerna ("Green Tavern"), an elegant restaurant on the "edge" of town (i.e. one hundred metres from the main market square), sit on the veranda in the fading September sun, and have a steak à la Béarnaise - as we did. It was a delight.

We decided to go on the small "train" that took you around the sights of Kazimierz-Dolny (the train is actually a tractor dressed up as a train that travels on the road and pulls a couple of carriages). Whilst it was now off-season, it did not augur well that this trip, at four o'clock in the afternoon, the last of the day, was also to be the *first* of the day - because there had not been sufficient customers to warrant the earlier journeys. Shades of Zakopane again, and I waited for the driver to start telling some dirty jokes.

However, on this occasion, it would be the conductor, travelling with the eight or so of us in the second of the two carriages (the first was empty) who would prove to be the most intriguing companion. Or, at least, the one who would spark the intriguing discussion that followed. It began about five minutes into the twenty minute journey when, already out of town, we saw on a hill close by a ten foot high wall constructed of six hundred well-preserved Jewish gravestones. The effect was moving, especially as the wall had a jagged, broken space in the middle, presumably symbolising what happened to the Jews of Kazimierz-Dolny during the war. At once, everyone was gripped by this sight. The conductor, seeing this, started to tell the history of the Jews of Kazimierz-Dolny: how many had lived here, what happened to them during the war, and so on. Once again I thought how, here in Poland, ordinary people seemed to know so much about the Jews compared to folks back home where, because there were never as many living there, most people remained unfamiliar. I felt warmed that this conductor, clearly no sophisticate, in his faded blue jeans and tatty T-shirt, a money bag drooped over his generous stomach, was so knowledgeable and felt so inclined to talk about matters Jewish.

Soon, however, I began to realise his commentary was taking a different tack - namely, what annoyed him about the Jews. First of all, he could not understand why they had built this wall of gravestones here, in Kazimierz-Dolny, when all the Jews died in concentration camps, anyway. Insensitive though such a comment was in respect of a town that had once been eighty per cent Jewish, at this point, I gave the conductor the benefit of the doubt. For one thing, I was aware that few knew, as I had discovered on my field-trip to Galicia, that half the Jews who died in the Holocaust were not executed in concentration camps. They were shot in forests, just like the forest in front of which the gravestones stood. But the conductor went on. What *really* annoyed him was that, when the Jews came to visit Kazimierz-Dolny, they came in two coach loads - accompanied by four coach loads of security guards. This, I decided, was somewhat less antagonistic toward the Jews, some of whom do seem to regard travelling through Poland as like travelling through a safari park. All of this encouraged conversation amongst the passengers. Two old ladies sitting together, and another passenger, somewhat Judaophile, correctly explained to the conductor that the Jews had constituted the bulk of the population of Kazimierz-Dolny, so why shouldn't a wall of their gravestones be constructed on the edge of town? Good on you, ladies, I thought. But the ladies formed only one of the two schools of thought present that day. Another three passengers began to swap endless stories along with the conductor about what it was *they* most disliked about the Jews. When one unpleasant old lady commented how she really disliked the way Jews picked up goods in the shops before they bought them (an opinion to which the three Judaophiles objected) I'd had enough.

"Look here!" I began, in broken Polish, addressing the whole carriage, which fell silent. "You should take care what you say about the Jews. Before the war, there were three and a half million Jews in Poland, and after the war only three hundred thousand. You should show some respect for them. I'm Jewish, and I'd hate to think you were prejudiced against the Jews or anyone else", I said. I was seething, but trying hard to retain my composure. This was the very anti-Semitism I had heard so much about, but so far encountered personally so little, something I thought lived on only in the form of mostly harmless jokes. Was I wrong?

Well, as soon as I mentioned I was Jewish, all heads immediately swivelled round to face the front of the carriage, eyes fixed on the wooden panelling there. It was like a classroom scene where the unruly pupils all dive back into their seats just before teacher enters the room. Actually, I felt sorry for my fellow passengers. An alien in their midst, listening to their raw emotion about the Jews! I also felt a warm glow of appreciation for Marzena who had kindly translated the more difficult words in my tirade, and stood strongly with me against this prejudice.

The conductor was clearly rattled. He approached, and sat down next to me, a hand on my knee, all cosy cosy. He explained he was not anti-Semitic at all - it was just that he had a bad experience once with a group of Jews, who promised him 300 złoty for a group trip, but gave him only two hundred and fifty. He confided in me.

"Look", he said, "as I say, I'm not really anti-Semitic. I have nothing whatsoever against the Jews - nothing at all. In fact", he beckoned me closer still, "d'you want to know who it is that really irritates me? It's not the Jews at all. *It's the blacks*".

I was genuinely upset after the trip at this display of anti-Semitism – something I had met so little in Poland until then - but I also saw the irony. I imagined a black person getting on at one of the stops on the train route, and the conductor sidling up to him and explaining that it wasn't really the blacks who he didn't like: *it was the gays*. Still, the strategic purchase of an Almond Magnum soon raised my spirits, and as the evening drew in, we set off for the spa town of Nałęczów, twenty kilometres or so from Kazimierz-Dolny, and scene of a handsome palace.

When we arrived in the town, we were directed to the palace and park by a woman, who spoke and acted a little strangely. She was accompanied by a friend who kept winking at us from behind this woman's back, as if to say - "my friend, she's a little cuckoo, you know". But the first woman's directions were sound, and we found the park. Inside, we saw the captivating chalet Podgórze, notable for the carved dark wooden alcoves featured at the front of the house. We also noticed the strange sculptures adorning the park, including unusual representations of humans and animals. But we could not find the most famous historical monument in Nałęczów park - the Małachowskis Palace. As it turned colder, we approached a young woman who was holding a painting bigger than her, and asked her the way. "Follow me", she said, and set off at a sprightly step. What a kind person, we thought! We followed, she asked where we were from, and we replied England and Poland respectively. How interesting, she said! Suddenly she stopped. Turning round to us, she held up in the air her huge canvas - of a vase of flowers - and asked, would we like to buy it? Marzena and I were taken aback. Something was starting to seem wrong, here. Well, it was very pretty, we replied - but we had to decline on this occasion. But thank you very much for the offer. Disappointed, our guide marched on, emphasising she would not take us *all* the way to the palace, but would direct us there - as we walked and walked and walked, and came to within a few steps of the palace itself. Now the young lady stopped again. Were we sure we didn't wish to buy her painting? We declined again. The young lady beckoned us forward. We were at the door, now. She pointed at the door, and whispered that the palace was in this direction. Unfortunately, she couldn't take us all the way there. She had to go. Not to worry, I whispered back, we'd probably find it from here. As she departed, she shouted:

"I wrote a letter to Prince Charles, and Lady Diana. He likes painting, you know! But I haven't sent it yet. Bye!"

This last comment was intriguing. I asked myself how it was the penchant for painting of a member of the British royal family had extended even to Eastern Europe. In fact, the royal family is well known in the East, but often as the butt of jokes aimed at our declining world influence. My friend Henryk could often be found at work asking me how the weather was today in "The United Kingdom of Great Britain and Northern Ireland and Her Majesty's Commonwealth", as he giggled out of one corner of his mouth. I suspect he felt he was in this way making his contribution to deflating that famous English superiority complex of which the Poles are so wary.

POLSKA DOTTY

I wondered about informing the young lady that, unfortunately, the Princess had been tragically killed in a car crash in Paris one year ago - but didn't. Even with my minimal powers of detection, I understood that she probably suffered from mental illness, and the news might not go down well. For as we had walked behind the young lady, we had read in our guide book that the palace at Nałeczow, with its water source and surrounding park land, was now a sanatorium as well as a tourist attraction, and I reckoned we had just met one or two of the guests.

We returned to Warsaw to spend the second week of our holiday at home. But we did so with urgency, in order not to miss a thanksgiving prayer service to which we had been invited. It was in aid of the opening of an Indian restaurant.

Marzena and I are very partial to Indian food. Unfortunately, there were only two or three Indian restaurants in Warsaw. Fortunately, one of them, run by a lively, friendly and interesting host - Charanjit - produced quite the most wonderful Indian food we had ever tasted. We could kill for Charanjit's chicken tikka. Because we went to his restaurant on the edge of town so often, we had been invited to the ceremonial opening of his new restaurant in the centre of town, to which otherwise mostly Indian guests had been invited. There were plenty of Indians in Warsaw, working in the textile industry, the centre of which, as we have seen, is in nearby Łódź.

We arrived at *Club Tandoor* late for the prayers, slipped off our shoes in traditional Indian fashion, and left them with the rest of the pile outside the restaurant. Inside, about twenty Sikhs (for, although the restaurant was termed "Indian", Charanjit was a Sikh from Singapore) sat around the edge of the room praying. Josticks burned, giving off a pungent smell. A long-bearded Sikh chanting behind a small, model temple, that had a classic Taj Mahal shape (szopka builders eat your hearts out) led the prayers. In between hymns, he explained in English to those gathered exactly what he had just been singing about, which was helpful. The ceremony came to a close with Charanjit waving a brush in the air, presumably to evict any evil spirits still foolhardy enough to be about the place, and the leader of the prayers handing out a brown fudge-like substance that tasted very sweet.

From time to time, as the service had gone on, passing Poles had stared fascinated through the windows at the ceremony inside. They seemed totally perplexed. One middle-aged man could not wipe an inane grin from his face, and eventually raised the yellow ice cream he had been licking in a gesture of "cheers" before departing. Later, an old lady, looking a little like a tramp, passed by the entrance and was equally fascinated by the pile of shoes outside. Suddenly, she slipped off her own shoe and attempted to insert her chubby foot into one of the more dainty women's shoes. Unsuccessful, she tried another, and another. Eventually, one of the waiters managed to move her on. But it was clear she had thought the shoes were part of the many street sales one encountered in Warsaw.

At the end of the prayers, I asked the leader if I could add to the good-luck cash donation a few worshippers had already put in front of the miniature temple. The leader corrected me. The money was not a symbol of good luck, he said. It was the third most important offering one could make in a ceremony such as this. Best of all was to pledge your mind to God. Second best was to pledge your body. Only third best was to give money. Knowing I was about to consume anything up to three portions of Indian food, which would amply demonstrate I had no control over my mind *or* body, I decided to add to the pile of 10 złoty notes in front of me. The food duly came, was duly tremendous, and I duly ate three platefuls. We thanked Charanjit for letting us witness this private ceremony, and looked forward in the future to partaking of our favourite Warsaw cuisine from this town centre branch of his burgeoning restaurant chain.

We seemed, in this Polish Golden Autumn, which is what Poles call a fair September, to be enjoying many of our favourite haunts in Poland: Cracow, the Tatras... and now, once again, the palace at Wilanów, with its exquisite architecture and manicured gardens. We had been to plenty of concerts in Łazienki, but never in Wilanów, so immediately following the ceremony and lunch at the Indian restaurant, we drove to Wilanów in the hope there would be a Classical music concert going on there. It would be the perfect way to drown out the noise of our stomachs digesting all that Indian fare.

We parked the car, and soon realised we would get something better than that, for we could hear what sounded like a brass band playing. As we approached the palace, and entered the main quadrangle, we could see it was a Polish army band. Resplendent in red, white and blue uniforms, wearing hats with red and blue plumes, they pumped out feet-tapping tunes as they marched along. We took up a place on the edge of the grass, on which the band was marching and playing, to watch. Then, more soldiers appeared, from the Polish army, navy and air force, wearing four-cornered hats, knee-length black boots, and carrying rifles with bayonets. They put on a marvellous display of gun wielding. They tossed guns through the air, and caught them impeccably, slapped their hands rhythmically and noisily onto their thighs in doing so, and marched in complex patterns. The by now large audience cheered and applauded. Finally, to end the display, but with no warning, the soldiers pointed their guns in the air and fired deafening shots - three times. Like thunder claps. Hearts raced in the crowd, and there was the smell of cordite. Little boys immediately raced onto the grass to pick up the spent cartridges, almost causing the band, which was marching back to its coach by now, to trip over them. A father of one of the boys argued with a security guard who wanted the lads to clear off the grass. The father told the guard in no uncertain terms that the grass was there to be walked on since the time of King Sobieski himself, pointing his finger at his head and revolving it in a "you're crazy" sign to the guard. He even pushed his bike, the handlebars of which he was holding, onto the grass momentarily, in defiance. The guard touched his baton. The father quickly removed the bicycle. Very soon, the area cleared. The band and the soldiers had gone, the band having played out all the way followed by a phalanx of excited children - Pied Piper style. The crowd dispersed, and Marzena and I were left in the now peaceful quadrangle – "spokój", as the Poles would say. We stood watching the sun light up the sand coloured walls of the palace, ourselves watched by the carved figures of ancient Gods that lined the palace roof. It was bliss, and it had also been all of Poland in ten frantic minutes.

That I recognised the peculiarly Polish nature of this tableau signified that, after one year of adventure here, I was finally beginning to know Poland. I could see what made Poland "Polish". What was left was for me to increase my involvement with the Poles, which meant partying with them more, enjoying their traditions. In other words, I needed to *integrate*.

15 INTEGRATING WITH THE POLES

In the ensuing six months, between October 1998 and March 1999, it would be two short trips I would make with my law office that would offer the best opportunity to become more involved with Poles. Furthermore, I was lucky: having been at my Polish law firm for the best part of one year when the first trip took place, I was already accepted as part of their scene. It meant the Poles could fully relax in my presence, involve me in their team-building, and help me move to the next level. The weekend events would also offer the possibility to visit two famous parts of Poland for the first time.

The first excursion took place at the end of October to Malbork castle, reputedly the largest in the world. The castle was the home of the Teutonic Knights in the Middle Ages – German crusaders who were the precursors to Prussian and then German militarism (though, initially, the Prussians were victims of the Teutonic Knights). It was originally established as a hospital for injured crusaders attempting to free the Holy Land from Moslem rule, later becoming a military castle.

We travelled up to Malbork on a Saturday morning. Once there, we found that our hotel - a former hospital for wounded soldiers - was pleasing enough, part of the outhouses of the castle mount or "Lower Castle". As for the main castle, it was spectacular - a magnificent series of red brick constructions that covered a vast expanse of ground, surrounded by a moat. On its edge was a formidable wall, punctuated by a series of watchtowers with slits for firing arrows, and holes, out of which, presumably, boiling liquids were poured. Walking across the moat via a drawbridge, and through this wall, we entered a large quadrangle known as the "Medium Castle", and then continued through a narrow passage at the far end of this into a small courtyard known as the "High Castle" – the centre of the complex. This was a romantic place of Gothic archways and cloisters on the ground and first floors, and above them an abundance of rooms beneath a steep brick roof. The castle also boasted the Palace of the Great Masters (the Great Master was the ruler of the Teutonic Knights) and a church that was at one time the most important in the state.

Saturday afternoon was unremarkable but enjoyable: the well-attended lectures resembled those given on such corporate outings back in England: how to improve revenue, profitability and the like. There was general good humour and plenty of joke-telling by everyone (including the bosses).

The first big event was dinner in the evening. It was held in a huge hall with a high vaulted ceiling. From the eves, various flags hung down, presumably standards of the Teutonic Knights. Standing suits of armour eyed us from the side of the hall. We ate at a great, U-shaped table, perhaps as the Knights had done in days of yore. The meal reminded me of my wedding feast, with course after course arriving. My colleagues, who had started drinking on the train the moment we left Warsaw, really got going now. They consumed everything, including whisky and wine, and the big favourite – vodka. A general feeling began to develop amongst my friends I was not participating enough. At first I protested, but soon realised there was nothing for it if I was to be accepted. So I filled one of the vodka tumblers, a small cup on a long stem, and made my way to the corner of the top table. Having requested and been granted silence, I made a speech in Polish thanking the firm for involving me - its first foreigner - in such a weekend. I then lifted the tumbler and downed the vodka in one, without touching the sides, in the traditional Polish way. As my stomach caught alight, a spontaneous round of applause burst out, and I heard the boss - a proud Pole, very protective of the Polish identity - utter something. A colleague later told me the boss had declared I was now a true Pole. I had arrived.

Following the previous night's excess, only about a quarter of the group attended the early morning lectures on the Sunday. They were uneventful except for the moment when one of the partners in the firm entered the lecture hall half way through the morning programme, looking far from his best, and received a hearty round of applause for his efforts. Afternoon lectures were cancelled to give people a chance to recover, and the day fell away. A few hardy souls walked into Malbork town in the rain, to report there was nothing there.

Everything now pointed, once again, to dinner. Apparently, we were going to have an unusual evening meal, preceded by a night time tour of the castle.

The tour was given by an ironic individual dressed in a monk's white habit complete with hood. He raised his voice to a boom when he wanted to make an impression - for example, when attempting to recreate the atmosphere of when the castle had been inhabited by the Knights - with considerable effect. The interiors of the castle were opulent - plenty of marble floors and faded frescoes on the walls - but in a state of disrepair. Most impactful of all was when we entered the courtyard of the High Castle. It was dimly lit with burning flames, and we could hear the high-pitched sound of monks' choral singing (recorded, it turned out). The effect was moving. Suddenly, we were drifting back in time half a millennium. We began to feel like Teutonic Knights. This transformation continued. We entered an antechamber just off the High Castle courtyard, and were asked to put on white vests with black crosses embroidered on them. Now we even looked like Knights! This "audience participation" changed the mood remarkably. There was a buzz of anticipation. What next? We were not let down. We filed through a corridor, and walked out into a feasting chamber that completed the time travel experience. The hall contained a T-shaped table, placed between thick brick pillars, laid out with endless dishes of food. To one side of the T, a piglet was roasting on a spit. Meats and sausages hung down from a kind of interior arbour next to the spit. They were all fresh - not plastic for effect. Next to this was a table containing a smorgasbord of fresh meats and salads. A band played lyres and old drums, and a lady sang an ancient song. The low ceiling bore down on the scene, increasing its intensity. I had never seen anything like it. I had completed my journey back in time to the Middle Ages, and it was a remarkably escapist feeling. All that seemed important now, as in days gone by, was to eat, drink and be merry.

Perhaps as a result of the romanticism of this scene, I indulged in a little more drinking myself. It helped that the staple alcohol on the second evening was beer not vodka - an easier proposition for an Englishman. Besides, most of my colleagues were still feeling delicate from the previous night's celebrations, giving me a chance to catch up. The evening was rowdy nonetheless, and the Poles continued drinking prodigiously. They seemed to have an infinite capacity for alcohol, which on this evening worked on them musically. The band had packed up and gone home quite early. So, all the Poles began singing traditional songs. Everyone joined in (except me, as I did not know any of the words). Inevitably, I was asked to give a rendition or two, and so, with some embarrassment, as the room suddenly fell silent, I started singing the Beatles number, "Michelle, ma belle". It was all I could think of at the time, and a pretty pathetic effort because it was not boisterous enough. But I need not have worried. After the first four notes, all the Poles joined in as well, singing in Polish (the song was translated and became a hit a few years back). My colleagues were delighted by my participation, and I had to perform several more songs before the night was over. When we returned to Warsaw by coach the next day - and to my astonishment - people were still talking about my musical talent, and I half expected to be asked for my autograph on the way.

Six months later, I set off on another work weekend, this time with more of an outdoor theme. The timing of the trip was questionable: it was the end of March, and the Polish weather was capable of being just about anything. But the boss was optimistic. We would go to the Mazurian region, the largest wetlands area in Europe, a few hours north of Warsaw – known as the "Land of a Thousand Lakes". The hotel we would stay at was situated on a hill above one of the many interlocking lakes, and the scene would be idyllic if the weather were conducive.

The hotel, in the village of Stare Jabłonki ("Old Apple Orchard") was situated in the middle of a sparse wood. The main hotel building, typically, was painted brilliant white with a red tiled roof, and included a number of balconies and alcoves that gave it some character. Along with many other lawyers, however, I was staying in a long, two storey annex, a little way away - a more functional but perfectly adequate building. We all unpacked our things, and then, as it was already late (we had travelled up on a Friday afternoon) went straight for the evening meal. It was a typically reckless affair, involving plenty of toasts and letting go. But I preserved myself for the following day, which I knew from the programme would be a full one.

The main event on the Saturday, ironically considering the self-styled integration with the Poles in which I was now indulging, was an

"Integration Project". This was not only intended to integrate our own lawyers with each other. It was also meant to integrate us with a group of new lawyers who had joined our firm *en masse* (having defected from another legal partnership) and with our Big Brother American accountancy firm, several of whose members had also come to Stare Jabłonki.

It would take the form of a combined physical and mental challenge. We were split into six teams of eight, and told we had a number of tasks to complete outside in the woods. It was by now a warm and sunny day, so this would be no hardship. Each team had a clock ticking on which the minutes (beginning at twenty) were decreasing. The aim was for each team to complete as many of ten tasks as it could, receive money for doing so, and buy time to add to the clock. The aim was to keep all six clocks from falling to zero minutes over a period of two hours.

Our team performed its first task with relative ease. We had to find spots in the wood that were the same as photographs we had been given and make copies with a camera to hand back to the judges. Depending on the resemblance of our picture to the original, we would be given more or less money. In another game we had to jump through some ropes pinned above the ground at different angles without touching them. We scored reasonably well. But it was on two of the more difficult games that our team performed best, developing an effective Polish-British entente in the process.

One was a challenge to pass an oversize, three metre diameter blow up ball over as great a distance as possible up a hill. The rules stated that only three members of our team could touch the ball at any one time, and they must not move their feet when they were holding it. Our attempt began. It was chaos, involving no method whatsoever. Team mates attempted to toss the ball from one group to another, but the movement soon broke down and the ball rolled off in recalcitrant fashion down the hill. I was frustrated by such lack of organisation on the part of the Poles, but was not sure what to do. It would look superior for the only foreigner to tell them they were not taking the right approach. But after several more unsuccessful attempts, and as our twenty minute clock ticked apace to zero, I had to do something. I asked everyone to listen, and told them my plan. Two people would balance the ball at its side, and then roll it on to a third person standing right in the middle of the ball, and slightly in front of it, who would act as a fulcrum. By the time he had rolled the ball over himself, two more people would have positioned themselves either side of the ball further up the hill to balance the ball and continue the process. Then another fulcrum. And another and another. We began this process gingerly, and saw that it was working first time. Slowly the ball ascended the hill, and then faster and faster as we became more adept at the process. The Poles (and I) were delighted. We got the ball almost to the top of the hill before it fell away to one side. The judge of the game was astounded. She said it was the best technique she had seen for the game. She gave us money for completing the task, a bonus for the distance we had covered with the ball, and an extra bonus for our technique.

For the next task, we again did well, managing to pick up a magnetic object which was lying on the ground surrounded by a canvas wall, without entering an area of about five metres square around the object. We did this with the use of ropes, wheels, pulleys and a magnet we had been given. However, on this occasion, and despite my protestations they were again not going about it the right way, it was my Polish colleagues who devised an elegant solution, suspending the equipment from trees that overhung the site. I should have had more faith in them: one of the Poles' favourite sayings about themselves is "Polak potrafi", which roughly translates as "A Pole can do". The judge of this challenge was also impressed. Again, she awarded us a bonus for technique, and said she would make a point at the concluding plenary session of how well we had co-operated.

Though a series of lectures were scheduled for the afternoon, most people wanted to spend time in front of the TV watching an important qualifying match for the 2000 European Football Championships. The teams? England and Poland. So the firm duly cancelled the lectures to everyone's delight. However, as the only Englishman amongst fifty or so patriotic Poles, I was a little nervous. My colleagues had hinted on the coach journey up that, if England won, I could find myself in the nearby lake. But apart from this isolated show of bravado, the attitude of the Poles to the match was generally subdued. Poland has never had a world-beating football team, but at certain moments in the past it has achieved significant international success, at one point coming third in a World Cup. Also, the present Polish team was on a run of around a dozen games unbeaten. Nevertheless, most of the Poles were already resigned and brow-beaten. We always lose to England, they said. We always lose the important matches. What hope did we have now?

I bought a round of beers for most of my friends who were watching the match with me, hoping to appease them. If England did win, which I was not sure I wanted them to in the circumstances, perhaps I would avoid a dousing.

Within a few minutes of the match beginning, Poland was two goals down. Now their resignation took concrete form. My colleagues hurled insult after insult at the players. There then followed a general discussion on how Poland always loses all of the big games. This done, most of the Poles sloped off. Only the die-hards remained. Poland then got a goal back, and the loud cheer from the TV room brought many of those who had gone away back in. *Now* the Poles were excited. The banter became more good-natured. I was gently mocked for England's conceding of a goal. I waited for a second and equalising Polish goal.

But a third England goal went in, near to the end of the game, and that was it. The room virtually emptied. I was left with a good friend of mine – Stefan - who remained, paradoxically enough, because he was not so keen on football, so Poland's losing did not bother him. I asked Stefan about the Poles' attitude to this match, and he was honest with me. Though it hurt him to say so, there was definitely a strong element of defeatism in the Polish character, he said. Stefan agreed with me about this being in part a consequence of centuries of subjugation, but added today's match was not a good example: often Poles have more mettle than this, but in the football match scenario, as I well knew, the risk of despair was an ever-present.

It was a subdued bunch of Polish colleagues who travelled with me for the final set-piece dinner of the weekend, as I tried to keep the grin of victory from my face. But their melancholy did not last long. We entered a traditional Polish inn ("karczma") and the scene that greeted us instantly reminded me of the feast in the High Castle at Malbork. This time, we began outside, and gathered round a wild boar that was being spit roasted. We were handed two or three metre long sticks, onto which we skewered sausages that we then poked into the fire. On either side of us, covered tables and benches ranged down what looked like former stables. Jugs of beer were laid out on the tables. We ate the sausages, and the wild boar, which was a delicious combination of crispy meat and a little fat, and drank the beer. We devoured thick slices of fresh, crusty bread, and various delicious salads and chose from a variety of mustard sauces to add to the meats. Then we had more. We were well and truly sated. It was at this point the inn's hosts invited us in for the evening meal...

We moved inside to long narrow tables all joined together and winding around the pillars of the karczma. The setting was similar to the evening in the High Castle, except this room was more capacious and airy, less crypt like. The food and drink began again, including of course vodka – but also mead, a sweet alcoholic honey drink from old times. However, it was the music and dancing that were to take centre stage on this evening. As soon as we sat down, a folk band of six members struck up a tune. They were a motley crew, wearing a variety of traditional folk costumes, each playing a different instrument. One played a violin, one a double bass and one a clarinet, two played accordions, and one simply tapped a tall stick that had bells attached and a rag doll stuck to its top. Then, on came a beguiling female singer in a frilly blue dress. She sang a number in which she evidently was refusing to dance with a young man vying for her attention. When this song ended, she moved to join the band, and more dancers in traditional Polish folk costumes took to the floor. The men whirled the women around spectacularly, and I was just beginning to enjoy this display when the audience participation began. I protested successfully for most of the evening, relying (as I had at my wedding) on my lack of a dancing education, until eventually one young lady dancer, evidently the cheekiest of the bunch, grabbed my hand. Fortunately, she then proceeded to get the rest of the dancers, members of the audience and me to begin a giant conga - steps even I could manage. She whisked us in and out of each other faster and faster, like a caterpillar getting twisted up in itself, for what seemed like an eternity. We finished, arms outstretched above us and screaming with delight, exhilarated but exhausted.

I was shown the way in the dancing by a colleague at work - Dariusz. Dariusz was a man simply brimming with enthusiasm for all Polish traditions – including Polish folk dancing. During one song, for example, when there was no available girl to dance with, Dariusz simply jumped up from his chair and started dancing with a couple. Singing was also within his repertoire. He took the unofficial prize for this at Malbork, and here at the Mazurian Lakes, defended his crown with aplomb. If ever there were a moment when the group fell silent during the evening, you could be sure Dariusz would fill the void with another number. I found this out to my cost. I was seated next to Dariusz throughout the evening, and as I liked him very much, I had tried to get chatting with him. However, as Dariusz always had one ear out for those cussed silences, we had not got far. He would tend to break off periodically from our conversation in order to reinvigorate the singing. If he was at a loss for a tune, he would simply revert to that old Polish favourite, "Jeszcze jeden i jeszcze raz" – "once again and one more time" - sung in a drunken drawl. Nevertheless, it was precisely because of such dedication that I nominated Dariusz my archetypal traditional Pole, and decided that, in being fortunate enough to have sat next to him for the duration of the evening, I had come a long way in my Polish integration.

16 DEPARTURE

And then, no sooner had I integrated, than we were leaving. It was May 1999. Marzena had completed her doctorate at the Jagiellonian University in Cracow, where she now had an opportunity to lecture - but work for lawyers was still only to be found in Warsaw. We therefore decided to return to London. There, we could live and work together, rather than be split between two Polish cities. In any case, the opportunities for foreign lawyers in Poland were already decreasing. Though they had been useful in introducing Western technique and know-how into the Polish legal market, it was now clear Polish lawyers could continue for themselves. They had the added advantage they knew Polish law and language. Nevertheless, my colleagues were sorry to see me go. They all accepted my career should progress faster in England. But who would they now speak English with, they asked? The boss, or "Pan Prezes" (literally, "Mr. President") as I used to call him to his delight, also had a question. Namely, who amongst his staff, once I had gone, would have the guts to remark repeatedly, "Pan Prezes powiedziała że...", which was supposed to mean, "Mr. President said that...", but which inadvertently feminised the verb and him!? As for me, I was extremely upset to leave, and tearful on departing the office for the last time when Antoni - the colleague with whom I had shared an office - gave me a huge, treasured pot of thick honey. It had been given to him by his parents, having been collected fresh from the hives in the Bieszczady region of south-east Poland where he grew up.

As the time for leaving Warsaw approached, we found ourselves cramming in as much last minute sightseeing as we could. On our penultimate weekend in the capital, we had a strange experience in the botanical gardens. These were not the botanical gardens in the centre of the city, that we had already visited a year or more ago, but the more extensive gardens on the edge of town that our landlord had forever been telling us to go visit. With time running out, we decided we had better do so, especially as there would be an outdoor Chopin concert there at noon on the Saturday. We left our flat in sunshine, although it was a little chilly, even in early May. Arriving at the gardens, we parked the car next to the entrance, and asked the attendant where the concert would take place. In the dwórek over there, he replied, pointing roughly in the direction of some buildings to the right of the entrance. We made for the buildings, but could never quite get there because we were separated from them by a wide, ornamental stream.

Never mind, we had half an hour to go before the concert started. We decided to follow the crowds, who were probably also headed for the concert. We walked with them down a wide, concrete path along which the wind swept relentlessly. It was getting really cold now, and neither Marzena nor I were dressed for the occasion. Marzena asked a passer-by where to go for the concert, and he gave us a thorough, five minute explanation of how to get there. Evidently noting something Anglo-Saxon in my comportment, he then repeated the explanation in English. We followed his directions, but did not appear to be getting any nearer to our destination. We asked another passer-by, who told us to leave the gardens by a side exit: the dwórek was just outside the garden complex. On the point of leaving by said exit, we asked another attendant if we were now headed for the dwórek, and she replied in the negative. We should stay in the gardens and head down one of the main thoroughfares, just ahead of us, which would take us to the concert.

By now we were despairing of ever making it on time. We shuffled speedily down the road, noting the beauty on either side of us: ferns, several arboretums, and a colourful display of early spring flowers set in the immaculate grass. Striding along, we at least warmed up, though it was by now drizzling, and then came upon the man who had advised us to leave the park. *Ah, there you are, there you are,* he said to us breathlessly, as if encountering old friends. *I've been looking for you everywhere! I gave you the wrong advice, you know. I'm so terribly sorry. The dwórek is over there. You're going the right way now. Good luck!*

We found the dwórek, in front of which benches had been laid out in a semi-circular garden parlour set against a backdrop of tall trees. It was picturesque. It was also twelve o'clock, and there was not a soul to be seen! A few prospective spectators entered the arena, then thought better of staying upon seeing how wet the benches were. A boy of about ten arrived looking handsome in black tie. He would definitely be the smartest member of the audience, I decided, until I realised he was the pianist. He began to play, and it was immediately clear he was a virtuoso. He cruised through polonaises and études for the twelve or so hardy souls who had now gathered in the rain – none of them daring to move for fear of reducing the size of the audience by a significant fraction. Then, abruptly, he stopped and asked his parents, avidly videoing him from the front row, whether or not he should go on. This was strange, I thought. Certainly there were not too many of us watching and listening, but I guess we deserved to hear the whole concert. Mother and father disagreed. Father thought he should go on, mother not. This was becoming an embarrassment! The audience began to murmur. The boy pianist left, and returned a second later to begin the concert. He had only been warming up.

The boy, who it said in our programme was a child prodigy, and who had already won competitions all over the world, produced a wonderful forty-five minutes or so of music. But the following weekend – our last in Warsaw - we attended a concert by the kind of pianist the prodigy must have aspired to be. It was at the National Philharmonic, and once again gave us the chance to see something we had managed to miss in the previous couple of years in Warsaw. Namely, the main concert hall of the Philharmonic, not the basement where we had listened to the Kaliningrad Folk Orchestra.

Unfortunately, all the seats were sold out, and we were forced to buy standing tickets. Never mind, the usher said. There were 500 or so season-ticket holders, and they never all turned up. The usher was right. We managed to get prime seats on the front row of the balcony, although not before I had opportunistically taken the seat of an elderly season-ticket holder, who shooed me out of his seat with raised eyebrows and a thundering look of which Mussolini would have been proud. We then stared past the neo-Classical, half-pillared walls at the front stage, awaiting the first piece. It was an abstract composition conducted by the composer of the piece himself, an elderly Pole. He continued to conduct for the next piece, which was more accessible, and in which the brilliant Georgian virtuoso Dmitri Bashkirov played the piano. He was magnificent. His hands floated over the ivories like butterflies. After this piece, the sheer enthusiasm of the audience brought him back on stage, and he played a short composition which showed off fully his abilities, a piece not unlike Rimsky-Korsakov's "Flight of the Bumble Bee". The evening then rounded off in fine style with a stirring rendition of Beethoven's Fifth.

We packed up and sent off most of our possessions to England with the removal people, and when it was finally time to go, found ourselves more emotional at having to say goodbye to our spacious flat and warm-hearted landlord than to anything or anyone else. We knew we would rent a box in London for the equivalent money when we returned to live there, owned by some ogre. Our landlord, as if sensing this, gave us a small, yellow elephant for good luck, which only made us more regretful. After all, where else in the world do landlords buy you yellow elephants? When we also considered we would no longer attend Chopin concerts in Łazienki park, or productions at the National Opera, or skip around Wilanów gardens, or even eat chicken tikka at Charanjit's restaurants - it seemed almost churlish to leave.

We bombed down to Cracow by car, the first leg of our drive across Europe. We spent three days with the family, before having to say farewells which, though not quite tearful, were wearing, because I felt like the villain of the piece for taking Marzena away from her family. If I had learnt nothing else, it was of the strength of the knot that tied the family, and as we left, we were already planning our next trip back to Poland.

We then set off for England, almost getting lost as soon as we left Cracow by following road signs that, though directing us where we wanted to go, only appeared at intervals of tens of kilometres, by which time we had lost faith as to whether we were going the right way. We got stuck behind long, smoking lorries that gave out more dirty emissions than a small factory, but which we were nervous to overtake because of unclear road markings. More signs sent us on numerous diversions through tiny villages unprepared for the traffic convoys sent their way. All the while, beady eyed police watched us from tricky vantage points at the side of the road that offered them maximum opportunity to hold up one of their red wands and begin their interrogation. When we finally reached the Polish border at Zgorzelec, having bumped the final kilometres along what we termed the "boom-boom-boom" motorway - a road barely repaired by the Poles since Nazi Germany first laid it in the 1930s, constructed from ill-fitting slabs of concrete - we were tired and dazed. We showed our passports, and immediately passed onto the new German autobahn, stretching the 100km or so from the border to Dresden, miraculously completed in the two years since we had arrived in Poland. Our VW jumped joyously onto the smooth tarmac and purred as it cruised westwards, accompanied now by its exclusive Mercedes and Audi friends. It was clearly happy at the improvement in conditions, but we were not. There was silence in the car, and the feeling we had left our hearts at the border – perhaps with the child prodigy in the botanical gardens, or maybe with Dmitri Bashkirov, or maybe someplace else.

Then Marzena said she would miss Poland. It was exactly what I had wanted to say, but had been waiting for her to say first. After all, it was her country. She knew so much better than me, with my relative handful of experiences and observations, all there was to miss about this place. It was for her to say it first, therefore. But when she had said it, I had agreed, for I felt deeply emotional to be leaving it all behind. Some time in the future, we both vowed there and then, we would return to live in Poland.

ACKNOWLEDGEMENTS

My great thanks to:

Wiesiek Kisielowski for his evocative sketches;

Mark Halper for his incisive editing;

Grzegorz Nowak for his construction of the *Polska Dotty* website;

Susie Williams for her marketing advice;

All the people in Poland who made us so welcome during our stay
- and to those who didn't! - without which this book would not
have been possible; and

My family – *never forget* the family - especially my parents and
children.

But most of all, thank you to Marzena, my love, muse, and endless
source of good counsel.

Jonathan Lipman
December 2012

ABOUT THE AUTHOR

Jonathan Lipman was born in Oxfordshire, England in 1968. In the 1980s he encountered many temporary émigrés from Eastern Europe - including Russians, Romanians and... Poles. They were visitors to his father's team that pioneered wind energy in the UK. Conversations with them would range far and wide, from the flaws in Capitalism to the evils of Communism, from the corrupt West to the post-Communist "Wild East", from Keynes to Marx and Engels. Little did Jonathan know this would stand him in good stead when, at the age of 25, he'd meet a variety of Eastern Europeans on a course at Oxford University, and fall in love with one of them - a Pole.

After qualifying as a lawyer in 1997, Jonathan married Marzena in Cracow, Poland, and they spent the next two years getting to grips with Warsaw. Jonathan worked for a renowned and very Polish law firm; Marzena completed her doctorate. In 1999 they returned to England, where Jonathan could continue to practice in English law. He is currently UK Legal Director of a large motor manufacturer moonlighting as an author, or maybe the other way around. Marzena works in consumer affairs. They live in Buckinghamshire, England, where they are slaves to two girls, three fish, and various generations of ipod.

Please visit the Polska Dotty website:
http://polskadotty.wordpress.com/

CHAPTER NOTES

[1] I recently took an unusual, educational and entertaining tour of Nowa Huta with "Crazy Tours". I was driven through the town in a yellow Trabant, and shown the gates of the steelworks, the church the townspeople built, and an old Soviet tank. Michael Palin did the same in his TV series *New Europe*.

[2] Things have improved since: for example, there are now impressive cinema multiplexes and aqua parks in the capital.

[3] The Warsaw roadworks authority did eventually decide to install a traffic management system in the city centre, and begin construction of a ring-road for the capital.

[4] Redevelopment of Plac Defilad – right at the heart of Warsaw – has been postponed time and again. There are now plans for a spectacular reconstruction.

[5] Even now there are only around 900km of motorways in Poland, but this does represent significant progress, and there are plans for many more routes.

[6] The death rate on Polish roads, though it has reduced, remains very high - at about three times that of the UK per capita.

[7] Poland did pass tough legislation on drink driving. The legal alcohol limit is very low, and offenders face up to 2 years in prison and loss of their driving-licence for up to 10 years.

[8] Inevitably Metro expansion will be slow, but construction has now began on a second line, to run east-west (the current one runs north-south).

[9] John-Paul II, Pope 1978-2005, credited with playing a major role in the downfall of Communism as an inspiration for the Solidarity

movement, to which he gave tacit support. But criticised for his conservative approach to issues such as contraception. Certainly one of Poland's most famous sons.

[10] AWS has since become defunct, its leading members having joined other political parties. SLD has continued, though with a generally reduced influence.

[11] Visitor numbers did indeed increase greatly in 1999, to at least double the average.

[12] Until now there has apparently been no such remake of "Killer".

[13] "With Fire and the Sword" was snubbed at the Oscars.

[14] Even now, the cost of such a meal will be in the region of only £20-30.

[15] Sanitary facilities are now greatly improved in Poland, along the lines of the facilities beneath Hawełka i.e. you have to pay, but it's not a lot, and worth every penny!

[16] Polish labour productivity remains well below the European average, by and large at the same level as the other countries that acceded to the European Union in 2004. But this hasn't stopped companies such as Cadburys moving large parts of their operations to Poland.

[17] That was in 1999. Transparency International's Corruptions Perception Index for 2010 places Poland back in joint 41st place ie the 41st least corrupt country in the world – keeping company with Oman and Costa Rica.

[18] President of Poland 1995-2005.

[19] Maximilian Faktorowicz, Polish Jewish cosmetician (1875-1938).

[20] Praga has recently reinvented itself as a centre for arts and partying.

Pre-war factories and warehouses have been converted into trendy bars, clubs, galleries and restaurants.

[21] Poland has been slow to promote gender equality which, though enshrined in the constitution, has not been sufficiently implemented in legislation. This eventually resulted in a complaint to the European Commission. Latterly efforts have been made by the Polish government to push this issue higher up the political agenda.

[22] In 2011 the ruling political party in Poland suspended one of its MPs for homophobic comments.

[23] Churchill said of the Poles: "There are few virtues which the Poles do not possess, and there are few errors they have ever avoided".

[24] In 2011 there is talk of a film being made of Karski's life, to complement republication of his book recounting his wartime experiences, "Story of a Secret State". It is a brutal but gripping read, and a must read for anyone who wishes to understand life during wartime in Poland.

[25] The sign was stolen in December 2009 and soon after recovered. It had been cut into three pieces. Three Poles were sent to prison for the offence, and other individuals may also be prosecuted.

[26] This site has now been turned into a huge arts, culture and retail complex, appropriately enough named "Manufaktura".

[27] A 2010 survey by the Polish Public Opinion Poll Institute claims that 6% of Poles asked about influential minorities mentioned the Jewish people, down from 20% in 2002.

Printed in Poland
by Amazon Fulfillment
Poland Sp. z o.o., Wrocław